D1602450

SKIRMISHES
AT THE
EDGE OF EMPIRE

The United States and International Terrorism

David Tucker

PRAEGER

Westport, Connecticut
London

Library of Congress Cataloging-in-Publication Data

Tucker, David, 1951–
    Skirmishes at the edge of empire : the United States and
international terrorism / David Tucker.
        p. cm.
    Includes bibliographical references and index.
    ISBN 0–275–95762–4 (alk. paper)
    1. Terrorism. 2. Terrorism—Prevention—Government policy—United
States. I. Title.
    HV6431.T83   1997
    303.6′25—dc20   96–41391

British Library Cataloguing in Publication Data is available.

Library of Congress Catalog Card Number: 96–41391
ISBN: 0–275–95762–4

First published in 1997

Praeger Publishers, 88 Post Road West, Westport, CT 06881
An imprint of Greenwood Publishing Group, Inc.

Printed in the United States of America

The paper used in this book complies with the
Permanent Paper Standard issued by the National
Information Standards Organization (Z39.48–1984).

10 9 8 7 6 5 4 3 2 1

Copyright Acknowledgments

The author and publisher gratefully acknowledge permission for use of the following material:

Excerpts from "Bearing Witness" by R. H. Price, 1989. *American Journal of Community Psychology*
17, no. 2: 151–167. Copyright 1989 by Plenum Publishing Corporation. Reprinted by permission of
Plenum Publishing Corporation.

To my Mother and Father

CONTENTS

Preface   ix

Introduction   xi

  1. History   1

  2. Definition   51

  3. Methods   71

  4. Organization   109

  5. Strategy   133

Conclusion   185

Notes   191

Selected Bibliography   215

Index   219

PREFACE

Some time ago, a young man who thought he might be a scholar sat down to write what he was sure would be the definitive account of Thomas Jefferson. At the same time, incidentally, he began to read about the Vietnam War. This reading soon led him to make comparisons between Jefferson, the greatest revolutionary and insurgent leader in history, and his assorted, ultimately failed, progeny. This led in turn to an abiding interest in revolution and insurgency and its modern accessories: subversion, terrorism, and guerrilla war. This interest soon became more than just scholarly. One result is this book.

The book about Jefferson has never been finished. Readers of this book will note, however, the degree to which Jefferson has influenced these pages. For providing a would-be scholar with an uninterrupted summer to read and write about Jefferson, I must thank belatedly the Earhart Foundation. The end notes record other debts to scholars, journalists and the former and still-serving named and unnamed government officials I interviewed for this book. To the latter, I am particularly grateful for the time they gave me. In various ways, a number of other people helped. I am grateful to Neal Weiner at Marlboro College and George Simmons for their instruction and encouragement and to Mr. and Mrs. Clyde J. Deitz for their example and support. Robert Dawidoff reintroduced me to Jefferson at the Claremont Graduate School. Although nothing in this book represents the views of the Defense Department or any other agency of the U.S. government, much of what is written here I learned through working with Chris Lamb in the Office of the Assistant Secretary of Defense for Special Operations and Low-Intensity Conflict. Chris also read and commented on an early draft, as did Chris Harmon. My wife, Ellen, read various drafts and discussed all the arguments, patiently pointing out problems. For not benefiting more from this varied tuition and for the faults that remain in this book, I have only myself to blame.

INTRODUCTION

As American troops prepared to deploy to Bosnia in December 1995, the press reported growing concern among political and military leaders that terrorists might target the troops. The leaders were concerned because the operation in Bosnia had limited support in Congress and with the public. Casualties from terrorist attacks might tip the balance of support against the mission, officials feared, undermining the ability of the United States and the North Atlantic Treaty Organization (NATO) to carry out the complex task of stabilizing Bosnia. Even if terrorist attacks did not undermine the effort, the need to counter the terrorist threat consumed valuable resources, diverting time and energy from the pressing problems associated with the mission in Bosnia and complicating an already daunting task. According to press reports, officials feared that several different groups might carry out these attacks: Bosnian Muslims, radicalized by four years of war; Muslim veterans of the war in Afghanistan against the Soviets, eager to fight the next battle against Islam's enemies; members of Islamic terrorist or subversive groups, eager for the same battle; and members of various Iranian government organizations, fighting for a mix of Islamic and geostrategic reasons. All viewed the United States as the enemy of Islam and the principal author of a peace disadvantageous to the Muslims of Bosnia. All were willing to use terrorism—car bombs, assassinations, and hostage takings—to attack their enemy.[1]

Bosnia thus became the latest setting for the confrontation between the United States and international terrorism, that is, terrorism involving the citizens or territory of more than one country. The confrontation, in a concerted and effective manner, had begun about thirty years before. It was several years after that, in the early 1970s, that the U.S. government began to treat terrorism as a priority of some significance. Rhetorically, it became a top priority in the final year of the Carter administration, as the Iranian hostage drama unfolded, and even more so in the first years of the Reagan administration. It was not until the mid-1980s, however, as terrorist attacks headed for a crescendo in 1985, that practice matched rhetoric.   Only then did the highest levels of the U.S. government, especially George Shultz and William Casey, focus on the threat and demand more effective ways to deal with it.   Yet, as U.S. policies and strategies began to have some success, the Iran-Contra affair discredited them, particularly with U.S. allies and, within the U.S. government, made them a political liability.   The special interagency group established to deal with terrorism was tainted by its association with Oliver North and in the last years of the Reagan administration, throughout the Bush administration and in the first years of the Clinton administration, combating terrorism became less of a priority rhetorically and practically. This change was appropriate. American policies, the crumbling of the Soviet Union and the Warsaw Pact, falling oil prices, and a changing political environment in the Middle East all contributed to a decline in the threat from international terrorism and in the need for the United States to oppose it publicly, frequently, and vehemently.   The Clinton administration listed combating international terrorism as one of its priorities when it came to office but not until 1995 did international terrorism in fact become a priority of the administration. In that year, in addition to the terrorist threat to the troops in Bosnia, a poison gas attack occurred in the Tokyo subway and bombings in the Middle East took American lives and threatened the peace process.   Following even more deadly terrorist attacks in 1996, the government's concern with terrorism has remained higher than in the Bush administration but lower than it was at the high tide of America's counterterrorism effort, during the mid-1980s. Again, this appears appropriate. Although U.S. casualties from terrorism were increasing in the mid-1990s, they had not reached the levels of the mid-1980s.[2]

Today, as both attacks on Americans and the attention paid them increase, officials are reportedly conducting the same debates their predecessors held ten years ago about how to respond to terrorism.[3] Such debates need not recur in a vacuum. The U.S. government's efforts to deal with terrorism over the past twenty-five years provide a wealth of experience to help settle many questions. If we are to handle terrorism effectively in the future, at whatever level it threatens us, we should pause now and assess the experience we have already had with it. Such reflection is particularly important as we adjust to a post–Cold War world that calls into question the suppositions that have guided our thinking about security and foreign policy.

The following pages attempt this assessment, but they also attempt something more. They try to place terrorism in a wider context. Terrorism is neither solely a political problem nor solely a military problem. Instead, it inhabits what the *National Military Strategy* calls "the gray zone between peace and war." Historically, the United States has had difficulty dealing with this gray area. We do well in peacetime, and we win our wars. But in that broad band of activities that is more than just the usual competition between states but less than war, we have not, typically, done so well.[4] The following pages discuss terrorism in this larger context, as an example of the political-military problems with which we have trouble. They seek to explain why we have difficulty with these problems and suggest some possible ways we might improve.

One might well ask whether it matters: as the saying goes, two out of three ain't bad. Why is success in war and peace not sufficient? Indeed, one might argue that, precisely because we are not good at handling ambiguous political-military problems, we should ignore them, counting on our ability to trump our enemies when the real fighting starts. This is certainly the approach preferred by most of our military establishment. U.S. Army planning, for example, continues to be dominated by what one critic has called the Army concept, "a focus on mid-intensity, or conventional, war and a reliance on high volumes of firepower to minimize casualties." To gauge how embedded this concept is, we should consider that in the mid-1990s, when one of the Army's most provocative thinkers looked ahead, he saw the Army continuing to operate according to its traditional concept, even though he explicitly presented himself as one who was trying to break the molds of Army thinking. He saw the Army battling what he called new warriors in an increasingly anarchical and technologically sophisticated world, but he wanted the Army to do so by ignoring the State Department, the skills of whose diplomats are unsuited to this world, he contended, and by directing "irresistible violence . . . against the warlord(s) and the warriors." This is the Army concept triumphant, as it was in the era of the insurgent, as it will be in the age of the new warrior. Although denying, rightly, that their skills are not suited for it, most diplomats would no doubt be happy to discover that in the future the military will continue to focus on warfighting, so that they can get on with their own business.[5]

Even if one accepts, as one should, that the ability to win our wars, whether against armies or hordes of warriors, must remain the principal task of the U.S. military—as representing our interests abroad must remain the principal task of our diplomats—one can still ask whether this is all our soldiers and diplomats must do, whether success at war and peace is sufficient. The study of terrorism suggests that it is not. The violence of terrorism clearly marks it as different from the routine jostling of international politics. About this there is no dispute. But its violence and its use as a tool of statecraft have led some to argue that it is really a kind of warfare. This argument resonates harmonically with the traditional American approach, which sees conventional warfare as the standard, preparation for which necessarily includes preparation for all other kinds of violent conflict. This was not just a Cold War view. Secretary of Defense William Perry reiterated it in 1995. Today, he remarked, we plan "to deal with two major regional conflicts. . . . [T]he other activities are now the lesser included cases. . . . [A]s long as we're capable of dealing with the two major regional conflicts, we almost automatically have the force capability we need to do" other things.[6] One of the principal tasks of this book is to demonstrate that this view is wrong. To the contrary, it argues that terrorism is representative of a kind of political violence that differs from war not in degree alone but in kind as well. Countering this political violence does not require massively different "force capability"—in this Secretary Perry was right—but it does require an approach to political violence and a strategy different from those we have traditionally pursued. Failure in this regard in the past has cost us significantly and, in the future, for reasons we will discuss, may cost us even more. Hence we must conclude, two out of three ain't good enough.

By saying that terrorism is representative, we are implicitly arguing that it is not unique, as some terrorist experts contend.[7] It may be the most dramatic form of political violence and, in its disregard for the lives of innocents, the most brutal, but this does not make it unique. In fact, to argue that it is so is to fall into the trap set by terrorists of making more out of their actions than is necessary. It is to give way to a kind of panic, which achieves one common terrorist objective. Holding the view that terrorism is unique may have another bad consequence: it may lead us to think that dealing with terrorism requires a unique response. On the contrary, or so we will argue, it is only when we treat terrorism in the context of a comprehensive national strategy, one formed in part by reflecting on political violence like terrorism, that we can have any hope of success with this persistent problem.

To accomplish its various purposes, this book offers a brief history of our experience with terrorism, an analysis of our response, and a strategic assessment. The history is neither exhaustive nor definitive. It aims, rather, to highlight the character of international terrorism as we have experienced it over the last thirty years and to present the ways we have responded to this threat in a context that will help us analyze the effectiveness of our response. This analysis is divided into three chapters, which discuss definition, methods, and organization (Chapters 2, 3, and 4, respectively). It may seem unnecessary to define a phenomenon we all recognize instantly when news of it breaks on our television screens. But we must discuss the definition of terrorism if we are to avoid the mistake of seeing it either as another kind of warfare or as a unique form of violence. Discussing the definition of terrorism also allows us to glimpse the array of political, legal, and moral problems associated with the use of violence for political purposes outside what we have customarily understood to be war. Having defined with some degree of precision what we are talking about, we are prepared to discuss the ways in which we have tried to combat terrorism: a policy of not making concessions to terrorists; a judicial response; economic sanctions; military retaliation; prevention; disruption; and, for the sake of completeness, preemption, which has been much discussed in and outside government but seldom used. The analysis of these varied responses presents their advantages and disadvantages, attempts some assessment of their effectiveness, and offers recommendations for ways to improve them. Chapter 4 deals with how we are organized to combat terrorism, since all government efforts take place through organizations. These different organizations are not transparent mediums but affect our efforts as they make them possible. It is in Chapter 4 that we look most closely at the traditional dichotomous approach of the United States to national security problems.

The history and analysis are largely retrospective, whereas what follows is more prospective. In Chapter 5 we take up the issue of national strategy because analysis of our policy and organization for combating terrorism leads to the conclusion that these can be effective only within the framework of a sound national strategy. It is at this level, too, that we can begin to address the broader issues raised by seeing terrorism as representative of a group of problems we confront in our international life. In this regard, Chapter 5 develops further an underlying theme of this book: terrorism and the American way of war. Most commentators argue that the United States cannot respond patiently and subtly to ambiguous threats. We prefer to use decisive and overwhelming force to win wars fought for grand objectives, like making the world safe for democracy. Yet the history of our response to terrorism reveals this criticism as something of a caricature, since for over twenty-five years, under the administrations of both parties and with only occasional lapses, we have pursued terrorists and their sponsors with patience and have learned to live with, if not to accept, ambiguous and inconclusive results. To the extent that in the post–Cold War world threats like terrorism will predominate, learning from what we have done over the past twenty-five years against terrorism is essential to our future national security.

The conclusion of this book offers an assessment of the strategic significance of terrorism, including its supposedly new forms, and explains why our fight against it, even at its most fearsome, is best understood to be a skirmish at the edge of empire.

1

HISTORY

At mid-century, because of its preeminence and principles, the United States and its diplomats, military personnel, and businessmen around the world became targets for political violence. In 1956, rebels fighting for the independence of Cyprus threw a bomb into a restaurant, killing the American Vice Consul in Cyprus, William P. Boteler, and wounding three other Americans. On June 28, 1958, Cuban rebels, led by Raul Castro, Fidel's brother, took twenty-nine U.S. servicemen hostage to gain attention for their cause, to shield the rebels from Cuban government attacks, and to press their demand that the United States not supply weapons to the Cuban government or allow supplies to reach the government through the Guantanamo Naval Base. The rebels eventually released the hostages. On July 8, 1959, Vietcong guerrillas sprayed automatic weapons fire into a room where American advisers were watching a movie, killing Major Dale Buis and Master Sergeant Chester Ovnand, two South Vietnamese guards, and an eight-year-old Vietnamese boy. In 1960, the home of the U.S. Ambassador to Bolivia was bombed, and a year later dynamite was thrown at his parked car. On May 1, 1961, the first American plane was hijacked. The hijacker claimed he wanted to fly to Cuba to warn Fidel Castro about an assassination plot. In the fall of 1962, explosions damaged U.S.-owned oil facilities in Venezuela; authorities suspected the Venezuelan Army of National Liberation (FALN). In 1964, Congolese rebels took Americans, including U.S. diplomats, and other foreign nationals hostage, holding them for several months in an effort to prevent Congolese government attacks. Belgian paratroopers, with U.S. assistance, eventually rescued over two thousand hostages, although 101 were killed. On December 24, 1964, Vietcong guerrillas exploded a car bomb at the Brinks Hotel in Saigon, where American officers were billeted, killing two and wounding fifty-eight.[1]

These attacks and others like them did not lead the U.S. government to develop special policies or organizations to fight terrorism. Indeed, these attacks were not generally or consistently called terrorism; nor were those who committed them generally or consistently called terrorists. They were bandits, rebels, guerrillas, or, later, urban guerrillas, revolutionaries, or insurgents. During the Kennedy administration, the United States developed policies and organizations to fight insurgency or wars of national liberation. What we now generally call terrorism was seen as part of such conflicts, which it was in the vast majority of cases. Hostage takings, shootings, and bombings were a tactic in wars of national liberation because they got publicity for the revolutionary cause, intimidated or eliminated opponents, and (or so revolutionary theorists speculated) would help mobilize the masses by showing that the power structure was weak or, by provoking the authorities to take stringent security measures, that it was oppressive.[2]

After World War II, so-called wars of national liberation occurred throughout the world, but more attacks against Americans occurred in Latin America than elsewhere because of America's often antagonistic historical connections to the region and pronounced presence in it. Throughout the 1960s, Latin American groups, often factions splintered from long-established communist parties, acted on the supposed connection between violence and liberation. In 1963, members of the FALN kidnapped Colonel James K. Chenault, Deputy Chief of the U.S. military mission in Caracas, to get publicity for their cause. He was released unharmed. A year later the same group kidnapped another member of the military mission for the same reason, also releasing him unharmed. In May 1965, urban guerrillas in Uruguay, the Tupamaros, bombed the offices of All-American Cable and Western Telegraph. In 1966, the FALN fired a machine gun at a school for American children. In January 1967, the Tupamaros bombed the U.S. consulate in Montevideo. In January 1968, the Rebel Armed Forces in Guatemala ambushed and killed Naval Attaché Lieutenant Commander Ernest A. Munro and the chief of the U.S. Military Assistance Advisory Group, Colonel John D. Webber, wounding two other members of the military mission as well. Eight months later, the same group ambushed and killed the American Ambassador, John Gordon Mein, the first American Ambassador killed by terrorists. In 1969, in Brazil, National Liberation Action and the October 8 Revolutionary Movement (the latter named in memory of the day Cuban revolutionary Che Guevera was killed) kidnapped the American Ambassador, C. Burke Elbrick, releasing him three days later when their demands were met. A similar incident occurred in March 1970, when leftists in the Dominican Republic kidnapped Lieutenant Colonel Donald J. Crowley. He, too, was released when the terrorists' demands were met. Not all such incidents ended so happily, at least for the kidnapped. For example, in Uruguay, in July 1970, Tupamaros terrorists kidnapped an American police advisor, Dan Mitrione, whom they eventually murdered, and attempted to kidnap two American diplomats. There were many other such attacks on

American personnel and property in Latin America during this period, all part of a larger pattern of political violence that eventually attracted the attention of American officials. In February 1971, for example, in remarks prepared for a Special Session of the General Assembly of the Organization of American States (OAS), Secretary of State Rogers noted that twelve kidnapping incidents involving foreign officials (not just Americans) had occurred in the preceding seventeen months. Secretary Rogers referred to "the kidnapping of foreign officials by private groups for ransom purposes" as "a phenomenon new to the history of international relations."[3]

Secretary Rogers's remarks are noteworthy because they represent the emergence in the U.S. government of an awareness that terrorism and guerrilla warfare were not identical. Traditionally, guerrillas waged war indirectly, avoiding direct confrontations with the authorities because the guerrilla forces were too weak to survive such battles. Guerrillas ambushed military units, organized hit-and-run attacks on government officials and installations and sabotaged infrastructure. Urban guerrillas or terrorists, on the other hand, were attacking people not directly involved in the conflict, even carrying out their violent attacks in other countries. They attacked not only noncombatants but even innocents or those who would be considered as such by all those not subscribing to various Marxist interpretations of the world capitalist system.

In response to the increasing frequency of attacks on foreign officials in Latin America, the United States worked to have the OAS adopt a "Convention to Prevent and Punish Acts of Terrorism Taking the Form of Crimes Against Persons and Related Extortion that Are of International Significance." This convention was approved by the OAS General Assembly on February 1, 1971. On February 3, a State Department spokesman said of the convention that it represented "the first time that any international agreement has specified that the murder or kidnapping of representatives of states are not to be considered as political offenses whose perpetrators are sheltered by asylum." The issue of asylum or, more generally, how to distinguish political acts from common crimes, had been a subject of debate during preparation of the convention. The United States took the position, as the OAS General Assembly had in June 1970, that terrorist acts were common crimes and not political offenses. Although acknowledging that terrorism might arise from poverty, ignorance, discrimination, and other "social and political ills," the United States still insisted that such causes could not excuse terrorist attacks. Such attacks fell outside acceptable political protest and were nothing more than common crimes.[4]

The U.S. government's first response to terrorism, then, as something related to but separate from insurgency, was to define it as criminal and use international organizations to establish and enforce a regime of international agreements that would outlaw certain acts as terrorist and promote the cooperation necessary to capture and punish the perpetrators. The OAS convention of 1971 was not the first such agreement (for example, conventions negotiated in Tokyo, 1963, and at The Hague, 1970, covered various aspects of hijackings), but it is representative both of this approach and of the problems that plague it: lack of consensus, first, on whether terrorism is a criminal, political or humanitarian problem and on the degree to which a cause or grievance could justify it and, second, on whether to focus on the supposed causes of terrorism or on the acts of terrorists. These problems help explain in part why the draft convention on terrorism introduced by the United States at the United Nations (UN) in September 1972 was not accepted by the UN's members. Despite the rejection of this draft and continuing debates over the circumstances that justify political violence, the pursuit of international conventions has remained one of the methods the U.S. government uses to combat terrorism. In doing so, the U.S. government has always preferred to define terrorism as criminal activity and to focus on generating international cooperation to stop these criminal acts. From the beginning, it has insisted that trying to define terrorism is counterproductive and even harmful, since the debates generated in framing a definition of terrorism would only detract from efforts to combat it.

In November 1972, in an address to the American Bar Association, State Department legal advisor John R. Stevenson gave a clear account of the American policy of considering terrorism criminal and focusing attention on specific terrorist acts. Noting that political differences made trying to define terrorism counterproductive, Stevenson explained that the U.S. government sought international condemnation of certain acts "because of their grave and inhuman effect on innocent persons or because of their serious interference with the vital machinery of international life." He cited as examples hijacking and sabotaging civilian aircraft and kidnapping and assassinating foreign diplomats and officials. Again showing the new awareness in the U.S. government that the violent attacks on its personnel and facilities were different from guerrilla warfare, Stevenson singled out for criticism the "export of terrorism to countries not involved in the conflicts which spawned those acts of terrorism."[5] The views articulated by Stevenson remain U.S. policy. In July 1993, for example, in response to UN General Assembly Resolution 46/51, passed on December 9, 1991, which asked that a conference be convened to define terrorism and to differentiate it from struggles for national liberation, the United States argued that such an effort would not help the struggle against terrorism and might harm it, siphoning attention and resources from efforts to stop terrorist acts.

While kidnappings and assassinations in Latin America first focused the attention of U.S. officials on terrorism, attacks were also occurring in Europe, the Middle East, and Asia. Attacks on officials more than doubled worldwide between 1969 and 1970. Other terrorist activities were also becoming more prominent. On August 29, 1969, the Popular Front for the Liberation of Palestine (PFLP) hijacked a Rome–Tel Aviv TWA flight to Damascus. All the passengers were released, except the Israelis, who were released later when the government of Israel freed two Syrians. The plane was destroyed. This was the first hijacking involving a third party. The PFLP had previously, beginning in 1968, hijacked El Al planes. In December 1969, the Baader-Meinhof group, West German terrorists, placed a bomb at the El Al office in West Berlin, which was defused, and another at a U.S. officer's club, which exploded. In March 1970, the Japanese Red Army (JRA) hijacked a Japanese airliner from Tokyo to North Korea. In September 1970, the PFLP organized the first terrorist spectacular, hijacking several passenger jets at the same time, including a TWA and a Pan American plane, eventually blowing them up on the ground, three of them at Dawson Field in Jordan. All the passengers were eventually released.[6]

The PFLP was an Arab version of the national liberation movements that were active in other parts of the world. Organized in 1967 in the aftermath of the Israeli victory in the Six Day War, espousing Marxism and Pan-Arabism, and until 1993 a member of the Palestine Liberation Organization (PLO), it received support from Syria and other Arab states, like the PLO itself. Like all the elements of the PLO, the PFLP was unable to conduct operations in the land it wanted to liberate; uniquely, the PFLP decided in the late 1960s to make its terrorism campaign international. It was to this new aspect of terrorism that the State Department's legal advisor was referring when he spoke in 1972 of the "export of terrorism to countries not involved in the conflicts which spawned those acts of terrorism." Terrorist groups like the Baader-Meinhof gang, the Tupamaros, and the JRA were also Marxist in orientation but more vaguely so than national liberation movements like the PFLP because their Marxism was suffused with nihilism. Their principal purpose was destruction because, in their view, only after the old order was swept away would people be truly free to imagine what they and the world might be. This nihilistic revolutionary violence was made fashionable by the support and encouragement of such intellectuals as Jean Paul Sartre, who argued that "the only true culture is that of the revolution; that is to say it is constantly in the making" and that the "irrepressible violence" of a war of national liberation "is man recreating himself" into "a different man; a man of higher quality." True to those he had helped inspire, Sartre visited members of the Baader-Meinhof gang when they were imprisoned. Although fashionable, these groups were no less deadly for being so. In May 1972, the Baader-Meinhof gang bombed U.S. Army Fifth Corps Headquarters in Frankfurt, killing Colonel Paul Bloomquist and wounding thirteen others. Also in May 1972, members of JRA, working for the PFLP, attacked Lod Airport in Tel Aviv, killing twenty-six and wounding more than seventy. Most of those killed were Latin American pilgrims.[7]

The attacks in Frankfurt and at Lod Airport occurred in the midst of an outbreak of intense international terrorist activity, an outbreak triggered by a terrorist attack. The hijacking of the planes to Dawson Field convinced Jordan's King Hussein that the PLO, with its revolutionary rhetoric, reprisal-generating raids into Israel, and international terrorism, could no longer be tolerated in Jordan. Ten days after the planes were hijacked, Hussein ordered his army to attack the PLO. After some fierce fighting and mopping-up operations, the PLO was driven out of Jordan. The PLO responded with a terrorism campaign, assassinating Jordan's Prime Minister in Cairo and attempting to assassinate its Ambassador to London. Having suffered a devastating loss of prestige and the loss of fighters and other cadre, as well as a good base from which to attack Israel, Fatah (Yasir Arafat's group and the largest component of the PLO) decided to join the PFLP in using international terrorism to press its war of national liberation. It had previously restricted its use of violence to targets in Israel. To carry out its international terrorism, Fatah created a cover organization, Black September (in memory of the defeat in Jordan) headed by Abu Iyad, one of the most important leaders in Fatah. In addition to assassinating Jordanian officials, Black September blew up oil storage facilities in Rotterdam and hijacked Jordanian aircraft. No terrorist attack in this period by Black September (or any other group, for that matter) had a greater effect, however, than the attack on the Israeli athletes at the Munich Olympics on September 5, 1972. Eight members of Black September broke into the athletes' quarters at the Olympic Village, killed two of them and took nine hostage. The hostages, five terrorists, and one policeman were killed at the airport, the shoot-out broadcast live on television.[8]

Fatah did not consider any of these attacks to be terrorism. Echoing arguments heard during the preparation of the OAS convention, which in fact were commonplace by the early 1970s, Arafat, Abu Iyad, and other PLO spokesmen contended that killing civilians was justified because it was part of the armed struggle to free their homeland. All Israelis were guilty, Arafat told an interviewer in 1972, of wanting to destroy the Palestinian people, so all were legitimate targets. In his autobiography, Abu Iyad distinguished between "revolutionary violence" and terrorism. The former was a political act, the latter merely "an individual act committed outside the context of an organization or strategic vision." He rejected such individual acts "dictated by subjective motives" but considered revolutionary violence acceptable as long as it was "part of a large structured movement." Such violence "serves as a supplementary force" to mass struggle "and contributes, during a period of regrouping or defeat, to giving the movement a new impetus. It becomes superfluous when the grass-roots movement scores political successes on the local or international scene." Abu Iyad thus summarized various strands of revolutionary theorizing about the role of violence, applying it to the period of regrouping, if not defeat, through which the Fatah and PLO passed after their expulsion from Jordan.[9]

Whatever PLO leaders may have thought, it appeared to the United States that the PLO was regrouping through terrorism. The day after the Munich massacre, President Nixon called for measures to deter international terrorism in the United States and abroad. On September 9, 1972 the U.S. government announced the formation of an intelligence committee that would work with other nations to deter international terrorists. The committee consisted of representatives of the Central Intelligence Agency (CIA), the Federal Bureau of

Investigation (FBI), and the State Department. It was headed by a Deputy Assistant Secretary of State for Near Eastern and South Asian Affairs (a Deputy Assistant Secretary is a low rank in the bureaucratic hierarchy, suggesting the low priority the committee had on the government's agenda) and was to have the assistance of other U.S. government intelligence organizations, in addition to the CIA and FBI. The administration also announced that it was taking steps to increase protection of diplomats and "official guests" in the United States.[10]

A few weeks later, on September 25, the United States took another step in response to Munich when President Nixon created the government's first combating-terrorism organization, the Cabinet Committee on Terrorism. The Cabinet Committee consisted of the Secretaries of the State Department (Chairman), Defense, Treasury, and Transportation; the Directors of the CIA and FBI; the Attorney General; the Ambassador to the UN; and the Assistants to the President for National Security Affairs and Domestic Affairs. The President directed the Cabinet Committee to coordinate the fight against terrorism, including such activities as the collection of intelligence and the physical protection of U.S. personnel and installations abroad and foreign diplomats and diplomatic installations in the United States. The committee was also to evaluate all counterterrorism programs and activities, and, where necessary, recommend ways to make them more effective, devise procedures for reacting swiftly and effectively to acts of terrorism, make recommendations to the Director of the Office of Management and Budget concerning proposed funding of counterterrorism programs, and report to the President, from time to time, regarding the foregoing. Ambassador Armin Meyer was appointed to serve as the Chairman of the Committee's supporting Working Group, which was to consist of "personally designated senior representatives of the members of the Committee." Meyer was given the title Special Assistant to the Secretary of State for Combating Terrorism.[11]

In discharging its duties as directed by the President, the Working Group addressed a number of issues, including which government agencies should handle various terrorist incidents, visa reform, intelligence sharing within the government, consultations with allies, security of U.S. facilities abroad and of aircraft and "foreign guests" within the United States, standard operating procedures for kidnappings and other terrorist incidents, security of nuclear materials, the "tagging" of explosives and weapons for tracking, and, in the aftermath of a Pakistani discovery that Iraq had shipped weapons through its diplomatic pouch, counteracting the abuse of pouch privileges. Although these issues are recognizable for the most part as the stuff of current counterterrorism agendas, some progress has been made since these early days. This is evident if we consider the elementary initiatives that the Working Group undertook in 1972–1973. For example, an early success in improving intelligence sharing and interagency cooperation was the installation of secure communications between the Immigration and Naturalization Service and other agencies, so that inquiries about possible terrorist suspects could be handled confidentially.

Again, a major improvement in U.S. border security occurred when the Working Group arranged for the suspension of the regulation that had permitted visitors to transit the United States for up to ten days without prior approval or screening. In the past, the Working Group reported, as many as 600,000 people a year had taken advantage of this transit status.[12]

Given that the number of terrorist attacks against Americans had been growing steadily since the late 1960s (from 71 in 1968 to 225 in 1972),[13] the Nixon administration's counterterrorism efforts may appear belated and insufficient. This criticism is less compelling, however, when we remember the context in which the administration was acting. During the late 1960s and early 1970s, it was attempting to carry out a full and complex foreign policy agenda. It initiated Strategic Arms Limitation Talks with the Soviets in 1969, which led to the first U.S. Presidential visit to the Soviet Union in May 1972. It was also developing an opening to China, the initial phase of which culminated with Nixon's visit there in February 1972. As if this were not enough, it was attempting at the same time to end American involvement in the war in Vietnam through negotiations with the North Vietnamese, while dealing with growing domestic protest against the war and other domestic problems, including inflation, which led Nixon to impose wage and price controls in August 1971. Finally, there was Watergate, a scandal that began with the arrest of the Watergate burglars in June 1972 and grew to devour the Nixon administration over the next two years. It is testimony to the power of terrorism, exemplified by the televised horror of the Munich hostage-taking, that in the midst of all that the Nixon administration was doing and suffering, combating terrorism got any attention at all.

Apart from the emphasis on using international agreements to combat terrorism, the most important counterterrorism policy developed in the early 1970s was the U.S. government's insistence that it would make no concessions to terrorists. From its first experiences with hostage taking shortly after independence, the United States had tended to stand on the principle that such activities should not be rewarded by paying ransom or making concessions to the hostage takers. Both as Ambassador to France and later as President, Thomas Jefferson tried, with varying results, to avoid the common practice of paying ransom to the Barbary states. One hundred and fifty years later, when Cuban rebels took Americans hostage, John Foster Dulles announced that the United States would not give in to blackmail because doing so would only encourage others to take Americans hostage. The Eisenhower administration also refused to make concessions to East Germany to free American servicemen whose helicopter had strayed into East German territory. In both these cases, the hostages were eventually released. In 1964, when Congolese rebels took a large number of Americans and others hostage, the United States again refused to make concessions. The United States took a different approach in 1968, however, when the North Koreans seized the U.S. ship *Pueblo*. The United States eventually gave in to the North Korean demand that we admit that the ship had violated North Korean waters, although we attached to our "confession" the statement that this admission was not true. About this same time, when its diplomats were first kidnapped in Latin America, the United States, like all other governments at the time, encouraged the host government to meet the kidnappers' demands. This occurred, for example, when Ambassador Elbrick was kidnapped in Brazil in September 1969 and again in Guatemala in March 1970, when the labor attaché was kidnapped. The United States broke with the prevailing practice, becoming the first government not to request that another government ransom its personnel when the Tupamaros kidnapped and eventually killed the American police advisor, Dan Mitrione, in Uruguay in July 1970. At the time, this refusal to make concessions to Mitrione's kidnappers was seen as an exception and not a precedent that established a fixed policy. Over the next several years, however, in response to the growing number of kidnapping incidents, American policy gradually returned to its traditional position of refusing to meet hostage takers' demands. According to one commentator, this "no concessions" policy developed at the insistence of Henry Kissinger, in emulation of what was supposedly the Israeli policy. After first agreeing to terrorists' demands, the Israelis had decided beginning in late 1969 to stop making concessions.[14]

Whether or not Kissinger was its author, by early 1973, "no concessions" had become American policy. The Working Group prepared a message to this effect to be sent to U.S. diplomatic posts around the world, but neither Secretary of State Rogers nor any other senior official in the State Department would sign it, apparently because the policy of no concessions appeared too callous. At this point, however, "no concessions" had not yet been publicly announced as U.S. policy. This silence was maintained in order to preserve flexibility. As long as the policy was not public, concessions could be made, if particular circumstances warranted, without undermining the policy. The first kidnapping that took place after the no concessions policy was established occurred in Haiti. When Ambassador Knox was held hostage in January 1973, the Haitian government almost immediately decided on its own to make concessions, although later in the incident it was informed that this was not U.S. policy. In studying lessons learned from this episode, the Working Group decided to make it standard practice to notify a host government as early as possible in a hostage situation that it was not U.S. policy to make concessions to kidnappers.[15]

The new policy received an early and horrible test when Black September terrorists seized the Saudi Embassy in Khartoum on March 1, 1973, took several people hostage (including Charge Curtis Moore and incoming Ambassador Cleo Noel) and eventually executed Moore, Noel, and the Belgian Chargé, Guy Eid (some contend at the order of Arafat). According to one participant handling the U.S. response, the Sudanese government was informed right away that U.S. government policy was not to make concessions but was not pressured to adopt this policy as its own. The United States did talk with the terrorists through third parties, indicating that it had no objection to their receiving free passage to another country in exchange for the hostages but also indicating that it would not meet their demands, including the release of Abou Daoud (a Black September leader who had been captured in Jordan a month earlier heading a hit team that was to attack Jordanian and American targets) and Sirhan Sirhan (the assassin of Robert Kennedy). Talks with the terrorists through intermediaries continued, with deadlines being extended and various conditions for free passage being discussed. As these talks went on, President Nixon declared at a news conference that the U.S. government would not pay ransom or submit to blackmail. The terrorists later claimed that Nixon's remark influenced their decision to execute Moore, Noel, and Eid. Whether or not this was the case, soon after the remark, the terrorists announced that the executions had taken place.[16]

The tragedy in Khartoum caused some ill-feeling in the Foreign Service and raised questions about the effectiveness of a policy of no concessions but did not dissuade the United States from continuing it. In the years following Khartoum, "no concessions" was featured as a prominent part of U.S. policy. Then Secretary of State Kissinger was drawn into defending the policy publicly on two occasions in 1975: first, when the U.S. Ambassador to Tanzania was recalled after helping arrange for the payment of ransom to free Americans held hostage by Marxist guerrillas during the summer, and then again later in the year when Americans were held hostage in Ethiopia. In the Tanzanian case, Kissinger attempted to discipline the Ambassador for not following the U.S. government's policy of not making concessions or paying ransom. In both cases, he argued that concessions or ransoms would only encourage terrorists to target Americans again. Making concessions "may save lives in one place [but only] at the risk of hundreds of lives everywhere else."[17]

By the end of 1975, then, the U.S. government had defined terrorism as criminal; had in place two policies to combat it ("no concessions" and the use of international agreements and organizations); had made some rudimentary progress toward improving interagency coordination and security at facilities abroad and in the United States; and had set up a Nuclear Emergency Support Team (NEST) to handle the threat of terrorists using a nuclear device. In a further development of the no concessions policy, the United States now publicly urged this policy "on other governments, private companies, and individuals" but noted that it was the responsibility of the host nation to decide if it would make concessions. It also continued to acknowledge that there were underlying causes of terrorism, encouraging and assisting "other nations to alleviate the inequities and frustrations from which international terrorism mainly—though by no means entirely—arises." The U.S. government reckoned that terrorism, even for Palestinians, had been a failure but, looking to the future, feared that new weapons, such as portable missiles and even nuclear materials or chemical and biological agents, would increase the lethality of terrorism. This concern reflected the fact that terrorist groups had by the mid-1970s already tried to acquire these materials and agents and that technology was making it easier to make and use them. State-sponsored terrorism ("international terrorist groups for hire") was noted as an incipient development, a way for weaker states to gain their objectives without resort to open warfare.[18]

The contention that terrorism was a failure even for Palestinians reflected perhaps the fact that attacks against Americans had declined in 1974–1975 from the peak years of the early 1970s. But this was the first evidence of a pattern that was to emerge over the years—a period of increased terrorist activity followed by a lull. Apparently, this decline in terrorism in the mid-1970s suggested that the Palestinians realized that they could not get what they wanted through terrorism. This conclusion would only be half right, however. Fatah's terrorism campaign hurt the PLO by generating international sympathy for Israel and damaging the PLO's relations with countries, not least of all the United States, whose help it needed if it were ever to achieve its objective of destroying Israel. But the damage to the PLO's international standing was hardly overwhelming. Arafat was invited to address the UN General Assembly in November 1974, after all. In addition, by increasing Fatah's standing as a revolutionary organization, the campaign increased Fatah's prestige in the Palestinian movement. Since it and the PLO had regrouped by establishing bases in Lebanon from which to attack Israel, it no longer needed international terrorism as much as it had right after its ignominious expulsion from Jordan. Accordingly, Fatah decided in 1974 to deemphasize international terrorism, discontinuing the use of the cover organization Black September. An additional reason for this decision may have been the meeting in November 1973 in Morocco between a close associate of Arafat's and then Deputy CIA Director Vernon Walters. According to his own account, Walters warned the PLO to stop attacking Americans. Reportedly, Fatah subsequently disavowed an attack on a TWA plane carried out in the name of Black September and in 1974 executed a renegade member for conducting terrorist attacks contrary to Fatah's interests a few days after the renegade's group had blown up a TWA plane over the Ionian sea. It also reportedly even helped protect Henry Kissinger during a trip to Beirut in late 1973 and other American diplomats in Beirut after 1975.[19]

The meeting between Walters and the PLO casts a peculiar light on the claim that Palestinian terrorism was a failure. As Kissinger points out, in 1973, the PLO had not yet been recognized politically even by the Arab states; the UN treated Palestinians only as refugees. "Before 1973," Kissinger remarks, "the PLO rarely intruded into international negotiations." In addition, Israel, according to Kissinger, considered the PLO gaining "any legitimacy whatever" a threat to its survival. Yet on November 3, 1973, eight months after it had murdered two American diplomats in Khartoum, the PLO met with the Deputy Director of the CIA. In his account of this first meeting and subsequent contacts, Kissinger minimizes their importance. Walters only listened; no negotiations took place. Kissinger stresses that the United States took steps to make sure that interested third parties understood the limited nature of the contacts. But given the status of the PLO at the time, a meeting with an official of Walters's stature (he was known as an arranger of secret deals) had great significance even if all the participants did was exchange business cards. In fact, however, more than that happened. It is clear from Kissinger's account that, at a minimum, an implicit negotiation took place. Both sides wanted things the other side could give and both were willing to give up something in return. The PLO wanted a place in the Middle East negotiations and American help in achieving some of its goals. To encourage the Americans to give it these things, it could stop causing trouble in Arab politics and stop killing Americans. As Kissinger points out, "the PLO had a high potential for causing trouble all over the Arab world. We wanted it to be on its best behavior during the delicate early stages of our approaches to Egypt and while we were seeking Saudi support." A meeting with an official representative of the United States, especially with one from whose aura something more than a mere exchange of information could be spun, despite official U.S. explanations, was a gain for the PLO sufficient to make it promise to behave in return. In short, given the PLO's status and Israel's opposition, the meeting with Walters was a concession to the PLO and a success for its strategy of terrorism, the first success of terrorism against an important U.S. policy initiative.[20]

Even if Fatah had given up international terrorism and, of special interest to the United States, attacks on Americans, other groups in the PLO and other terrorist organizations had not. On May 4, 1973, the People's Revolutionary Armed Forces kidnapped the American Consul General in Guadalajara, Mexico, Terence G. Leonhardy. He was released after the Mexican government met the kidnappers' demands and Leonhardy's wife paid a ransom. In February 1974, the People's Resistance Organized Army exploded four bombs at a Dow chemical plant in Greece. In February 1975, the Arab Communist Organization bombed the Tyre, Lebanon office of the American Life Insurance Company. One of the leaders of this group remarked that she became a communist "after learning how much money Americans spend on pet food in a starving world." Fifteen days later, Montoneros guerrillas kidnapped John Patrick Egan, the U.S. consular agent in Cordoba, Argentina. When the government of Argentina refused to meet their demands, they killed him. In October 1975, the PFLP kidnapped Charles Gallagher and William Dykes of the U.S. Information Agency in Beirut, releasing them four months later. In December 1975, the Greek leftist group November 17, named for the date of a student uprising in 1973 against the military regime, killed CIA Station Chief Richard Welch in Athens.[21]

Given such terrorist attacks, the continuing problems with the U.S. government's counterterrorism effort were worrisome. Efforts to improve international cooperation against terrorism at the UN and other international fora continued to meet resistance based on the criticisms that terrorism for the sake of a just cause like self-determination could not be considered criminal and that states as well as subnational groups were capable of terrorism. Bilateral efforts against terrorism also ran into difficulty because European states, for example, feared retaliation or the loss of Middle East oil and markets. The Working Group had continued to meet (101 times by February 1976) and had grown in size (from ten members originally to twenty-two by February 1976), but the Coordinator for Combating Terrorism who chaired it had only a small staff (Meyer had one mid-grade officer and a secretary; Ambassador Quainton, the incumbent from 1978 to 1981, had a staff of six), no budget of his own, and "lacked sufficient rank to impose [his] will on officials in other departments." With such limited bureaucratic power, he could do little to get agencies to care about terrorism more than they did. In addition, critics argued that members of the Working Group were not sharing information and that the Group had become too large to promote effective coordination. Moreover, with the level of terrorist attacks having declined in the mid-1970s and no general sense that terrorism posed a great threat to the United States, there was little cabinet-level interest in combating terrorism and thus little top-down pressure to make the various agencies solve these problems. For example, the Cabinet- level committee met only once before it was disbanded in 1977. Another sign that the government's effort to combat terrorism lacked drive was the rapidity with which Working Group Coordinators came and went. A new one had been named almost every year from 1972 to 1978. Finally, one analyst believed that authority to respond during a terrorist incident had not been clearly assigned among the various agencies involved in combating terrorism.[22]

The Carter administration attempted to remedy some of these problems by reorganizing interagency counterterrorism mechanisms. After assuming office, it undertook a review of the government's counterterrorism organization and capabilities (Presidential Review Memorandum 30).[23] As a result, President Carter dismantled the Cabinet Committee to Combat Terrorism and its Working Group, transferring primary responsibility for counterterrorism to the National Security Council (NSC) and, for the management of crises, to what came to be called the lead agencies. These agencies were the State Department for international incidents, the Justice Department and FBI for domestic incidents, and the Federal Aviation Administration (FAA) for domestic aircraft hijacking. The NSC provided general guidance to the lead agencies through the NSC's Special Coordination Committee (SCC), which was chaired by the National Security Advisor. The SCC was not intended to be involved in managing individual terrorist incidents, except "in the event of a major terrorist incident requiring highest-level decisions." For more routine terrorist matters, the Carter administration established two interagency bodies: a senior interagency Ex- ecutive Committee and a Working Group on Terrorism. Established in September 1977, the Executive Committee consisted of senior representatives (Assistant Secretaries) from the Departments of State (chairman), Justice (vice-chairman), Defense, Energy, Transportation, and Treasury, and from the CIA and the NSC staff. Representatives from the FBI and the Joint Staff also "participate[d] on a regular basis." The Working Group had representatives from approximately twenty additional departments and agencies. It was chaired by the State Department.   The Vice-Chairman was the Justice Department representative.[24]

The Carter interagency plan gave each level of its counterterrorism hierarchy specific functions.   The SCC was responsible for supervising the Executive Committee, resolving jurisdictional disputes that might arise during a terrorist incident, and assuring that counterterrorism programs and plans were coordinated among the concerned agencies.   The Executive Committee was responsible for counterterrorism policy and contingency planning, particularly sorting out command and control arrangements.   The Working Group provided an arena for the exchange of information and for the development of working relationships among all the various agencies involved in counterterrorism, but it also did some "drafting and planning."   Neither the Executive Committee nor the Working Group managed terrorist incidents.   Both could provide staff support for those who did: the lead agencies and the SCC.   In addition, an intelligence coordination committee, similar to the one set up under the Nixon administration, continued to function in the Carter administration, focusing attention on terrorism, improving the flow of intelligence, and handling any special intelligence issues referred to it by the Working Group.[25]

According to participants in the Working Group, its large size was debilitating.   There were too many players for work to be efficient, let alone for coordination to be effective.   This problem was overcome to some extent by the Executive Committee, which consisted of only the key agencies involved in counterterrorism.   This made it more efficient than the Working Group and improved coordination between agencies.   The Carter administration also addressed the unwieldy size of the Working Group by dividing it, in 1978, into five standing committees to review preparedness and to develop policy recommendations for the full Working Group and the Executive Committee. The committees' names and their duties give some sense of how complex the counterterrorism effort had gotten in just six years.   The Research and Development Committee was responsible for coordinating federal antiterrorism research, responding to research proposals from private individuals and organizations, and carrying out projects assigned by the Working Group and member agencies.   The (Domestic) Security Policy Committee took care of border management, the exchange of operational information between agencies, and the vulnerability analysis of potential U.S. targets.   The (Foreign) Security Policy Committee worked to strengthen security at U.S. properties overseas, train U.S. government employees stationed overseas, provide assistance to American businessmen who worked overseas, and improve interagency cooperation in Washington and abroad.   The Contingency Planning and Crisis Management Committee was responsible for ensuring that all agencies had up-to-date contingency plans for incident management, training crisis managers, making available adequate intelligence for crisis management, and ensuring that there was adequate data storage and retrieval.   The Public Information Committee reviewed media guidelines for terrorist incidents, considered ways to prepare government officials to deal with the media during an incident, and identified the most useful way to respond to media interest in terrorism. The International Initiatives Committee explored new ways to improve multilateral counterterrorism efforts, including using international organizations and proposing new international conventions.[26]

This proliferation of committees was not simply a bureaucratic reflex. One might question the number of committees and how the Carter administration tried to organize its overall counterterrorism effort, but none of the committees or their aforementioned tasks were manifestly irrelevant to that effort. By the mid-1970s, the threat of nuclear, chemical, or biological terrorism was being studied and planned for; terrorists had used shoulder-fired missiles, supplied by Libya, to attack aircraft on the ground and suitcase bombs to blow them out of the sky; American personnel and businesses were still under attack; and American facilities were still vulnerable.[27] All of this was taking place under the scrutiny of media significantly more present and less respectful of authority than only a decade before. In addition, the three branches of the federal government, as always to varying degrees and in different ways independent of the others, could make conflicting decisions about terrorism policy or operations. Finally, our federal system of government meant that the national government shared power with state governments, who themselves had to work with local authorities. Terrorism and the business of responding to it had become complex, as complex as the committee and interagency structure developed by the Carter administration.

The Carter administration's reworking of the interagency process did not always produce well-coordinated efforts, as a hostage incident at the German consulate in Chicago demonstrates. On August 17, 1978, two men walked into the Consulate and took the staff hostage in an attempt to force the release of Stepjan Bilandzic, reportedly the founder of the Croatian National Resistance, who was being held in West Germany for the attempted murder of a Yugoslav diplomat. As the U.S. government began to respond, the State Department claimed the lead because foreign diplomats were involved, while the FBI claimed the lead because the incident was in the United States. The FBI eventually prevailed. In another example of a lack of coordination, a State Department official recalls receiving briefings from two different military units each of whom claimed to be the lead unit for military counterterrorism operations and disparaged the capabilities of the other. Once the military sorted out this problem, good working relations developed between the military counterterrorism unit and the State Department office responsible for counterterrorism, according to this official. During the Iranian hostage crisis, working-level cooperation between the State and Defense Departments was restricted by Secretary of State Vance's decision that the sensitivity of the crisis and the need to keep the State Department's role in it focused at the highest level required that certain information pertaining to the hostages be passed to Defense only by the Secretary's office.[28]

In addition to trying to improve interagency coordination and the management of terrorist incidents, the Carter administration also modified U.S. counterterrorism policy and methods in certain respects, while maintaining the emphasis on no concessions and on negotiating and enforcing international conventions against terrorism. Compared to the pronouncements of the Nixon-Ford years, those of the Carter administration put less emphasis on the criminality of terrorism and more on its political character. Correspondingly, the administration made a greater point than its predecessors of the need to address the underlying causes of terrorism, referring in congressional testimony to the Camp David Agreement and its efforts to foster a peaceful transition to majority rule in South Africa as examples of this policy in action.[29]

The Carter administration also presided over the addition of two new weapons to the U.S. government's counterterrorism arsenal: the use of economic sanctions and the decision to develop a hostage rescue capability. Sanctions developed as a way to combat state support for terrorism. Such support was not new in the mid- or late 1970s. Almost from the moment he led the coup that overthrew the Libyan monarchy in 1969, Muammar Qadaffi had begun supporting terrorists. In 1972, he set up his own group that subsequently targeted and killed Americans. At the time of the Khartoum murders in 1973, there were reports that Libya had supported the terrorists. The Soviet Union, Syria, and Iraq were also early supporters of terrorism (the latter two each bankrolled their own Palestinian terrorist organizations). As evidence of this support accumulated, official comments took note of it. In February 1976, the State Department's coordinator for counterterrorism said that state support for terrorism was in an incipient stage. But in April 1976, the CIA published a research report claiming that the Soviet Union had been supporting terrorism since 1969. By 1977, the State Department's coordinator was testifying before Congress that state support for terrorism "spans a wide spectrum of activities." Secretary Vance spoke of governments that supported terrorism and of others that refused to work against it in congressional testimony in 1978. Having acknowledged that states were supporting terrorism, the question was what to do about it. Neither of the two methods that the U.S. government first used to combat terrorism, "no concessions" and international conventions, made states pay for supporting terrorism. Sanctions promised to do that. Using sanctions to combat terrorism was not an administration initiative, however. Both in acknowledging the role of state support and in taking steps to do something about it, the executive branch lagged behind Congress. The State Department, for example, feared that sanctions would damage bilateral relations and thus the chance to use diplomacy to persuade states to pursue policies friendly to the United States. The Commerce Department feared the effects of sanctions on trade. In the absence of executive branch support, Congress became the driving force behind using sanctions as a tool to combat terrorism.[30]

The U.S. government had actually placed sanctions on Libya in 1973 (barring military sales) because of its support for terrorism, but this did not set a precedent. The Ford administration, for example, did not impose sanctions allowed under the 1974 Antihijacking Act, and both the Ford and Carter administrations allowed the sale of civilian aircraft to Libya. The Carter administration blocked such sales in March 1978 but allowed them again in November of that year, after consultations with Congress and the Commerce Department, when it received assurances from the Libyans that the planes in question would not be used for military purposes. Despite the administration's reluctance to use sanctions and its objection to congressionally mandated sanctions as an improper restriction on the President's authority to conduct foreign affairs, Congress pressed ahead throughout the 1970s with laws that imposed sanctions on state sponsors of terrorism. It prohibited foreign assistance (1976), security assistance (1977), and other aid (1977 and 1978) to states that supported terrorism, for example. These measures were considered largely ineffective, however, because state sponsors did not receive any American foreign or security assistance to begin with or because the sums they received were too small to give the United States any leverage. Consequently, as both the number of terrorist attacks and congressional frustration over what it felt were faltering efforts to counter them rose in the late 1970s, Congress turned to export controls. In 1979, it passed the Fenwick Amendment to the Export Administration Act, which required the Secretary of State to notify Congress before approving an export license for goods valued at more than $7,000 destined for countries that supported terrorism. The Secretary, to whom Congress had given the authority to designate which states sponsored terrorism, so designated Libya, Syria, Iraq, and South Yemen. Sanctions were imposed on all four following passage of the law.[31]

Recognizing the role of state sponsors and taking steps to put pressure on them was an important step forward in the efforts of the United States to combat terrorism. State support is what makes international terrorism the problem that it is. At least one terrorist has publicly acknowledged this. In response to an interviewer's remark that the "new terrorists" were "efficient and well-organized professionals," Abu Abbas, the organizer of the hijacking of the *Achille Lauro,* during which a crippled American, Leon Klinghofer, was shot and thrown overboard, noted that "it is impossible to organize costly overseas attacks without backing from a state's [intelligence] service." State support gave terrorists money, weapons, and training. It offered them the protection of diplomatic passports for their travel and diplomatic pouches for their weapons and explosives. It provided embassies as staging points for attacks and national territory as safe havens from prosecution or reprisal. Finally, it furnished terrorists with intelligence from the supporting governments and those allied or friendly with it. With this support, the terrorists built organizations that had resiliency and durability because of counterintelligence capabilities and training programs and, by the division of skilled labor, expertise in the destructive arts greater than any individual could muster. For these reasons, state-sponsored terrorist organizations became formidable adversaries. In the years following the 1973 Arab Israeli War, oil price increases gave several of the state sponsors of these groups all the financial resources they could use to support their terrorist allies. Although not a decisive weapon in the fight against terrorism, sanctions were a useful and necessary step to counter this state support. But the new weapon was not without its opponents. Imposition of sanctions on Libya in 1978 and again in 1979 brought immediate criticism from the businesses who were denied exports to Libya, their representatives and senators, and the Commerce Department.[32]

The second innovation in counterterrorism policy developed during the Carter administration was the option of using force to rescue hostages in the event their captors would not release them and their lives were in imminent danger. Impressed by the Israeli rescue at Entebbe (July 1976) and the German operation in Mogadishu (October 1977), the Carter administration encouraged the military's efforts to organize forces that could undertake similar operations. The U.S. military's capabilities in this regard became a matter of public record in May 1977, when that month's issue of *Army* carried an article describing the Army's two Ranger Battalions. The author quoted the First Battalion commander, who remarked that "the Entebbe thing is just what we're trained to do," described two hostage rescue training exercises (one a rescue of hostages from a desert camp, the other the rescue of hostages from an oil rig), and quoted a Pentagon directive ordering the Rangers to be ready to conduct operations "against nuclear storage sites, missile sites, [and] key enemy personnel or resources," as well as to rescue "political hostages." Later that year, "Pentagon sources" told the *New York Times* that the Ranger Battalions had the mission of "dealing with terrorist incidents involving Americans abroad." Pentagon officials told the *Times* that the United States had a specially trained unit, drawing on all the services, to combat terrorism but the sources explained that Air Force and Navy involvement in counterterrorism was primarily to transport the Rangers. It was to such capabilities, by then resident in special units other than the Rangers, that the State Department's Director for Combating Terrorism referred when in 1979 he listed for the first time as part of the U.S. government's counterterrorism strategy "selective and flexible tactical response capabilities," and spoke of "readily available special units to be deployed on rescue or other missions" and "FBI and military . . . teams, skilled in the use of special weapons and tactics, which can be used in the event an incident cannot be resolved by negotiations."[33]

Near the end of its time in office, the Carter administration offered what was in effect a summary of its accomplishments in the effort to counter terrorism. In testimony before Congress in May 1980, Ambassador Quainton listed those areas in which progress had been made. He mentioned increasing adherence to international conventions and agreements, reinforcing the policy of no concessions, improving security at U.S. facilities abroad and infrastructure targets at home (such as the electrical power system) improving intelligence and interagency coordination, and examining possible responses to terrorist use of weapons of mass destruction (WMD). These were all areas in which the U.S. government had been at work since 1972 and would remain at work through the next decade. Indeed, Ambassador Quainton stressed that more work needed to be done in each of these areas.[34]

Critics of the administration's efforts agreed. As early as 1978, newspaper articles appeared recounting the views of various unnamed civilian and military officials to the effect that the administration was not doing enough to prepare the U.S. government to combat terrorism. According to these experts, neither the military nor the FBI hostage rescue teams were adequately trained, nor did they have sufficient intelligence support. The critics also complained that the administration's reorganization had not increased the interagency coordination necessary for success at countering terrorism. They cited the fact that different agencies had responsibility for different terrorist incidents as proof that U.S. government efforts were not coordinated. In addition, they pointed out that those in charge of counterterrorism at the State Department and the NSC had no previous experience dealing with terrorism and that they had not bothered to attend capabilities exercises to gain a better understanding of military and FBI operational capabilities. Finally, they opined that the administration had not given the threat from terrorism high enough priority, noting that the Director of the State Department's counterterrorism office had changed three times in three years in the mid-1970s. The questioning at congressional hearings in the late 1970s suggested that many Congressmen and Senators shared some of the views of these critics.[35]

Judging by the rate at which international terrorist incidents were occurring in the late 1970s, the critics seemed to have a point. There were more attacks in 1978 than in any year since recordkeeping had begun in 1968. More attacks occurred in 1980 and 1981 than in any other years except 1972 and 1978. More of these attacks were causing casualties than earlier in the 1970s, and they targeted Americans more often than any other nationality. In 1980, two out of every five terrorist attacks were against American persons or property. In these years, there were more attacks on private citizens and businessmen and their offices and other facilities than in the early 1970s and somewhat fewer (except in 1980) on diplomatic or military personnel, suggesting that efforts to improve the security of official representatives and facilities abroad were having a beneficial effect. Still, American officials were targeted successfully by terrorists or caught up in their attacks. On February 14, 1979, Ambassador to Afghanistan Adolph Dubs was kidnapped in Kabul and then killed when the Afghanis tried to rescue him. On the same day, "urban guerrillas" seized the U.S. Embassy in Tehran, holding the Ambassador, Arthur Sullivan, and 101 members of the staff hostage for two hours before militia loyal to the new government of Ayotollah Khomeini fought the guerrillas and won the Americans' release. A year later, in Bogota, M-19 terrorists took Ambassador Diego Ascencio and other diplomats hostage at a reception. Ascencio was held until April 27, when he and the other remaining hostages were released in return for a ransom and safe passage to Cuba for the terrorists. Six months later, unknown assailants fired at the car in which Ambassador to Lebanon John Gunther Dean was riding. Also in these years, domestic turmoil in Turkey and Iran led to a number of attacks on American officials and businessmen.[36]

Although the rising number of terrorist attacks in the late 1970s appeared to support the critics of the Carter administration's efforts against terrorism, their criticisms were misleading. For example, some criticism of governmental organization appears based on ignorance of what came to be known as the lead agency concept. Designating different agencies to take the lead in different kinds of terrorist incidents may or may not be a good way to organize a government to combat terrorism, but it is not necessarily a sign of disorganization. Nor should such a criticism be made without pointing out the long-standing American tradition of dividing the powers of government and limiting the involvement of the military in law enforcement. Moreover, some of the criticism, such as that directed by name at the commander of the military's newest counterterrorism force, appears to have been the result of professional jealousy. Finally, by the time it left office, the Carter administration had done a good deal to improve the U.S. government's counterterrorism capability. In addition to the organizational changes and tactical response capabilities already mentioned, the Carter administration connected the military's new hostage rescue capabilities to the Executive Committee, sending the State Department's Counterterrorism Coordinator on exercises with the military units and providing him with a direct communications link to the NSC; organized terrorist incident exercises (in response to the somewhat flawed handling of the kidnapping and execution of Ambassador Dubs in Afghanistan) that included the State Department, the NSC, and the Joint Staff; began counterterrorism training programs for other countries; increased support for the NEST; and conducted planning and exercises to examine possible responses to terrorist use of WMD.[37]

Although contemporary criticisms of the Carter administration's counterterrorism efforts were largely misguided, in retrospect one criticism can be made with some accuracy, although the fault was not peculiar to the Carter administration. The reorganization of the counterterrorism apparatus in 1977 and further refinements in 1978 never produced a fully responsive, efficient organization. According to the Carter administration's plan, the highest-ranking officials regularly attending counterterrorism meetings were Assistant Secretaries, a step higher in the bureaucracy than the official in charge of the interagency counterterrorism group in the Nixon-Ford years. But even if these officials attended as planned, this was still not sufficient clout to get the bureaucracy to respond smoothly on difficult issues. Making matters worse was the absence of a central authority to organize all the agencies and departments that had a hand in counterterrorism. The State Department could not impose its views or decisions on other agencies. The NSC, which might have played some sort of organizing or managing role, did not do so, for several reasons. First, until the Iran hostage incident, there was not enough cabinet-level interest in counterterrorism to make it an issue of overriding importance for the NSC staff. Second, the individual responsible for counterterrorism at the NSC was skeptical of the claims made about terrorism by many so-called terrorism experts. He believed that what was called terrorism was either a crime, when committed within the United States, or, when committed overseas, a political-military problem. In either case, it required no special arrangements. Established procedures for dealing with both crime and political-military problems were sufficient in his view. Finally, he wanted to keep management of counterterrorism away from the White House to protect the President from involving himself in counterterrorism incidents. Any direct involvement by the President, the NSC official thought, would give terrorism too high a profile, only encouraging terrorists to attack Americans. For these reasons, the NSC did not have as strong a role in the Carter administration's counterterrorism effort as it did in the Reagan administration's. The interagency organizations, the Executive Committee and the Working Group, functioned but were handicapped by the lack of cabinet-level interest that would have given the efforts of lower-ranking officials more momentum. All agencies accepted the lead agency concept, but working out the details was an ongoing process, as the incident at the German consulate in Chicago suggests.[38]

Central authority in national security matters has been a problem for all administrations. Nor is confusion between agencies necessarily a sign of incompetent management in a government whose agencies have unavoidably overlapping responsibilities and respond to complex problems. The Carter administration's national security organization had anticipated conflicts between agencies and, as we have noted, gave the SCC the job of sorting them out. Inevitably, this had to be done as problems arose because no one could have anticipated all the possible issues associated with institutionalizing the lead agency concept. Indeed, working out the details of this concept continued for years after the Carter administration left office and is still, in some respects, a work in progress. The problem, then, was not, as the critics contended, the lead agency concept itself or the Carter administration's NSC structure, but a typical national security problem. Until the Iran hostage crisis, there was not enough cabinet-level interest in terrorism in the Carter administration to provide strong central guidance to counterterrorism efforts or a motive for all levels of the bureaucracy to cooperate. The highest-ranking members of the Carter administration did not consider combating terrorism a higher priority than negotiating a strategic arms agreement with the Soviet Union, peace in the Middle East, or a new Panama Canal treaty; renewing the opening to China; encouraging respect for human rights; protecting the environment; rejuvenating NATO and deciding whether or not to deploy the neutron bomb; articulating a new strategic doctrine; and responding to upheaval in Iran, the Soviet invasion of Afghanistan and a number of other crises and events, from Cuban soldiers in the Horn of Africa to eroding Communist Party control in Poland.[39] Should the Carter administration have given counterterrorism a higher priority than these issues and initiatives? Not self-evidently. Moreover, terrorism had this lower priority not because Carter administration officials were blind to the results of terrorism but because they tended to see it as a problem that grew out of other problems. In this sense it was a peripheral or secondary problem, best treated by attacking the primary problems which generated it. Dealing with these problems is where the Carter administration put its emphasis. Terrorism would not have a higher priority until an administration came along that saw terrorism as a problem in itself, as a primary weapon in a war being waged against the United States, a view that prevailed among some of the key officials of the Reagan administration.

In addition to problems generated by a lack of cabinet-level interest, the Carter administration's counterterrorism effort also suffered from an inability to adhere consistently to its policy of making no concessions to terrorists. The Ford administration had had a similar problem. Although Secretary of State Kissinger had tried to punish the U.S. Ambassador to Tanzania for bargaining with terrorists, the Ambassador's perceived success led officials in the State Department to rethink the policy of not negotiating with terrorists. In early 1976, U.S. government officials revealed that a confidential conference at the State Department had discussed a more flexible policy of responding to terrorist demands and that this revised policy would probably be put into effect. When the Carter administration came to office, it insisted, as the Nixon and Ford administrations had, that the U.S. would not pay ransom or make concessions to terrorists. But the debate on this issue continued. A Defense Department memo from 1977 responded with strong support for the no concessions policy to a RAND report being discussed in interagency circles that argued for a flexible response to terrorist demands. While "no concessions" remained official U.S. government policy, it was not always followed. When Diego Ascencio was taken hostage, the U.S. government urged the Colombians to talk with the terrorists in order to resolve the crisis, although no pressure was brought on the Colombians to make specific concessions, according to a State Department official. The *Washington Post* reported that Secretary of State Vance told the Austrian government, whose Ambassador was also being held by M-19 terrorists, that the United States had asked the Colombians to negotiate with the terrorists.[40]

Whatever one ultimately concludes about the Carter administration's counterterrorism effort—and it had some significant accomplishments—this effort and everything else that the administration achieved was overshadowed by the seizure of the U.S. Embassy in Iran on November 4, 1979 and the ensuing hostage drama. From having been too disengaged with terrorism, the highest levels of the Carter administration, including the President himself, became too engaged. Carter publicly put himself in charge of the hostage crisis, making his Presidency hostage to the fate of the hostages. In keeping with its approach to similar situations, the administration initially focused on negotiations. To gain some leverage on the Iranian government, it imposed a series of sanctions, such as prohibiting the importation of Iranian oil and freezing all Iranian assets in the United States. As the chaos of internal Iranian politics made a negotiated settlement increasingly unlikely, the Carter administration considered the use of force more seriously. When finally undertaken, the effort to rescue the hostages resulted in a spectacular failure. The sight of burned-out helicopters and the charred remains of American servicemen was a sharp contrast to the successes that the Israelis and Germans had enjoyed in their rescue efforts.

In a review of the major developments of the 1970s, published in late 1979, the *New York Times* called terrorism "almost a commonplace," describing it as a leitmotif of the age. Against this background, according to the *Times*, the seizure of the American Embassy in Tehran on November 4, 1979 had only one novel element: the unambiguous use of terrorism as a weapon of state. The *Washington Post*'s reporting agreed with the *Times*' commentary. In an article published eighteen days after the takeover, the *Post* summarized the views of various terrorism experts. According to several of them, the hostage crisis showed that terrorism had become a form of "surrogate warfare." The article quoted a RAND study prepared for the State Department in 1976 as arguing that as conventional and nuclear war became too terrible or, for smaller powers, impractical, terrorism would become a form of "surrogate warfare." With the embassy takeover, according to the *Post*, this had now happened. "Terrorism," the *Post* informed its readers, "has apparently become a weapon not only of isolated groups but also of nations."[41]

Of course, as administration officials and others had been saying for some time, terrorism had been used during all of the 1970s as a weapon of state. The *Times* article was more accurate in this regard. The seizure of the Embassy in Tehran was more of what had been going on around the world for some time, except that state support for terrorism was now unambiguous. Since the mid-1960s, states had supported and sponsored terrorist attacks against the United States in an effort to undermine American policies in Europe, the Middle East, Latin America, and Asia. But the takeover did have a novel element, at least to Western observers. In the 1970s, terrorism, according to a State Department official, meant for the United States primarily Palestinian terrorism.[42] It meant terrorism in the service of a struggle for so-called national liberation. This changed with the hostage crisis. Terrorism was no longer in the service only of national liberation. It was now the tool of militant Islam and brought the United States and the West face to face with this powerful force for the first time.

As the hostage crisis continued into 1980, however, it took on another significance, for 1980 was a Presidential election year. Both the Embassy takeover and the issue of terrorism more generally were discussed in the Presidential debates. Undoubtedly, the hostage crisis helped defeat President Carter in the November election. At a minimum, it gave to terrorism a political profile that it had not had before and assured that it would have the interest of the highest levels of the U.S. government in the next administration.[43]

The higher priority that the Reagan administration accorded combating terrorism was evident from the beginning. When welcoming home the hostages on January 27, President Reagan promised that terrorists attacking Americans would suffer "swift and effective retribution," more pointed rhetoric than any President had previously used. The next day, in his first press conference, Secretary of State Alexander Haig accused the Soviet Union of supporting terrorism, as he had when leaving command of NATO, and stated that "international terrorism will take the place [in our foreign policy] of human rights [in Carter's foreign policy] . . . because it is the ultimate abuse of human rights." Three weeks later, after studying the agreements that the previous administration had made with Iran, the Reagan administration announced that it would abide by the them but made clear that it thought its predecessor had been wrong to negotiate with the Iranians, even though the agreements did not give Iran any ransom, merely returning to it Iranian money the United States had held during the crisis. The Reagan administration took the occasion of this announcement to repeat that "future acts of state-sponsored terrorism against the U.S. will meet swift and sure punishment," although it did not explain what this would mean in practice. The administration also took action. On May 6, 1981, it closed the Libyan People's Bureau or Embassy in Washington. This was the continuation of a series of actions initiated by the Carter administration to indicate to the Libyans that their support for terrorism would have a price. Other such actions included the imposition of sanctions in 1978 and 1979 and discussions in Tripoli in 1980 between a ranking State Department official and the Libyan Foreign Minister about Libya's support for terrorism.[44]

The administration's early pronouncements set the themes of the public discussion of terrorism for the first year of its tenure. Both former Secretary of State Edmund Muskie and former Deputy Secretary of State Warren Christopher, for example, responded to the new administration's rhetoric by publicly questioning "the wisdom of the Reagan administration's newly declared policy of not negotiating with terrorists," and other experts and commentators joined in. But by far the loudest and most heated discussion centered on Haig's claim that the Soviets supported terrorism. This sometimes vitriolic debate raged throughout the year. It was fueled by the slowly leaking news that William Casey, the new Director of Central Intelligence (DCI), had requested an intelligence estimate of Soviet support for terrorism after Haig's remarks. Casey rejected the first version. Apparently accepting the argument that violent acts committed in the name of national liberation were justified, its authors used a definition of terrorism that excluded violent acts with a political motive. Since the Soviets were supporting "national liberation," this meant they were not supporting terrorism. Going to the opposite extreme, the second version seemed to count all violent acts as terrorism, which allowed the conclusion that the Russians supported terrorism but implicitly required labeling George Washington a terrorist as well. A third version, using a definition much like the one now in use (that terrorism is politically motivated violence against noncombatants intended to influence an audience), concluded that the Soviet Union did support terrorism but that its support did not alone explain the prominence of terrorism. The controversy within the intelligence community and the government sparked by the estimate featured prominently in press coverage, as did the views of assorted editorial writers and academics, one of whom, skeptical of administration claims about Soviet involvement, "urged that 'rigorous scholarly scrutiny' be applied to suggestions that Soviet leaders had overcome doctrinal inhibitions about terrorism as a revolutionary technique."[45]

Scholarly skepticism about Soviet support for terrorism followed from taking seriously the orthodox Marxist view that revolution would come about inevitably as the result of historical processes and did not need to be coaxed into existence prematurely by "infantile leftists," as they were called by the orthodox. Perhaps we can ascribe scholarly gullibility in this matter to certain academic prejudices, but the controversy over Soviet support for terrorism in the intelligence community and the U.S. government in 1981 is harder to understand. The CIA's 1976 research paper had elicited no such controversy. The difference between 1976 and 1981, however, was an administration that had publicly reached a conclusion critical of the Soviets and then appeared to ask for an analysis to support it. This seemed to some analysts to violate the fundamental rule that analysis should be separate from policy and political influence. Perhaps they were reluctant, therefore, to give the administration what it wanted. Some of this resistance may also have been what always arises as a new administration sweeps into power, contemptuous of its supposedly bumbling predecessors. Those who make up the permanent government are seldom pleased to be classed with the bumblers or the untrustworthy, as they invariably seem to be by their new political bosses, and they react accordingly. Finally, some critics of the U.S. intelligence community would point to the ethos and outlook of analysts to explain why some were reluctant to conclude that the Soviets were supporters of terrorism. According to these critics, the CIA's analysts tend, because of their upbringing, education, and professional associations, to be liberal internationalists, who, when looking at the Soviets, see themselves. The Soviet use of terrorism, like the Soviet refusal to accept mutual assured destruction, would destabilize the world order. Since this makes no sense from the perspective of the liberal internationalist, it must not be Moscow's policy.[46]

Whatever may have caused the controversy, it should now be put to rest, since the Soviets' own documents have proven them to be supporters of terrorism. As part of his effort to discredit the Communist Party, Russian President Boris Yeltsin, in 1992, released Central Committee documents proving Soviet support for terrorism. One document from May 16, 1975 recorded the Central Committee's decision to give arms to the PFLP. According to the document, the weapons were "to continue the 'oil war' by special means, accomplishing actions against U.S. and Israeli personnel in third countries and conducting terrorist activities." The collapse of the Soviet empire has also allowed its former European members to release documents detailing their support for terrorism. Various Eastern European countries provided training, equipment, and safe havens for terrorists in transit to or from their operations during the 1970s and 1980s. For example, a German newspaper has published minutes of a meeting in 1979 between members of the East German security service, the Stasi, and Abu Iyad, who was then Chief of Security for the PLO. Accepting the PLO's position that the "main blow . . . has to be directed against the United States," the East Germans agreed at the meeting to give the PLO explosive charges for ships, grenades, Western sniper rifles, other explosives and cadre training. Another court case in Spain has revealed that the Communist government of Poland provided arms, training and medical care to Palestinian and other terrorists.[47]

The collapse of the Soviet empire has also allowed us to put to rest another controversy of the first year of the Reagan administration: the argument over whether there was a terrorist network. Such a claim was implicit in Secretary Haig's description of the Soviet Union's sponsorship of terrorism. But the notion that there was a terrorist network received its biggest boost from the publication of Claire Sterling's book, *The Terror Network,* in 1981. Caricatured by its opponents as the view that there was a Terrorist International, with a board of directors, who had mapped out a plan and were acting on it, the terrorist network, at least as Sterling presented it, was no such thing. The evidence, she concluded, "does not prove a closely planned and centrally commanded worldwide conspiracy." But it did show that the various terrorist organizations were linked. The "network" consisted of governments and terrorist groups with compatible ends who were willing to use or to support others in the use of certain violent means in hopes of achieving these ends. For example, according to some of the German Red Army Faction terrorists who participated, the government of what was then called South Yemen provided training facilities and safe haven for a variety of terrorist groups in the 1970s, including the Irish Republican Army (IRA) and Basque separatists. Through the Stasi, the East Germans supported this work, in part by training South Yemen's "fraternal" intelligence service.[48]

Information revealed in a German court case in 1994 gives some sense of how this network functioned and the attitudes of some of the participants. To intimidate the French government into freeing some of its members, the terrorist organization headed by "Carlos" conducted a series of bombings against French targets in 1982 and 1983. One of these targets was the Maison de France in West Berlin, which was bombed in August 1983. Carlos and his associates were given the explosives for the attack by the East Germans. They staged the attack from East Berlin, which was at this time, according to the testimony of former East German security officials, a hub of terrorist activity, where various groups met and exchanged information and bought weapons. After receiving the explosives from the East Germans, the Carlos group stored them at the Syrian embassy, which was itself very active in the East Berlin terrorist world.

Syrian intelligence officers stationed at the Embassy served as liaison and support officers for terrorists. Members of the Carlos group stayed in apartments and used cars provided by the Syrians. They traveled on Syrian passports and took refuge in Damascus, the Syrian capital, after the bombing. Syrian embassies in Prague, Sofia, and Budapest provided similar support to terrorist groups, support that was known to and warily tolerated by the authorities in these countries, who, while willing to use the terrorist groups, never really trusted them or the other states that supported them. Based on information found in Stasi files, the Berlin Public Prosecutor's Office issued in summer 1994 an international arrest warrant for a former Syrian Ambassador to East Berlin because of his complicity in the bombing of the Maison de France. Arrested while on official business in Vienna in October 1994, the Ambassador was subsequently released when an Austrian Court determined that he had diplomatic immunity. The press in Austria and Germany reported high level-pressure on the Austrian government from Syrian and other Arab governments to release the Ambassador.[49]

As the various terrorism controversies of the early Reagan years raged on, the government's routine bureaucratic policy statements on terrorism changed in small but significant ways. They mentioned, as had most such statements in the 1970s, the need to improve border and visa controls, crisis management, and support for the international conventions that sought to outlaw terrorist acts. The Reagan administration's statements differed from past statements, however, by putting more emphasis on state-sponsorship. They now also contained remarks such as that the U.S. government "will use all appropriate resources at our disposal, be they diplomatic, political, economic, or military, to respond to" acts of state-sponsored terrorism. This was, in effect, the explanation of what the new administration meant by "swift and effective retribution." This struck a new note, inasmuch as the Carter administration had restricted talk of the use of military force to hostage rescues. The new administration appeared willing to use it to punish states as well. According to a State Department official involved in the counterterrorism efforts of both the Carter and Reagan administrations, this was in fact a change in policy. During the Carter years, there had never been any thought of using military force to take punitive measures against state sponsors. Secretary Haig changed this.[50]

As the Reagan administration settled into office in 1981, terrorist attacks both in general and against Americans in particular declined. Still, in that year, terrorists killed six and wounded thirty-one Americans. Attacks on Americans occurred in Costa Rica, Egypt, El Salvador, France, West Germany, Guatemala, Honduras, Italy, Lebanon, Lesotho, and Peru.[51] Of these incidents, the most important for the development of the U.S. government's counterterrorism capabilities was the kidnapping by the Italian Red Brigades of Brigadier General James Dozier, the senior U.S. officer in NATO's Southern Command, in Verona, Italy, on December 17, 1981.

Dozier was eventually rescued when Italian police work located the apartment where he was being held and an Italian counterterrorism force burst in and found him, capturing five terrorists. The U.S. government's efforts to assist the Italians revealed that the interagency process did not work. A few days before the General was kidnapped, the Reagan administration had established the Special Situation Group (SSG) to deal with crises. Chaired by Vice-President Bush and consisting of the Secretary of State, Secretary of Defense, the Counsellor to the President, the DCI, the Assistant for National Security Affairs, and the Chairman of the Joint Chiefs of Staff, Reagan's SSG was identical in composition to the Carter administration's SCC, except for the addition of the Counsellor to the President and the substitution of the Vice-President for the National Security Advisor as the group's chairman. It was this organization that proved inadequate when General Dozier was kidnapped. It did not effectively integrate the activities of the different agencies or provide a clear sense of who was in charge. One official recalls that it took a while before the CIA became an effective player in the Washington machinery during the Dozier crisis and that both the State Department and the military wanted to be in charge of the effort to rescue the General, although the State Department did not seem to have clear mechanisms in place to exercise its authority as the lead agency and the military had a tangled chain of command.[52]

There were several reasons for these problems. In its first months in office, the administration was focusing on domestic issues. In foreign policy, its principal concerns were the Soviet Union and Central America. Despite the administration's rhetoric, the NSC at this point did not consider counterterrorism a high priority. It had not pushed for any consensus on counterterrorism policy. The phrase "swift and effective retribution" had been inserted into the President's speech by a staff member, without discussion about what it meant or how, in fact, the government would visit such retribution on terrorists or their sponsors. The new members of the counterterrorism interagency organization did not know one another and had not done any exercises together. According to a Defense Department official, an interagency exercise had been proposed for October 1981 but the State Department had objected, arguing that the interagency process worked fine, and the exercise was not held until January 1982, as the efforts to find and rescue Dozier continued. According to an official who worked on the NSC staffs of both the Carter and Reagan administrations, the latter's interagency confusion was in part a self-inflicted wound. Refusing to believe that the Carter staff had developed any effective mechanisms to handle counterterrorism, the Reagan administration did away with the Executive Committee, an interagency body that might have helped with coordination. As far as counterterrorism was concerned, then, the departments and agencies were on their own. This lack of coordination had become painfully obvious prior to Dozier's kidnapping. Several months before the Red Brigades took him prisoner, the United States held a bilateral meeting with Great Britain to discuss combating terrorism. The American representatives had not coordinated their positions. In response to British questions about how the U.S. government would respond in certain situations, the Americans had to work out their position on the spot, revealing their disagreements and confusion. The Americans heard later through "back channels" that the British found the experience deeply disturbing. They wondered how they would be able to work with such amateurs.[53]

In this confused situation, the interests of the various departments and agencies asserted themselves when Dozier was kidnapped. For example, the Defense Department had a personal interest in the rescue of Dozier, since he was a military officer. It wanted to take charge and get its man back, just as the CIA would over two years later when the CIA station chief in Beirut, William Buckley, was kidnapped. The State Department resisted this because, according to the lead agency concept, the Department was in charge of managing terrorist incidents overseas. This difference of opinion was similar to one that had emerged several years before between the State Department and the FBI, except that the roles were now reversed. Then, when the incident involved foreign diplomats in the United States, the State Department had wanted to violate the letter of the lead agency concept and take the lead from the FBI. Although the lead agency concept had been part of the U.S. government counterterrorism response for years, clearly it was not working as effectively as its proponents hoped.[54]

As far as the Defense Department was concerned, the Dozier kidnapping raised a critical point related to the effectiveness of the lead agency concept. According to this concept, as noted, the State Department was in charge of managing terrorist incidents overseas. But the State Department is not part of the National Command Authorities (NCA), the President and Secretary of Defense, who can order the use of military force overseas. The State Department's management of terrorist incidents overseas suggested, then, either that military force would not be used against terrorists or that some way had to be found to connect the State Department to the NCA, which could authorize its use. This was not a problem, of course, if the use of force against terrorists was not being considered, but it was a problem for an administration that had publicly promised "swift and effective retribution" or at least it was for those in the administration who took this promise seriously. Whether or not State Department officials supported the use of force, there were at least two incidents, both in Latin America, that indicated to Defense and CIA officials that the State Department did not understand the relationship between the NCA and the use of military force or how to run operations involving military and covert personnel. In one of these operations, or so CIA officials felt, the lives of personnel had been endangered. Defense officials felt that the only way to solve this problem was to have counterterrorism under the control of the NCA.[55]

In response to the interagency problems revealed by the Dozier kidnapping, the Reagan administration issued new instructions for handling terrorist incidents in spring 1982. The administration codified the lead agency concept, dividing responsibility among the State Department, the FBI, and the FAA according to the by then standard practice that the State Department had responsibility for terrorist incidents outside U.S. territory, the FBI for those within U.S. territory, and the FAA for airplane hijackings within the jurisdiction of the United States. In addition, the instructions established an interagency terrorism management organization that superseded the structure inherited from the Carter administration. The most important part of this structure was a new interagency group, a standing group, chaired by an NSC staff member, with representatives from the State and Defense Departments, the CIA, the FBI, and the Federal Emergency Management Administration, that was to provide operational support and interagency coordination for the SSG during a terrorist incident. This group was added to the original instructions because the Defense Department argued that as first written they simply codified the existing system, which was inadequate because of the NCA problem.[56] According to the Reagan administration's new instructions as finally promulgated, the lead agencies were supposed to manage terrorist incidents under the direction and coordination of the standing group and the SSG. This arrangement put the State Department, like the other lead agencies, in contact with the NCA, assuring the appropriate chain of command should the use of military force be considered. The significant innovation here was that unlike the Carter administration's counterterrorism organization, the Reagan administration's had an interagency structure to provide operational and policy support to the highest-level interagency committee that had ultimate responsibility for the U.S. government's response to a terrorist incident. The Reagan reorganization also continued the larger interagency counterterrorism working group, which it called the Interdepartmental Group on Terrorism (IG/T), chaired by the State Department, to develop counterterrorism policy.

The decision to set up a standing interagency group was reached only after some fierce interagency battling. The State Department opposed putting control of counterterrorism in the NSC. To officials at the Defense Department, it looked as if the State Department was merely defending its turf. But NSC and White House officials also opposed putting counterterrorism under control of the NSC. With the Carter administration's hostage experience freshly in mind, they did not want counterterrorism anywhere near the President. The need to have the NCA involved in managing incidents that might include the use of force eventually overrode the concern with insulating the President from "the negatives" associated with counterterrorism, however. The standing interagency group acting under the authority of the SSG was the resulting compromise. The lead agencies still managed the incidents, but they did so under the direction of the standing group, which in turn worked for the SSG, whose members included part of the NCA. In practice, however, the new interagency system did not function in this way. According to a Defense official, the NSC, which had not wanted management of counterterrorism in the NSC or White House, turned the chairmanship of the Working Group meetings over to the State Department representative.   In this way, it won bureaucratically a battle it had lost officially.[57]

By mid-1982, then, the Reagan administration had a counterterrorism organization in place that, at least on paper, was adapted to the use of force. It also had at its disposal special counterterrorism forces organized under the Carter administration but strengthened, as was all of the Defense Department, by the Reagan administration's defense build-up. This organization and these forces were best suited for hostage-barricade situations. In these incidents, terrorists take hostages and hold them in a building or plane. This gives police or military units the opportunity to break into the area where the hostages are being held and rescue them. The hostage rescues at Entebbe and Mogadishu were the models for these operations. The Italian rescue of General Dozier had reinforced their preeminence. Yet, even as the U.S. government improved its ability to handle such situations, they were becoming less frequent. As early as 1977, U.S. officials had reported that over the past two years there had been "a decline in the more complicated and risky hostage-barricade type of operation and a marked increase in simpler but more lethal attacks such as bombings, assassinations, and armed assaults." The pattern that was emerging in the mid-1970s continued to develop over the following years, with bombings outnumbering kidnappings and hostage-barricade situations by six or seven to one. Indeed, the bombings of the U.S. Embassy and Marine Barracks in Beirut, Lebanon in 1983 and 1984, in which 260 Americans died, and of Pan Am Flight 103 (1988) and UTA Flight 772 (1989) proved to be the most spectacular and, in the case of the Beirut bombings that drove us out of Lebanon, the most effective terrorist attacks of the 1980s. Forerunners of the plane bombings had occurred in 1970 or 1971, and of the U.S. Embassy and the Barracks bombings in 1981, when the Iraqi embassy in Beirut was destroyed by a car bomb on December 15.[58] In these cases and in the case of assassinations (e.g., Lieutenant Colonel Ray, U.S. military attaché, in Paris, on January 18, 1982), the military response capability that the U.S. government had at its disposal and the incident management organization that the Reagan administration put in place were of no use. For in such cases, there are neither hostages to rescue nor ongoing incidents to manage. This leaves two possibilities for the use of military force: retaliation or preemption.

Both retaliation and preemption were discussed by U.S. government officials in the aftermath of the Beirut bombings in 1983. The Long Commission, appointed by the Defense Department to examine the Beirut Barracks bombing, argued that terrorism as it had developed by the early 1980s had to be countered by "an active national policy which seeks to deter attack or reduce its effectiveness. . . . A reactive policy only forfeits the initiative to the terrorists." While it may be true that discussion of such an active policy had actually begun before the bombings in Beirut, these events focused attention on terrorism in a way that had not been true before and permitted discussion of a new preemptive policy to go forward in the interagency arena. As this discussion continued, the very aggressive language of what became the new terrorism policy was toned down to avoid giving the impression that it sanctioned assassinations. Echoes of this discussion appeared in the press, however, where journalists citing unnamed sources reported that the U.S. government was considering "hit teams" to take out the leaders of terrorist organizations. According to a Defense official involved in these discussions, there was virtually no support for such activity. The State Department and NSC opposed it as likely to produce retaliatory strikes on U.S. officials and as unlikely to get necessary congressional support, while the Joint Staff opposed "hit teams" as being incompatible with the military ethos. According to newspaper accounts, the CIA was opposed because of the adverse publicity that the Phoenix program had generated in Vietnam. (The Phoenix Program involved the CIA, the Defense Department and the government of South Vietnam in an effort to destroy the Viet Cong infrastructure. It was widely reported to include assassination as one of its tactics.) The only support seems to have come from civilian officials in the Defense Department, one of whom now rejects the approach as an "Israeli model" not appropriate for the United States. As for retaliation, discussion of it focused on the need to avoid indiscriminate revenge, the costs of terrorist counter-retaliation, and the safety of the airmen who might be shot down in any retaliatory mission and fall into the hands of the terrorists or their sponsors. The military was cautious in its approach. According to one Defense official, the Joint Staff did not prepare targeting plans for retaliating against a terrorist attack for fear that, if the plans were ready, the civilians would order the attack without thinking through all its possible repercussions.[59]

Pushed through the interagency community by the impetus of the bombings in Beirut, the new terrorism policy was signed in April 1984. Despite being moderated in draft, the final version was without doubt the most aggressive counterterrorism document the U.S. government had yet produced. Those most supportive of an aggressive approach to combating terrorism came to believe that the new policy had little effect. In general, this seems to have been the case, even though the document stipulated that the improvements to U.S. counterterrorism capabilities that it listed were to be made before the end of 1984. Virtually all of the institutions involved in the counterterrorism effort had opposed or had been suspicious of the new approach, and this opposition and suspicion did not disappear just because the document had been signed. In addition, bureaucratic problems impeded implementation at some of the key agencies. For example, counterterrorism in the Operations Directorate at the CIA was still the preserve of the individual regional divisions, where it was not always as high a priority as it was in the minds of William Casey or certain other high-level officials in the Reagan administration. The CIA's Directorate of Intelligence produced little finished intelligence on terrorism at this time. At the State Department, the regional offices had more clout than the office for counterterrorism, so much so that it was difficult to get sufficient funds out of the bureaucracy to improve security at embassies. It was also the case that key personnel were not attuned to the new policy. This began to change, however, with the appointment of Robert McFarlane as National Security Advisor in October 1983 and of Ambassador Robert Oakley as Director of the State Department's Office for Counterterrorism in October 1984.[60]

Whatever its practical consequences, the new approach to counterterrorism represented a further development of U.S. counterterrorism policy. Through the 1970s, U.S. policy had focused on defensive measures, such as improving security at embassies, and on applying indirect pressure on terrorists through the promotion of international conventions whose signatories agreed to prosecute or extradite those accused of terrorist acts. In the late 1970s, U.S. policy came to include direct action on the terrorists themselves to rescue hostages. The Reagan administration, in addition to continuing to support defensive measures and the use of international conventions, carried the notion of direct action against terrorists and their sponsors a step further by advocating "swift and effective retribution." The new terrorism policy of April 1984 represented the next step on this road by authorizing preemption.

A series of speeches given by Secretary of State George Shultz in 1984 and early 1985 gave further evidence of the gathering momentum for a more aggressive approach to counterterrorism. The first of these speeches, "Power and Diplomacy in the 1980s," was delivered on the day that President Reagan signed the new policy, April 3, 1984. The Secretary followed this effort with speeches on June 24 and October 25, 1984 and February 4, 1985. While mentioning, as did all official pronouncements, that better security at overseas facilities, improved intelligence, and better international cooperation were essential for more effective counterterrorism, in most respects, the argument of these speeches broke new ground. For example, Shultz emphasized that terrorism was political violence, as others had done, but argued for the first time explicitly that there was indeed a difference between freedom fighters and terrorists because democracies, which allowed for peaceful change, were not the legitimate target of political violence, while totalitarian states, which did not, were. In making this argument, Shultz was joining the debate over the definition of terrorism that had complicated the intelligence community estimate of the Soviet Union as a state sponsor. The Secretary also pushed the notion of terrorism as political violence further than other officials had by declaring, like the Long Commission, that state-sponsored terrorism was a kind of warfare used to gain strategic advantages that could not be obtained by conventional means. This was a notion that experts had been discussing for several years, but Shultz was the highest ranking and one of the few U.S. officials to espouse this idea. Finally, Shultz stressed the importance of Soviet support for international terrorism but added the idea that such terrorism was part of the worldwide struggle between democracy and totalitarianism. In response to this threat, Shultz argued that we had to use force, take "preventive or preemptive actions against terrorist groups before they strike," and be prepared to take such measures without "the kind of evidence that can stand up in an American court of law."[61]

As Secretary Shultz was making this series of speeches, he also took other opportunities to discuss terrorism publicly. For example, during a speech in Miami on drug trafficking, he discussed the "disturbing interrelationship" between "narcotics traffickers, terrorists, and communist revolutionaries," who "increasingly make common cause in their separately destructive activities." Referring to information revealed in the indictment of four "high-level Cuban officials" by a Miami grand jury, Shultz went on to describe how the Cuban government had assisted Colombian traffickers in getting cocaine to the United States, assistance that earned them "hundreds of thousands of dollars" and, as another part of the deal, got weapons to the M-19 terrorist group in Colombia. Shultz also described the involvement of Nicaraguan officials, including an assistant to then Interior Minister Tomas Borge, in similar activities. According to Shultz, traffickers parked their plane on a Nicaraguan military airfield and had the help of Nicaraguan troops in loading it. Shultz noted that "the link between narcotics, terrorism, and communism [was] not confined to Latin America," mentioning Italy, Turkey, Burma, and Bulgaria as countries affected by or involved in this linked activity. Connecting it to the larger themes he was exploring in his speeches on terrorism, Shultz argued that the links between terrorists, drug traffickers, and communist nations were "part of a larger pattern of international lawlessness" by these nations aimed at "legitimate governments." The nations that aided traffickers financed themselves—to make up for "their failing economies"—and their terrorist allies—who targeted legitimate governments—at the same time that they helped "weaken the fabric of Western democratic society" by supplying it with massive amounts of narcotics. Other government officials had made similar arguments about what came to be called narcoterrorism, but Shultz was the highest-ranking official to do it in such detail.[62]

As the Secretary has noted in his memoirs, his speeches advocating an aggressive response to terrorism caused considerable debate both within and without the administration. To some extent this indicates, as noted previously, that although the President had signed the new counterterrorism policy, its more aggressive stance was not yet effective policy throughout the government. Some evidence of policy differences in the government appears in a speech given by the State Department's Director of the Office for Combating Terrorism, Ambassador Robert M. Sayre, in August 1984, in the middle of the series of speeches that the Secretary was giving. Echoing Shultz, Sayre argued that terrorism was "low-level warfare" and that to combat it we had to use force and diplomacy "in ways that reinforce each other." But he insisted that combating this low-level warfare "is essentially a police matter and not a military matter" and that we had to deal with terrorism's "root causes," this last point one that Shultz considered misleading. Finally, Sayre argued that "it is possible to deal with terrorism on a legal basis. There is no need to resort to extralegal measures." While a typical official remark, in the context of the debates over the new policy and in light of Shultz's remark about the standard of evidence that had to be met, this comment about legality can be seen as an implicit caution to the supporters of an aggressive approach to counterterrorism that they might be going too far. It is possible to overstate the importance of the reaction to Shultz's speeches for counterterrorism policy, since much of the debate they occasioned focused on the use of military force in general and not in counterterrorism as such. But there was opposition in the executive branch both to the new counterterrorism policy and to Shultz's version of it.[63]

Shultz's insistence that terrorism was a form of warfare probably arose from the fact that state-supported terrorism had undone our policy in Lebanon, which Shultz had strongly supported. The Embassy and Barracks bombings, which forced our virtual withdrawal from Lebanon, were carried out with Iranian support by Hizbollah, a Shia organization inspired by the Iranian revolution that wanted to establish an Islamic state in Lebanon. After the Israeli invasion of Lebanon in 1982, the Iranians had dispatched fifteen hundred of their "revolutionary guards" to Lebanon's Bekka valley to train members of Hizbollah. Many of these guards had been trained in Lebanon themselves, by the PLO during the Shah's reign. Most of Iran's support for Hizbollah, which included money, training, and weapons, was organized through the Iranian Embassy in Damascus, because Syria controlled the Bekka area of Lebanon. Involved in a war with Iraq and, in any case, too weak in conventional military means to oppose the United States, the Iranians were using terrorism to achieve their objectives. Although inspired by religious ideas, these objectives were still political: the destruction of America's influence in the Middle East and the spread of Iran's. Thus, while America's growing confrontation with militant Islam introduced it to new tactics (suicide bombings), terrorism itself had not changed. It remained politically motivated violence.[64]

In addition to Shultz's speeches, there were other indications in 1984 and 1985 that the U.S. government was beginning to focus more attention on its ability to respond to terrorism. In January 1984, for example, the Defense Department established a special organization to improve its counterterrorism and other special operations capabilities. Shultz himself did more than just talk about terrorism. He made clear that it was a priority, meeting every morning with the State Department's new Director for Counterterrorism, Ambassador Robert Oakley, as the Secretary reported in a speech in February 1985.[65] With Shultz's approval, the position of Director was elevated to Ambassador-at-Large for Counterterrorism in the fall of 1985. This level of attention began to have an effect on the bureaucracy, as did the interest in terrorism of the National Security Advisor, Robert McFarlane.

Nothing did more to bring terrorism and the need to counter it to the attention of senior officials, however, than the actions of terrorists themselves. The number of terrorist attacks increased as the 1980s wore on, reaching a high point in 1985. As usual, more of these attacks targeted Americans than any

other nationality.   On February 2, 1985, in Glyfada, Greece, a group calling
itself the National Front bombed a nightclub frequented by U.S. military
personnel, injuring sixty-nine, to protest U.S. support for Turkey's position on
Cyprus.   Four days later, the Che Guevara Faction of the National Liberation
Army and the Ricardo Franco Front, a faction of the Revolutionary Armed
Forces of Colombia, bombed several U.S. businesses in Medellin, Colombia.
In April, a bomb destroyed a restaurant frequented by U.S. military personnel
near Madrid.   Basque separatists and Islamic Jihad, a name used by Hizbollah,
both claimed responsibility for the attack.   The authorities eventually credited it
to Islamic Jihad.   On June 19, six to ten men opened fire on a cafe crowd in San
Salvador, El Salvador, singling out a group of American Marines, killing four,
and two U.S. businessmen.   An element of the Farabundo Marti Liberation
Forces claimed the attack.   On July 1, the Abu Nidal Organization (ANO)
bombed TWA's offices in Madrid.   Three weeks later, Islamic Jihad claimed
credit for a bomb attack on the offices of Northwest Orient Airlines in
Copenhagen.   On August 8, the Red Army Faction, using the name "George
Jackson Commando," after the Black Panther killed in a prison escape in 1971,
set off a car bomb at the U.S. Rhein-Main Air Force Base in West Germany,
killing 19-year-old Airman First Class Frank H. Scarton and 22 year-old Becky
Jo Bristol.   On September 16, the ANO organized a grenade attack on a cafe
near the U.S. Embassy in Rome.   The resulting explosion injured forty people,
including some Americans.   In early November, Major Michael Snyder was shot
while riding to work in Puerto Rico.   Two different revolutionary groups took
credit for the attack.[66]

These and other attacks like them were the normal stuff of modern terrorism.
But 1985 distinguished itself with three terrorist incidents that were out of the
ordinary.   In June, TWA Flight 847 from Athens to Rome was hijacked, setting
off a spectacle that lasted seventeen days and featured numerous American
hostages, the murder of one of these (U.S. Navy diver Robert Stethem), the
aircraft's movement back and forth between Beirut and Algiers, intensive media
coverage (including interviews with the plane's crew and some of the hostages),
the use by the hijackers and the U.S. government of a Lebanese faction leader as
a go-between, the involvement and intercession of other faction leaders and of
the highest ranking officials in the governments of the United States, Israel,
Greece, and Syria, a farewell dinner for some of the hostages, and a final news
conference by some of the hijackers, after which they were allowed to walk
away.   Hizbollah appears to have been responsible for the hijacking.   In
October, the Palestine Liberation Front, with weapons supplied by the Polish
government, hijacked the cruise ship *Achille Lauro* in the eastern Med-
terranean, killing Leon Klinghofer.   The terrorists eventually surrendered to
Egyptian authorities, who flew them out of the country.   The plane was
intercepted and forced to land at a NATO air base in Italy.   American troops
were prevented from seizing the terrorists by the Italian authorities, who arrested
the terrorists but released two Palestinian officials accompanying them,

including Abu Abbas, who had masterminded the attack. On December 27, members of the ANO attacked the airports in Rome and Vienna. Five Americans were killed in the Rome attack, including an eleven-year-old girl, Natasha Sophie Simpson. The terrorists had been trained in Lebanon's Bekaa valley and had traveled to Europe from Beirut and Damascus, via Budapest and Belgrade.[67]

On the calendar of terrorism, then, 1985 was distinguished both by the number of incidents that occurred, more than in any previous year, and by their spectacular nature. The result was an embarrassed Reagan administration. Following the hijacking of TWA Flight 847, for example, the *Wall Street Journal*, normally supportive of the administration, published a front-page article on its counterterrorism efforts that slammed it. "Ronald Reagan," it began, "for all his tough talk, has failed to develop a coherent anti-terrorism policy. The impotence of the U.S. policy has been dramatically demonstrated by the hijacking of TWA Flight 847." Senior officials involved with counterterrorism at this time recall the pressure generated by the deluge of calls to the White House and the collapse of tourism to Europe, with planes flying empty across the Atlantic.[68]

In the aftermath of the hijacking of TWA Flight 847, President Reagan appointed a task force headed by Vice-President Bush to evaluate U.S. policies and programs for combating terrorism. Although establishing a task force or commission is a hackneyed response to a problem, this task force accomplished something, according to a number of officials who either worked on it or helped implement its recommendations. The most immediate consequence of the Task Force was a comprehensive counterterrorism policy signed in January 1986, which incorporated all of the task force's recommendations. This document, like the task force report, did not alter any established policies, arguing that they were sound, but suggested ways to improve their implementation. It made only one change to the interagency structure, establishing a small interagency group to oversee noncrisis operations and activities. As for the use of military force against terrorists, the task force acknowledged that for a number of reasons this would not often be done. Nevertheless, it concluded that military force was a valuable tool and recommended that this capability should be maintained.

By itself, the comprehensive policy might have had no more effect than its predecessor signed in April 1984. But times had changed. Higher-level interest in counterterrorism was beginning to improve U.S. efforts. According to officials involved, the change was apparent in the response to the *Achille Lauro* hijacking. The State and Defense Departments and the intelligence community fused their various capabilities better than they had before, according to participants, in the effort to force down an Egyptian aircraft carrying the hijackers. While the outcome was not what the participants intended, several of them cited this operation as a benchmark indicating both how counterterrorism capabilities had progressed and how effectively they could be combined. Another important step forward that resulted from high-level interest was the creation of an integrated approach to counterterrorism at the CIA. Although the concept for this approach was evident in two of the task force's recommendations, the CIA's new organization was formed in early 1986 primarily in response to William Casey's outrage at the bloody attacks on the Vienna and Rome airports. The new approach brought together a variety of CIA specialists, as well as representatives from a number of government agencies involved in counterterrorism in a Counterterrorism Center (CTC). Opposed by the CIA's regional offices, the new office was set up only because of Casey's support. According to officials involved with the organization of the CTC, it was designed to help implement the new more aggressive counterterrorism policy. With a National Intelligence Officer for terrorism (appointed in March 1985) supervising the U.S. government's intelligence analyses, by early 1986 the CIA had focused significant resources on terrorism.[69]

The best indication of how much things had changed was the success of the small interagency group set up to oversee noncrisis operations and activities. Convened in early 1986, meeting weekly thereafter, this organization brought together policymakers (the State Department, the Office of the Secretary of Defense [OSD], NSC) and operators (CIA, FBI, Joint Chiefs of Staff [JCS]). Its original members shared similar views on terrorism and how the United States should respond to it and appear to have quickly developed a mutual trust. The meetings were informal; no notes were taken. The participants set meeting agendas, which Oliver North, the NSC representative, coordinated. Several officials who participated in these meetings mentioned that there were no leaks from their discussions, a remarkable accomplishment in their experience, which encouraged sharing of information and frank discussion. One NSC member of the group said that its frequent meetings allowed the participants to "calibrate one another." They learned who would overstate or understate a problem. This "calibration" helped the group manage day-to-day issues but was most important for organizing the interagency support of operations and terrorism incidents, a job the group assumed. Perhaps the critical factor in the success of this group was the support of and access to their cabinet-level superiors that its members enjoyed. This increased the effectiveness of the group by increasing its ability to cut through the obstacles presented by the interagency bureaucracy.[70]

According to its members, this interagency group served several functions, in addition to coordinating policy and operations. The exchange of information among its members allowed them to prepare their Principals for higher-level interagency meetings, accomplishing informal coordination in advance of the formal meeting. This information exchange also helped the State Department representative, with the support of the Secretary of State, prepare his colleagues for bilateral meetings, keeping terrorism on the agenda with allies and other nations. The group also helped refine command and control arrangements for incidents overseas and organized exercises to practice these and other counterterrorism procedures.

According to its civilian members, the JCS representatives to the interagency group were not as forthcoming as their civilian counterparts from the OSD. They believe that there may have been several reasons for this. Some of the reticence may have been due to traditional military reluctance to share operational information with civilians for fear that it might be leaked or might allow civilians to meddle in military matters or get the military involved in situations that it did not want to get involved in. One NSC representative thought that the military was not comfortable with the informality of the interagency group. Noting that the military was more forthcoming in counternarcotics than in counterterrorism, he pointed to another source of the Joint Staff's reserved participation in the deliberations of the interagency group. Counterterrorism, more than counternarcotics, involved Special Operations Forces (SOF). The traditional military did not trust these units. An NSC representative quoted a senior Joint Staff officer in charge of operations as saying that SOF "could get you into trouble, but couldn't get you out." Whatever the reason, in the eyes of civilian members, Joint Staff participation in the interagency group was less collegial than civilian participation. While one civilian went so far as to describe JCS participation as unsatisfactory, all agreed that when tasked with a specific requirement, the JCS responded professionally and competently.[71]

The improved interagency cooperation that the interagency group encouraged did not mean that all proposals for operations met with agreement or were properly coordinated. William Casey went directly to President Reagan, for example, to get approval for operations. On one occasion, Casey got approval from the President to capture a notorious Shiite terrorist from the streets of a European capital so that he could be brought to trial in the United States. When the State Department official in charge of counterterrorism found out about this, from the representative of another agency to the interagency group, he was able to enlist Secretary Schultz's support and stop the operation. On another occasion, a proposal was put forward for the use of military force against a state sponsor of terrorism in the Middle East. Again, the State Department intervened to stop the operation, arguing, as it had with the plan to grab the terrorist, that the operation would do more harm than good to broader, long-term U.S. interests, even though it might be a blow to terrorism.[72]

There was, of course, one use of force against a state sponsor of terrorism that the State Department strongly encouraged: operation El Dorado Canyon, the raid against Libya in April 1986. This was perhaps the most visible counterterrorism measure the Reagan administration took. Coming only ten days after the Libyan-organized bombing of a discotheque in West Berlin frequented by U.S. military personnel, it appeared to be, fourteen years after the Nixon administration spoke of responding swiftly and effectively to terrorism and five years after President Reagan spoke of "swift and effective retribution," the kind of aggressive response many had long called for. We now know, however, that contingency planning for such a raid began long before this bombing, in response to Qadaffi's interventions in Africa, particularly Chad, and his efforts to counter U.S. diplomacy in the Middle East, as well as his support for terrorist activities in Europe. A remarkable military operation, the raid had beneficial political effects. It focused the attention of foreign officials on the terrorism threat and increased the leverage of American diplomats dealing with these officials, even as it irritated and dismayed them. It made even Syria's leader, Hafez Asad, pay attention. It also apparently got the attention of the East Germans, although American diplomats did not know it at the time. Recently released East German security documents contain a memo reporting that American officials had approached the East Germans in May 1986, a few weeks after the raid on Libya, with the information that Abu Nidal, who had Libyan backing, was planning a terrorist attack at a book fair in West Germany that several well-known Western personalities, including Henry Kissinger, were planning to attend. Noting that they did not want to give the Reagan administration any excuse "to pursue the policy of force against sovereign states and national liberation movements," the East German memo concludes that "it would be in our common interest if the friends would use the opportunities available to them to influence the Palestinian groupings known to them to prevent the carrying out of any terrorist actions in Europe." Last but not least, the raid had an effect on Qadaffi. Following a series of immediate revenge attacks, Libyan-sponsored terrorist attacks ceased for approximately twelve months. They picked up after that, and if we count the bombing of Pan Am Flight 103 in 1988 as a response to the raid, we can see that its effects were not all positive from the American viewpoint.[73]

At about the same time as the raid on Libya occurred, a less-publicized counterterrorism operation was developing against the ANO. This Palestinian terrorist group broke from the PLO in the early 1970s, after Yasir Arafat decided to restrict PLO terrorism to Israel and the occupied territories. Supported at various times by Syria, Iraq, and Libya, with administrative and training facilities in these countries and Lebanon's Bekaa valley, it developed into one of the most deadly terrorist groups in the world, targeting Israel and the United States (because it supports Israel), Britain and France (because they have prosecuted and imprisoned its operatives), any Palestinians or Arab states that do not have as their chief priority the armed struggle against Israel, and Arab states that are the enemies of its current sponsor, whoever that may be. From 1974 to 1994, the ANO "has carried out over 90 terrorist attacks . . . in 20 countries, killing or injuring almost 900 people." In addition to its facilities in Middle Eastern countries, the ANO has developed infrastructure, including financial support, in Europe, Latin America, and North America.[74]

Based on intelligence developed by the CIA, the U.S. government was able to attack the ANO's infrastructure. According to analysts who worked on this case, this intelligence allowed them to connect disparate pieces of information on the ANO brought together by the fusion of terrorist intelligence in the new CTC. The new intelligence, developed with the assistance of analysts in other agencies, also provided a number of leads that the CTC pursued with the help of these other agencies. The result was a new and fuller understanding of how the ANO worked, particularly its relationships with Eastern European governments. For example, according to a press report based on a leaked State Department document, the ANO and the Polish government agreed in 1979 that the ANO could operate out of Poland. A few years later, the ANO set up an export-import company in Warsaw that traded in weapons and other goods. This gave the ANO ready access to weapons, as well as profits from the company's business activities. This ANO company in Warsaw also coordinated the activities of ANO enterprises in other European countries. Armed with this information, the CTC organized operations against the ANO and worked with the State Department to pressure the Polish government to curtail the terrorist group's activities. As these efforts developed, additional dèmarches were made to Yugoslavia and East Germany, where the ANO was also operating with the knowledge of authorities. According to those involved, the combination of diplomatic protest and public pressure generated through press reporting caused Poland and Yugoslavia, but not East Germany, to close down ANO facilities or limit the group's activities, significantly disrupting its ability to carry out terrorist acts.[75]

The operation against the ANO confirmed for its supporters the value of the CTC. The first break in the case was a matter of luck, but the CTC structure allowed analysts and ultimately operators to exploit it, according to these supporters. The analysts benefited from the fusion of information from a variety of agencies made possible by the CTC, while the fact that analysts and operators worked together in this new organization meant that the operators were able to exploit leads that in turn fed into and improved the analytical process. Those skeptical of the CTC believe that the analysts would have exploited the lucky break under the old order. Whether this is true or not is hard to say. The answer may depend most on the quality of the analysts involved in either organizational arrangement. In any event, an analyst from another part of the intelligence community, while not questioning the good work done in the case of the ANO, has raised an objection to the idea behind the CTC: combining analysts and operators in the same office. According to this analyst, such an arrangement violates the rationale behind the separation of analysts and operators that has governed the structure of the CIA from its beginning. If the two work together, there will be bureaucratic pressure for the analysts to defend the quality of the reporting that the operators' sources produce. If the two are in separate organizations, then the analysts can maintain a critical distance from the sources. If they are combined, skepticism about the worth of a source's reporting may appear to be disloyalty to the organization, which will not enhance an analyst's career prospects. This pressure may be particularly acute if the leadership of the CTC comes from the Directorate of Operations, as it does. The analyst claimed that in fact the analysts at the CTC had taken to defending their sources' reporting no matter what other information contradicted it. This had led to other elements of the intelligence community disregarding to some degree the analysis of the CTC.[76] While there may be truth to this criticism, at the time, the operation against the ANO validated the CTC for those in the counterterrorism business and highlighted some of the new counterterrorism capabilities that the government had developed under the Reagan administration. These improved capabilities had developed because of the interest of high-ranking officials like Shultz and Casey and because their subordinates knew that combating terrorism had become a high priority, which allowed the government to focus attention and resources on it. This concerted effort was about to be undermined, however.

As the operation against the ANO gathered speed, the Lebanese magazine *Al-Shiraa* reported on November 3, 1986 that Robert McFarlane had secretly visited Tehran, after he had resigned as National Security Advisor, and that the United States had sold arms to Iran. On November 25, Attorney General Edwin Meese announced that money from these sales had been passed to the Contras. On the same day, McFarlane's successor as National Security Advisor, John Poindexter, resigned and the President fired Oliver North. The Iran-Contra scandal, as it came to be called, had several consequences for the U.S. government's counterterrorism program. It brought suspicion on the standing interagency group, since North had been its NSC representative. The special prosecutor became suspicious of this group's activities, and Justice Department lawyers and the NSC Counsel began to attend its meetings regularly. According to FBI, State Department, and CIA officials, when the lawyers began to attend, leaks began as well. The Justice Department's lawyers reject the inference that they were the ones who leaked, pointing out that the content of news stories at the time indicate that it was the operational agencies that leaked to the press. In any event, because of the leaks and because the interagency meetings were now bigger, the operational agencies became less willing to share information. In the longer term, according to NSC and other officials, the result of Iran-Contra was to diminish the NSC's role in counterterrorism, which to some extent made interagency coordination more difficult. Iran-Contra also caused problems with all the nations the U.S. had worked so hard with over the years in hopes of getting them to both cooperate in counterterrorism efforts and adopt the no concessions policy. According to one official involved in the process, it took the U.S. government almost two years to recover its credibility in the international counterterrorism arena. Finally, Iran-Contra helped shift U.S. counterterrorism policy to a greater emphasis on a judicial response to terrorism. Having made a deal with terrorists, the U.S. government could no longer talk to other nations about not making concessions to terrorists. Nor could executive branch officials promote this policy in congressional hearings or to the American public. To replace "no concessions" as the pillar or cornerstone of U.S. counterterrorism policy, officials began to emphasize, more than they had before, the identification, tracking, apprehension, and prosecution of terrorists. Even as our pledge not to deal with terrorists slowly regained credibility, following President Reagan's public admission that dealing with Iran had been wrong, this judicial approach remained more important than it had been prior to Iran-Contra.[77]

In a certain sense, as indicated by the emphasis on international conventions and the extradition of suspected terrorists, the judicial or legal approach to counterterrorism had been an important part of the U.S. government's policy from the beginning. What officials emphasized after Iran-Contra was something different and something new, however. It was a method of combating terrorism that had been slowly developing quietly while debates about military retaliation and preemption had been getting all the attention. Early in 1984, as part of its effort to improve U.S. counterterrorism capabilities, the Reagan administration proposed several laws dealing with terrorism. One aimed to set up a reward program to encourage people to come forward with information about terrorist activities. Another proposed making a conspiracy in the United States to commit a terrorist act overseas a crime. The most important of the proposed laws, however, was one to implement an international convention on hostage taking. This became law in October 1984 as the Act for the Prevention and Punishment of Hostage Taking. This law made it a crime in U.S. law to take an American hostage overseas. It gave the FBI the authority to investigate such a hostage taking and arrest the hostage takers overseas for trial in the United States. Although extraterritorial jurisdiction had existed before this law, the 1984 Act and the 1986 Omnibus Anti-Terrorism Act expanded this jurisdiction and made the use of U.S. law overseas against terrorists a higher priority for the FBI.

The idea for such an expanded grant of authority to the FBI originated in the Justice Department. A prosecutor who had worked on terrorism cases involving Armenian attacks on Turkish officials in the United States was impressed with the effectiveness of U.S. law enforcement in gathering evidence and in its ability to penetrate and disrupt terrorist groups. When this prosecutor joined the Justice Department, he sought to apply this lesson to terrorists overseas, adding impetus to the process that resulted in the 1984 and 1986 laws. According to one senior FBI official, the interest in extraterritorial jurisdiction also derived from frustration in the government over the failure of multilateral conventions and international law to do more to curb terrorism.[78] Whatever its origin, the application of U.S. law outside U.S. territory and, consequently, the capture of indicted terrorists overseas or their extradition or rendition to the United States became after Iran-Contra an increasingly important weapon against terrorism.

Both FBI and Justice Department officials say that the Bureau and the Department moved aggressively when they got extraterritorial jurisdiction. Following passage of the 1984 law, the FBI investigated hostage incidents overseas. Its efforts were frustrated, however, by what seemed to the Bureau to be a lack of cooperation from the State Department and, to a lesser degree, from the CIA. Part of the problem, at least in the beginning, according to officials from all agencies (including the FBI), was that the Bureau tended to conduct its activities overseas as it did at home. The difference, of course, was that whatever U.S. law might say, other nations did not recognize the FBI's jurisdiction. In short, the FBI was not sufficiently diplomatic or, as one of its own officials said, in the eyes of the State Department, appeared to act like "a bull in a china shop." This did not endear it to the State Department. In addition, some of its activities seemed to infringe on the responsibilities of the State Department's Regional Security Officers, which became another bureaucratic problem. The CIA felt that posting FBI attachés at U.S. embassies confused foreign governments about which U.S. agency was, in fact, responsible for intelligence and security overseas.[79]

In addition to these bureaucratic problems, there were practical problems with the extraterritorial judicial approach. The U.S. government had either to get other countries to extradite or hand over accused terrorists to the United States or capture them. Extradition was difficult because of the so-called political exception rule. Many countries refused to honor extradition requests for those who could plausibly be said to have committed political rather than criminal acts. The United States, for example, at this time granted such exceptions to members of the IRA. Other countries were reluctant to hand over suspected terrorists because they feared domestic or foreign reaction. Seizing terrorists was problematic, the *New York Times* reported, citing various U.S. government officials, because such operations could make FBI agents liable to suits for false arrest or for indictment on kidnapping charges in the country where the seizure occurred. In addition, such acts might set a precedent for other countries to seize Americans or damage relations with the country where the seizure occurred, as the State Department argued in the case of Casey's plan to seize the terrorist in a European capital. Moreover, officials told the *Times,* they had trouble getting the indictments they needed to authorize capturing suspected terrorists because much of the information in the cases they were developing was based on intelligence and the intelligence agencies were reluctant to release it. Nevertheless, officials felt that eventually the U.S. government would succeed in capturing a terrorist for trial.[80]

Twenty-one months after the *New York Times* reported this prediction, it came true. On September 13, 1987, the FBI arrested Fawaz Yunis in international waters in the Mediterranean, thereby avoiding several of the problems cited in the *Times* article, and brought him to the United States for trial. This was the first time that U.S. law enforcement officials had arrested a suspected terrorist overseas. Yunis had been indicted for his participation in the hijacking of a Jordanian passenger plane, among whose passengers were four Americans. From the viewpoint of one law enforcement official, the operation was of questionable worth. He described the arrest of Yunis, which required the diversion of elements of the sixth fleet and a good deal of other logistical support, as the most expensive apprehension in the history of law enforcement, noting that if Yunis had been a member of the Mafia in the United States, the FBI would not have bothered with someone of such low rank. While this is undoubtedly true, it does not mean that arresting Yunis was not worth the cost. Counterterrorism officials justified it as part of an effort to deter terrorism. Citing intelligence reports indicating that arresting Yunis had made other terrorists more cautious about their travel, they argued that inhibiting travel in this way made it more difficult for terrorists to carry out their attacks. The arrest of Yunis was perhaps most significant, however, for demonstrating the increasing ability of the U.S. government to bring off complicated counterterrorism operations that required close interagency cooperation. Intelligence, military, and law enforcement officials all had key roles in the arrest, which required extensive interagency cooperation in planning and executing an operation that had many components.[81]

The arrest of Yunis also suggests that by late 1987, there was a wider acceptance of the judicial response to counterterrorism and of the role of the FBI outside the United States. This was true, according to an FBI official. Cooperation between the FBI, CIA, and the State Department improved steadily during 1986–1988. The State Department's counterterrorism official, for example, using his access and influence with Secretary Shultz, helped the Bureau get its legal attachés into Embassies over the objections of the State Department's Regional Bureaus and some of the ambassadors concerned. According to this same Bureau official, this pattern of cooperation was broken in the U.S. government's response to the assassination of Pakistani President Zia. For reasons that are not clear to Bureau officials, neither the State Department nor the U.S. military commander for the region wanted the FBI to investigate the plane crash that killed Zia in August 1988, even though the American Ambassador was on the plane with Zia and it was destroyed in flight by what might have been a terrorist act. (To this day, no clear explanation for the crash has emerged.) One FBI official speculated that there was fear in the State and Defense Departments that the Pakistani military had a hand in Zia's death and neither agency wanted this exposed. In any event, the Bureau did not get to conduct a proper investigation, no evidence emerged identifying those responsible for the incident, and Congress expressed dissatisfaction with the exclusion of the Bureau. The result, according to Bureau officials, was that only a few months after Zia's assassination, when Pan Am Flight 103 was blown up (on December 21, 1988), the State Department did not hesitate to let the Bureau get involved.[82]

The FBI did more than get involved. It eventually took the lead in the government's investigation of the Pan Am bombing because circumstances, material and political, dictated that the United States pursue a forensic and judicial response. Since no terrorist group made a credible claim of responsibility for the bombing, it was not possible in the first weeks and months following the attack to respond with diplomacy or force against a group or one of its state sponsors. According to an NSC official, during this time the United States was confused, following several false trails that he has come to believe were deliberately set. Intelligence suggested at first that it was the Popular

Front for the Liberation of Palestine-General Command that was responsible, but, according to this official, not enough evidence accumulated to justify a military response. As this official pointed out, success in the ongoing Mideast peace talks was a higher priority than a quick response to the Pan Am bombing and everyone feared that military action would scuttle the talks. Consequently, the example of the raid on Libya was not brought up. The response to Pan Am Flight 103, therefore, was forensic and judicial rather than political and military. The criminal investigation, aided by U.S. intelligence, resulted three years after the destruction of the Pan Am flight in the indictment of two Libyan officials. Evidence developed in this investigation, according to an FBI official, provided a firm foundation for the State Department to organize sanctions through the UN intended to persuade the Libyans to surrender its two officials for trial. Because of this, again according to this FBI official, the investigation of Pan Am Flight 103 established in the minds of State Department officials that the FBI and the judicial response to terrorism were effective and useful.[83]

The development of the judicial response and its rise to prominence among U.S. counterterrorism policies occurred during the Reagan administration because of Iran-Contra and Pan Am Flight 103. Such a development is ironic, perhaps, for an administration well known for its bellicose rhetoric. But the results of acting on such rhetoric must also be listed as one of the reasons why the judicial response rose to prominence. Twelve months after U.S. planes bombed Tripoli in retaliation for the dischotèque bombing, Libya again became active in sponsoring terrorist attacks. Early efforts to get the CIA involved in more aggressive covert or clandestine counterterrorism efforts resulted in or coincided with a car bomb explosion in Beirut, the publicity from which discouraged further such efforts. It is telling in this regard that the Vice-President's task force found many nongovernmental experts willing to testify that the use of force was a good way to respond to terrorism, but also found them willing to modify or even abandon this position under questioning by the task force, whose personnel were aware of the various practical considerations that any policymaker must keep in mind when trying to decide when to use force. In the end, then, what the Reagan administration contributed to counterterrorism policy was a nonmilitary approach to counterterrorism, the exact opposite of the approach its rhetoric suggested. By the early 1990s, both the State and Defense Departments were calling terrorists criminals and the Director of the FBI could describe the Bureau as "the U.S. government's main weapon in its fight against terrorism."[84]

Vice President George Bush was nominated as the Republican candidate for President on the day that Zia's plane was destroyed. Having won the election in November, he was in the midst of his transition when Pan Am Flight 103 was blown apart. When he took office in January 1989, he inherited a counterterrorism program whose policies, organization, and methods were much as his task force recommended they be. The policy mixed elements as old as the program itself, such as "no concessions" and international cooperation, with the new elements added in the Reagan years, retaliation and extraterritoriality. The standing interagency group, renamed in the wake of the Iran-Contra scandal, was an organizational innovation still proving its worth. The Bush administration also continued the more low-keyed approach to terrorism that had come to characterize the later Reagan administration. Indeed, it was even more low-keyed than its predecessor. The practical results of the aggressive, proactive approach to counterterrorism having tempered enthusiasm for it, a declining number of terrorist attacks in the late 1980s, and the gradually emerging effects of the end of the Cold War allowed the Bush administration to deemphasize counterterrorism. This lack of emphasis soon worked its way through the bureaucracy. The title of the State Department's principal counterterrorism official, for example, reverted to "Coordinator" from "Ambassador-at-Large."[85]

The lower profile of counterterrorism in the Bush administration contributed to one of its counterterrorism successes. On December 4, 1991, Terry Anderson, the last of the Americans taken hostage in Lebanon, was released from captivity, bringing to an end a terrorism problem that had bedeviled the Reagan administration. A number of factors contributed to the conclusion of the Lebanese hostage episode: the collapse of the Soviet Union, which changed the political dynamics in the Middle East, a change exemplified by the membership in the anti-Saddam Gulf War coalition of several Middle Eastern countries; a perception in Iran that it had gotten all it could out of holding hostages in Lebanon; and the intercession of a UN representative. All of this played a part but so did the policy of the Bush administration. Citing unnamed analysts in an article explaining why the hostages were being released, the *Washington Post* noted that "the Bush administration has been careful to avoid the mistakes of the Carter and Reagan years, when the plight of the hostages often preoccupied the president." This downplaying of the significance of the hostages explains, perhaps, why the Iranians began to conclude that they were no longer useful. This same approach to hostage-taking helped deprive Saddam Hussein of the benefit he hoped to gain from the hostages he took after his invasion of Kuwait and was part of the administration's strategy for dealing with Saddam.[86]

Another success against terrorism registered during the Bush administration was the effective international cooperation that blunted the efforts of Iraq to attack the Desert Storm allies through terrorism. Surveillance of Iraqi embassies and other organizations and facilities associated with Iraqi interests and the expulsion of Iraqi diplomats, techniques developed during earlier confrontations with Libya, disrupted the infrastructure of Iraqi terrorism overseas. These measures were part of a more general antiterrorism campaign that focused on increasing security measures and awareness in the United States and at U.S. facilities abroad. The success of these measures, the vindication of years of tedious, unglamorous work, was one of the U.S. government's greatest achievements in combating terrorism.

While the Bush administration did, in general, lower the profile of counterterrorism, it also prepared aggressive measures. For example, according to newspaper accounts, in June 1989, then Assistant Attorney General William P. Barr signed a memorandum, in response to a request from the FBI, stating that the President "may order the seizure of fugitives in foreign countries without the host governments' consent." In another example, the NSC staff requested that the commission appointed to study the Pan Am Flight 103 incident include in its report language that would encourage a strong response to terrorism. The issued report called for "vigorous policies" against terrorists and their sponsors, "including planning and training for preemptive and retaliatory strikes against known terrorist enclaves" and "where such direct strikes are inappropriate . . . covert operations, to prevent, disrupt or respond to terrorist acts." Using this as an opening, the NSC requested in June 1990 that the Joint Staff prepare unobtrusive ways to respond to terrorism. The Joint Staff did this, in conjunction with the NSC and CIA, developing a number of lethal and nonlethal measures to disrupt, preempt, or retaliate for terrorist attacks.[87]

When the group that had developed these measures first presented them to senior decisionmakers toward the end of 1990, they responded enthusiastically. This enthusiasm soon waned, however, leading one of the participants in the development of these measures to wonder if opponents of an active response to terrorism in the bureaucracy had prevailed. They may have, but their victory may not have been only another triumph for bureaucratic inertia. As the number of terrorists attacks against Americans declined, as the hostages were released, as the Iraqi terrorist offensive failed to develop, as Desert Shield became Desert Storm, as the Pan AM Flight 103 investigation led to indictments and the imposition of sanctions against Libya, and as the peace negotiations continued in the Middle East, opponents of aggressive measures against terrorism may have had an easy time convincing senior decisionmakers that such measures were no longer necessary and would even harm U.S. interests.

Counterterrorism maintained its lower profile in the first two years of the Clinton administration, whose documents and officials placed a high priority on fighting terrorism but which, as a practical matter, did not have to deal with much international terrorism directed at the United States and its citizens. In response to the assassination plot against President Bush, President Clinton ordered a cruise missile attack on an Iraqi intelligence building late at night, but this did not compare with the high drama of the Reagan counterterrorism campaign. The Clinton administration began to pay more attention to terrorism in 1995, when the religious cult, Aum Shinrikyo, launched a poison gas attack in the Tokyo subway, bombings in Israel threatened efforts toward peace in the Middle East, and a bomb killed U.S. servicemen in Saudi Arabia. The second bombing of a U.S. military facility in Saudi Arabia in June 1996, and reports that other attacks would take place, heightened concern about terrorism even more. At the end of its first term, the Clinton administration was paying more attention to terrorism than the Bush administration had, but less than had the Reagan administration.[88]

At the same time terrorism seemed to be changing in certain respects. The familiar groups, such as the ANO and Hizbollah, continued to operate, but they were being joined by loose associations of individuals, such as the group that bombed the World Trade Center in February 1993. These so-called ad hoc or autonomous groups have little or no hierarchical structure, coming together under the influence of a religious leader or other individuals who move from country to country with some expert knowledge and financial backing from different states, nongovernmental religious or social organizations, or individuals. Such associations also differ from the more familiar groups in having less specific political agendas. In many cases, they seem motivated only by hatred of the West or the United States. Similarly motivated but more highly structured groups were also emerging, such as Aum Shinrikyo. However organized, such groups may be less inhibited in their use of WMD than other groups with political agendas, which, for this reason, do not want to undermine their political appeal by using WMD. But even organizations with political agendas were showing disturbing indications of renewed interest in WMD, as indicated by the planting of a harmless but portentous radiological device in a Moscow park by Chechen separatists in the fall of 1995. Although still too early to tell, if the new groups and renewed interest in WMD were an anomaly or a trend, U.S. officials reportedly were debating among themselves, as their predecessors had in the 1980s, about the best way to respond to the threat from terrorism. Once again, they were debating the relative merits of preemptive strikes, covert action, sanctions, and diplomacy and whether to target the states that sponsor terrorist attacks or the organizations and individuals that carry them out.[89]

Looking back over twenty-five years of U.S. government counterterrorism efforts in late 1993, a former State Department official who had been involved in them judged them a success. Such controversial measures as the raid on Libya had had benefits, he contended, acknowledging that no single component of the U.S. effort or all of them together had been decisive. At about the same time, another former State Department official, reflecting on this same twenty-five-year effort, with which he too had been involved, agreed in essence with the first official's assessment but argued that the decisive factor in the effectiveness of our counterterrorism program was not the program itself but the overall policies and strategies we pursued to protect and promote our interests. Indeed, he argued, ignoring this broader perspective was the greatest difficulty with our counterterrorism program. Terrorism is a threat, he argued, but only one of many we face and not the most important. Treating it as if it were had, on occasion, threatened to do us more harm than good.[90]

For those who emphasize the need to place counterterrorism efforts in a broader context, a coincidence of news reports in 1983 would be telling. On the same day in that year that the press reported the Long Commission's conclusion that terrorism was a kind of warfare and that the United States needed to respond to it with more active measures, it also reported that Yuri Andropov, chairman of the Communist Party and head of the Soviet State, had criticized the failings of the Soviet economy. Juxtaposed in these reports, although it would not have been evident to their readers, were the glimmerings of the Soviet Union's collapse and the beginnings of the U.S. government's hard line against terrorism. Given Soviet and Warsaw Pact support for terrorism, as well as the countries that sponsored it, this juxtaposition might make us wonder what deserves more credit for the decline in terrorism: U.S. efforts against terrorism or the Soviet Union's collapse (and collapsing oil prices in the late 1980s that adversely affected the Soviet Union and other states that supported terrorism). Even if it is true, as we are now told, that the United States tried to lower the price of oil in the 1980s as part of a comprehensive strategy to defeat the Soviet Union, this would only make us wonder if the State Department official was right that not our counterterrorism policies but our overall foreign and security policies and strategies deserve most credit for whatever success we have had against terrorism.[91]

We cannot really say how effective our efforts against terrorism have been or are likely to be in the future, however, unless we examine them in detail. Before doing so, we must consider how we have defined or understood terrorism, for what we understand terrorism to be will affect both how we combat it and our assessment of how successful we have been. If terrorism is criminal activity, as the U.S. government has insisted, then we will tend to combat it with legal means, as is now the case. If, however, defining or understanding terrorism as criminal activity is wrong or inadequate, then this approach to combating terrorism will be inadequate. Again, if terrorism is a kind of warfare, we should wage war against it. If it is not, doing so may not be to our advantage. Nor has the moral and political questioning ceased that has accompanied U.S. efforts against terrorism. In early 1996, an American citizen was sentenced to life imprisonment by a Peruvian court for aiding a terrorist group. In her defense, she called those she aided "'revolutionaries' fighting for the poor, not 'terrorist criminals.'"[92] How should the United States, birthed by the political violence of a revolution, respond to claims that others are merely doing what Americans did before? To answer these questions and to assess our struggle against international terrorism, we must consider what terrorism is.

2

DEFINITION

Above the gates of hell is the warning that all that enter should abandon hope. Less dire but to the same effect is the warning given to those who try to define terrorism. "It can be predicted with confidence that the disputes about a detailed, comprehensive definition of terrorism will continue for a long time, that they will not result in a consensus, and that they will make no noticeable contribution towards the understanding of terrorism." The author of this warning, undeterred by it, goes on to discuss the definition of terrorism at length.[1] In doing so, he follows an honored tradition. Every consideration of terrorism begins by discussing its definition and apologizing for doing so. The discussion arises from the commendable urge to know what we are talking about, the apology from the reasonable expectation that the complexity of the subject will defeat our efforts. Discouraged from defining terrorism by its complexity, we are urged by its monstrous character to get on with the job of combating it, whether we understand it fully or not, leaving the niceties of definition for a quieter time. This may particularly be the prejudice of so-called men of action. But we cannot take their advice, for, as we have just noted, how we define terrorism will determine how we combat it. Giving in to the urge to combat terrorism before trying to understand or define it, then, may give us some satisfaction in the short term, but only at the expense of frustration later on. With terrorism, as with everything else, acting before understanding is never practical. Without apology, then, we must consider what terrorism is.

This task is made less daunting by our practical purpose and our focus on the U.S. government. We want to understand what terrorism is not to develop a perfect definition but to gain the clarity necessary for effective action, and we are concerned with the actions of a particular government. The best place to begin, then, is with the various ways that the U.S. government has defined terrorism. Secretary of State Shultz, for example, who was the most visible spokesman on terrorism in the 1980s, defined it as politically motivated violence intended to impose the terrorists' will on a population or government, adding that it amounted to a form of warfare. While authoritative because of his position, this definition left government when the Secretary did. The various bureaucracies have spawned a number of definitions that, in the way of bureaucracies, endure. In response to a requirement made part of Title 22 of the U.S. Code by Congress, the Department of State defines terrorism in its annual report *Patterns of Global Terrorism* as "premeditated, politically motivated violence perpetrated against noncombatant targets by sub-national or clandestine agents, usually intended to influence an audience." Title 18 of the U.S. Code, containing the laws establishing the extraterritorial jurisdiction of U.S. authorities in terrorist incidents, defines terrorism as

activities that (A) involve violent acts or acts dangerous to human life that are a violation of the criminal laws of the United States or of any State, or that would be a criminal violation if committed within the jurisdiction of the United States or of any State; (B) appear to be intended (i) to intimidate or coerce a civilian population; (ii) to influence the policy of a government by intimidation or coercion; or (iii) to affect the conduct of a government by assassination or kidnapping; and (C) occur primarily outside the territorial jurisdiction of the United States, or transcend national boundaries in terms of the means by which they are accomplished, the persons they appear intended to intimidate or coerce, or the locale in which their perpetrators operate or seek asylum.

The FBI defines international terrorism "as the unlawful use of force or violence, committed by a group(s) or individual(s), who is foreign based and/or directed by countries or groups outside the United States or whose activities transcend national boundaries, against persons or property to intimidate or coerce a government, the civilian population, or any segment thereof, in furtherance of political or social objectives." The Defense Department actually has two definitions. A Department Directive defines terrorism as "the calculated use of violence or threat of violence to inculcate fear; intended to coerce or to intimidate governments or societies in the pursuit of goals that are generally political, religious, or ideological," while the Joint Staff defines it as "the unlawful use or threatened use of force or violence against individuals or property to coerce or intimidate governments or societies, often to achieve political, religious, or ideological objectives." Finally, the Intelligence Community has defined terrorism as "the threat or use of violence for political purposes by individuals or groups, whether acting for, or in opposition to, established governmental authority, when such actions are intended to shock or intimidate a target group wider than the immediate victims."[2]

These definitions make a number of claims about terrorism, not all of them compatible. They use terms such as *unlawful*, *political*, and *warfare*, for example, which we do not normally treat as synonymous. Yet despite their differences, they all rest on a core understanding of terrorism. Interestingly, it is a notion that corresponds to what one analysis has found to be the most common elements in 140 different definitions of terrorism. According to this analysis, the five most common elements are violence, political purpose, intention to influence an audience, an action that produces terror, and threat.[3] Of these five, one (an action that produces terror) does not tell us very much, if anything, since many things can cause terror, and another (threat) is implicit in the first three. If we discard these two elements, we are left with the core definition of terrorism common to all U.S. government definitions: politically motivated violence intended to influence an audience.

At first glance, this core definition may appear to be redundant. Are there any politically motivated acts that are not intended to influence an audience? When we speak of the *political*, we are referring to a realm larger than the interests and concerns of an individual: we are referring to a group's common life. To speak of a politically motivated act implies an intention to affect this common life and thus assumes an effort to influence an audience. While this may be true, the core definition emphasizes, perhaps to the point of redundancy, "influencing an audience" because terrorists care less about the individual targets of their violence than the audience which this violence affects. They use some people as targets to influence others. For example, they take hostages or blow up airplanes not because they want to hurt those particular hostages or passengers but because they want to influence or intimidate a larger public or government. This is why terrorists claim credit for their attacks or for the attacks of other groups. If no one claims credit for a violent attack or no claim appears to be credible, we may not be dealing with terrorism (that is, with politically motivated violence), but with an act of revenge. If Pan Am Flight 103 was blown up in revenge for either the raid on Libya or for the downing by a U.S. Navy ship of an Iranian Airbus, it may explain why no credible claim of responsibility was made. It is possible, of course, that violence may be committed to influence the politics of a terrorist group. In this case, violent acts might be committed without any general public claim of responsibility, as long as the members of the group or movement, the audience to be influenced, understand that one of their factions was responsible. At certain times, some Palestinian terrorism seems to be of this sort.

Understood in this way, as an effort to influence an audience, what we are calling the core definition of terrorism would appear to include some violent acts that we do not normally think of as terrorism. For example, this core definition would include most uses of force by states, since they use force for political reasons and often do so to influence an audience. The raid on Libya in response to the bombing of the discotheque in West Berlin, for instance, might be considered politically motivated violence intended to influence an audience. At least part of its purpose was to let an audience (e.g., terrorists and states that supported terrorism) know that we would respond to attacks. Thus, if we define terrorism as the use of force to influence an audience, the raid on Libya would be an act of terrorism. At the same time, the core definition of terrorism would exclude other violent acts that some might think of as terrorism. For example, such acts as the assassination of an individual or the slaughter of thousands, no matter how terrible, would not be terrorism if the killing did not have a political motive or was not intended to influence an audience. An extermination campaign against a religious or ethnic group might be intended simply to get rid of the group, not to influence others.

Of these two problems with the core definition, the second (that it excludes some terrifying, violent acts because they do not have a political motive or are not intended to influence an audience) raises a narrow technical question: does the criterion of influencing an audience distinguish terrorism from other violent acts in a way that helps us combat this particular form of violence? If it does, then we should keep it as part of the core definition. In fact, this criterion does distinguish terrorism from other violent acts in ways relevant to efforts to combat it. The objective of influencing an audience affects the kind and degree of violence that people are willing to perpetrate. Understanding this is relevant to combating terrorism. A madman who kills for the pleasure of killing does not worry about the effect of his acts on other people. Someone who kills for a political purpose, on the other hand, someone who uses violence but who wants to win new supporters or maintain those he has, must consider whether the violence he commits will alienate people. For this reason, concern for the opinion of an audience, whether a population or a government, can act to moderate or limit violence. Typically, for example, terrorism experts have argued that terrorists would not be inclined to use WMD because to do so would destroy the political support the terrorists hoped to garner, if only by depriving them of the vague sort of sympathy that the thought of the putatively oppressed arouses in some people. From the viewpoint of those combating violence, keeping in mind that some of their opponents seek to influence an audience is useful because it indicates a way of understanding the motivations of their opponents and might even be useful as a negotiating tactic or in planning a more strategic response. For these reasons, therefore, it is useful when refining the core definition of terrorism to maintain the idea that terrorism is violence that intends to influence an audience. Such an intention distinguishes what we call terrorism from other forms of violence, and keeping this distinction in mind may help us combat it.

The gas attack in the Tokyo subway system in March 1995 provides a useful illustration of this point. The group accused of perpetrating the attack forfeited any sympathy or even tolerance it may have enjoyed from the population at large. It became a pariah. It also became the object of a massive police investigation that eventually dismantled the group. This response to the group's alleged involvement in the gas attack is not surprising. Therefore, a group that had a political agenda would probably not commit such an act. In fact, the Tokyo group did not have a political agenda. As one investigator said, "it's not a political group as much as it is simply an anti-society group."[4] As such, it was less inhibited in its use of violence than would be those (e.g., the East German officials who supported terrorism or their Palestinian allies) who can attain their goals only if they are not seen as pariahs.

Arguing that pursuit of a political agenda and, therefore, influence over an audience will limit a terrorist's use of violence assumes, of course, that the terrorist is rational: that he or, less frequently, she can judge what are likely to be effective means to attain his or her ends. Either bad judgment or a psychological impairment may lead the terrorist to choose inappropriate means, either too much or the wrong kind of violence against the wrong targets. For example, Islamic terrorists in Egypt, who killed tourists as a way of attacking the Egyptian economy, miscalculated the effect their attacks would have on the local population, which relied on tourism for its income. News reports indicate that local populations who suffered economically from the attacks assisted the Egyptian authorities in identifying the Islamic militants who carried them out. Because of this cooperation and the stringent security measures applied by the government, the number of attacks sharply declined.[5] This requirement for sound judgment and rationality means that we cannot say that a group or individual with a political agenda will always limit the violence it uses to pursue its agenda. Like everyone else, terrorists make mistakes, and some people who use violence are irrational. But it is still useful to maintain the connection in our understanding of terrorism between the use of violence and the idea of influencing an audience. Since the rational vastly outnumber the irrational, the presence of a political agenda remains a useful way to distinguish among those individuals and groups that resort to violence. Those with such an agenda are likely to be more circumspect in their use of violence than those without one and are also more likely to make calculations of the costs and benefits of their violence, which those who combat them may be able to manipulate or take advantage of. For example, through effective public information campaigns we may be able to turn the violence terrorists use against them.

This traditional understanding of the importance of a political agenda has been called into question lately by people who wish to call "terrorism" the violence associated with ethnic conflict and certain so-called radical or fundamentalist religious movements, such as Islamic militants, right-wing Protestant groups in the United States, or the supposedly Buddhist group suspected of gassing the Tokyo subway system. Recognizing the origins of our current definition of terrorism in the political movements of the late 19th century that did use violent acts to influence a larger audience,[6] some want to challenge this understanding of terrorism as too limited for the new post–Cold War world we have entered.

It is hard to see why. In the first place, virtually all the ethnic and religious violence we have seen both during and since the Cold War has had political motivations. Ethnic groups fight for a homeland or regional autonomy, while religiously inspired terrorists, such as those in Hizbollah, pursue the establishment of Islamic states or their defense. These are political objectives. In this sense, there is nothing new in the phenomenon of ethnic and religious terrorism that would make obsolete the understanding of terrorism as politically motivated violence intended to influence an audience. Some religious or ethnic violence is carried out, of course, not for political purposes but simply to annihilate those who are from a different ethnic group or religion. Some Islamic militants, for example, see the United States as their enemy and want to destroy it. They commit violent acts not because they hope to influence an audience but simply out of hatred, as a way of punishing those they see as their enemies. Certainly, such violence can cause terror but this hardly seems a reason to call it terrorism. A great many things, from wars to earthquakes, cause terror. Should these, too, be called terrorism? In this case, *terrorism* would become merely a synonym for *terrible*. Violence for no purpose, as opposed to violence for a political purpose, would be real terrorism, as a news magazine has implied, because random violence is the most terrifying sort. No doubt such violence is terrible, as would be any use of a WMD, but for this reason should we call it terrorism? Undoubtedly, using *terrorism* as a synonym for *terrible* will increase the terrorism threat, giving terrorism experts more work, but it will do so at the cost of rendering the term *terrorism* analytically useless by making it too generic. Something like this is already happening. *Terrorism* is becoming just another way of saying that something is deplorable. A Justice Department spokesman, for example, described a particularly notorious hacker as "a computer terrorist," while a researcher called the sexual harassment of girls by young boys "gender terrorism." The President of Colombia called persistent rumors and allegations that his campaign had accepted money from drug traffickers "moral terrorism." A U.S. Congressman, apparently in earnest, called the stopping of traffic at rush hour by strikers "traffic terrorism." "They placed at risk the safety of hundreds of thousands of people who did them no harm," he explained, "and like other forms of terrorism this certainly involved the taking of hostages." Even the President's Chief of Staff could not resist the trend. As the President and Congress threatened each other with a shutdown of the government rather than compromise on the budget, he told reporters that "the Republicans are threatening the President. . . . That's a form of terrorism." A fine example of where this rhetorical, analytically imprecise use of the term *terrorism* leads was the call to action of one commentator who wove the perpetrators of the World Trade Center bombing, those who committed a hate crime, "frustrated ethnic minorities, . . . drug lords *and the like*" (emphasis added) into a "growing league of terrorist actors."[7] Apparently, we know enough about this heterogeneous collection of villains if we know they are "terrorists."

As we have argued to the contrary of such views, there is a reason to retain the notions of political motivation or purpose and, hence, the aim of influencing others in our definition of terrorism. As the analysts of what some have called "holy terror" have noted, the kind of violence committed depends on the motivation of those committing it. Religiously inspired violence may not be as self-limiting, for example, as political violence because religious violence is an end in itself rather than a means to some other objective, as is political violence.[8] For the sake of our understanding of and, thus, our ability to respond effectively to the various kinds of violence that confront us in the world, it would be better to preserve the accepted understanding of terrorism and refer to religiously or ethnically motivated slaughter as mass violence or, if appropriate, genocide. This approach would not deny that there are other forms of political violence besides terrorism or that such violence and other kinds we confront must be dealt with. It insists only that in the long run we will deal better with terrorism and violence generally if we do not confuse ourselves.

The usefulness of the idea of a political agenda as a distinguishing feature of the violence we call terrorism explains, at least in part, why the notion of influencing an audience, with which it is linked, appears in all of the U.S. government definitions of terrorism quoted previously. There is no such unanimity on the issue raised by the first problem with the core definition: it does not allow us to distinguish between the violence a state uses to respond to terrorism and the violence committed by terrorists. In the example we cited previously, both the Libyan-organized discotheque bombing and the U.S. raid in response might both be called terrorism because both were politically motivated violence intended to influence an audience. This is anything but a narrow technical issue. It leads, in fact, to the most significant of the reasons why all efforts to define terrorism are so controversial, for terrorism is not merely a descriptive word. Whatever its origins in the traditions of tyrannicide, it now has only pejorative connotations.[9] To be labeled a terrorist or a supporter of terrorists is to be branded as vicious in the court of public opinion. The *Washington Post*, for example, conforming to the standards of journalistic objectivity, when reporting on the case of the American sentenced to life in prison for aiding Peruvian terrorists studiously avoided referring to the woman's colleagues as terrorists. It called them guerrillas. Terrorism, whatever else it may be, is now identical in common usage with violence that is illegitimate, not merely damaging to our interests, as would be the military actions of an enemy, but unjustifiable and unconscionable. Defining terrorism thus unavoidably involves deciding what is the legitimate or just use of force, and nothing is more controversial than deciding what is just and unjust. Because it lumps together all uses of force for political reasons, and does not provide a way of distinguishing between legitimate and illegitimate uses of violence, the core definition is inadequate.

An obvious way to distinguish between legitimate and illegitimate violence comes from our own history. Our nation came into existence by using violence to overthrow an established government and its laws, yet we consider this violence to be legitimate and not terrorism, even though not all the violence occurred in the course of recognized military campaigns. Why was the violence of the American Revolution legitimate? The Declaration of Independence justified it as resistance to tyrannical government. Legitimate government, according to the Declaration, derives from the consent of the governed.

Governments that do not have this consent are illegitimate, tyrannical, or despotic and rightly resisted. In modern language, those who use violence to resist tyrannical government are freedom fighters, not terrorists, assuming that they do not intend to set up another tyranny should they be successful in overthrowing the one under which they suffer. Thus, as Secretary Shultz pointed out in one of his speeches on terrorism, while all governments will call violence directed at them illegitimate, only legitimate (i.e., nontyrannical) governments are right to do so.[10] Governments that are representative of the wishes of their citizens are not justifiably the targets of political violence. Such violence used against them, even if for a political purpose, is rightly classified as illegitimate. If you can vote, yet throw a bomb, you are a terrorist. Violence used against a tyrannical government, on the other hand, should not be considered illegitimate because the laws of the government in question are themselves illegitimate, not having been established with the consent of the governed, and the subjects of such a government are right to resist it. If you cannot vote and throw a bomb, you are a freedom fighter, as long as you actually intend to set up a free government.

Using the standard offered by the Declaration means that politically motivated violence is illegitimate and properly called terrorism if its purpose is to overthrow a legitimate government. Taking this qualification into account would produce a revised core definition: terrorism is politically motivated violence, intended to influence an audience as part of an effort to overthrow a legitimate government. This revised definition is an improvement over the core definition because it provides a way of distinguishing legitimate from illegitimate political violence, which we must do if we want to preserve the distinction between legitimate and illegitimate government that is at the core of our political life.

The Declaration's distinction between legitimate and illegitimate violence lies before us, yet no U.S. government definition of terrorism has picked it up. On the contrary, the intelligence community definition quoted previously rejects it. It defines as terrorism violence used against established government, whether or not the government is legitimate. As we saw in the previous chapter, such an understanding was part of the definitional problem that emerged when William Casey asked the intelligence community for an assessment of Soviet involvement in terrorism. By obliterating the difference between legitimate and illegitimate government, the intelligence community definition consigned our nation's founders to the ranks of the terrorists. Nothing could be further from the spirit of the Declaration, of course. Other U.S. government definitions do not so plainly contradict the Declaration; they simply ignore it.

In truth, it must be admitted that there are reasons to do so, all derived from the difficulties associated with the idea of legitimacy. In the first place, it is often difficult and controversial to decide when a government has become tyrannical and can be resisted with violence. This issue split Americans at the time of the Revolution, for example, and has today generated debate among historians about how tyrannical, in fact, British administration of the colonies was. The practical difficulties in deciding questions of legitimacy are enormous. How much fraud can occur in an election before its winner sacrifices his or her representative character? How much resentment or distrust of a government must exist in a population before the government loses its legitimacy? Or are there certain international norms, such as prohibitions against torture or other forms of repression, the violation of which make a government illegitimate? One might reject any effort to decide or even to discuss such questions because to do so concedes too much to the perpetrators of political violence. Since the standards of legitimacy are so ambiguous, raising questions about it merely affords some cover to those who bomb, assassinate, and kidnap. Such concerns were especially apparent during the Cold War, where we first encountered terrorism as an element of wars of national liberation. The political objective of the insurgents in these wars was to call into question the legitimacy of governments as part of an effort to overthrow them. For strategic reasons, since these governments were allies in the fight against the Soviet Union, we were not inclined to ask about either their legitimacy or the legitimacy of the forces that opposed them. In the course of these various struggles, as the character of these opposition forces became more evident, they should have been increasingly open to the objection that they merely hoped to replace one tyranny with another. Experience and argument was often not enough, however, to overcome Popular Front tactics and the American prejudice, deeply rooted in our history, to favor those fighting so-called wars of national liberation, without sufficient scrutiny of what they meant by liberation. Ho Chi Minh, it was said, was the George Washington of Vietnam.

Even though the Cold War has ended, the problem with using legitimacy as a standard to distinguish among acts of political violence has not disappeared completely. In the Middle East, for example, a government friendly to the United States that by the standard of the Declaration we could not call legitimate may come under attack from insurgents. To criticize the insurgents as illegitimate because they use force to settle a political issue will hardly be devastating to them. Where there are no elections or free speech, they can hardly do otherwise. Raising the issue of legitimacy will merely undermine the government we hope to defend. Admittedly, this problem will be easier to handle in such a case than it was during the Cold War, since the antigovernment attack is likely to come from Islamic militants, who will not be viewed sympathetically by educated Westerners. While the faults of the government may be apparent, it will be easier now to argue that they are preferable to those of their opponents, who are likely to be even less sympathetic to democracy and human rights than the established governments. The insurgents are unlikely even to appear to be freedom fighters. Their use of violence is, for that reason, unlikely to appear legitimate. Algeria provides a good example of this phenomenon. The reception of the Islamic Salvation Front has been less warm

among the democracies and in the U.S. government than was the reception of
the National Liberation Front during its earlier struggle with France. Still,
debates about legitimacy are unlikely to recommend themselves as a way of
supporting friendly Middle Eastern governments under attack. Outside of the
Middle East, without the Islamic militant as a convenient opponent, such
debates may recommend themselves even less. On the other hand, with the
collapse of the Soviet Union, the outcomes of these struggles should matter a
good deal less to us.

As if the difficulties of determining legitimacy and how we should deal with
this issue were not enough, the Declaration's standard of legitimacy poses
another problem: it does not express our sense of the restrictions that should
control any use of violence, including our own. The definition of terrorism
based on the Declaration (politically motivated violence, intended to influence
an audience as part of an effort to overthrow a legitimate government) sanctions
the use of violence against an illegitimate government. It says nothing about
what kind of violence may be used, however. Accordingly, blowing a
passenger plane out of the sky would not be illegitimate in the Declaration's
terms, if it were somehow part of a struggle to overthrow a tyrannical regime.
The Declaration, then, gives us at best only part of the standard we seek for
defining which instances of political violence are terrorism.

We might try to avoid the problems generated by using the Declaration of
Independence as a guide for distinguishing between acceptable and unacceptable political violence by using a standard that appears in three U.S.
government definitions of terrorism. These definitions distinguish between
legitimate and illegitimate violence by using the terms *unlawful* or *criminal*.
The definitions used by the FBI and the Joint Staff, for example, refer to "the
unlawful use of force or violence against persons or property." The Title 18
definition refers to acts that violate the criminal laws of the United States or
"would be a criminal violation if committed within the jurisdiction of the United
States or of any State."

The definition of terrorism by reference to our laws has several things going
for it, all derived from the fact that the issue of what is legal is less contentious
than the issue of what is just. For example, given the difficulty of the question
and what is at stake, it is better that bureaucrats take the law as a guide for what
is just or legitimate than that they rely on their own ruminations. While our
laws may not always derive from reflection on the just and unjust, they result at
least from a democratic process. Again, using a legal standard allows us to
avoid discussing disputable claims of legitimacy when dealing with friendly
governments that are under attack. The more straightforward notion of the legal
also removes an impediment to an international consensus against terrorism by
avoiding the politically sensitive issue of legitimacy. Finally, insofar as the
legal is less contentious than the just, it is probably more effective rhetorically to
brand someone a criminal than to stigmatize him as unjust.

This is an impressive list of reasons to refer to our laws when trying to define terrorism, but this approach is not without its own problems. First, we should consider a minor one: the erroneous idea that a legal standard and an insistence that terrorism is criminal can help build international cooperation to combat terrorism. This, in fact, has not happened. Cooperation has increased—even the United Nations General Assembly has condemned terrorism—but not because we have based our discussions of terrorism on the idea that it is criminal. Although nations act as they do for a variety of reasons, interest remains a powerful motivation. For example, in January 1994, the French ignored the extradition request of the Swiss government for two suspected terrorists because to do so, according to the French Prime Minister, was in the French national interest. Although the Prime Minister did not specify what these interests were, the French have often been reported as trying to avoid terrorist activity against French citizens and property by reaching certain agreements with terrorists. The French also have or wish to have extensive business dealings with Iran. When Great Britain and the United States criticized German contacts with Iran, including discussions between intelligence officials, German government spokesman Dieter Vogel told reporters that "we will naturally hold the talks with Iran that are required by German interests. . . . We will continue to do so. Iran is a trading partner of significant size."[11] These French and German officials may be criticized, with some justice, for having an insufficiently enlightened view of their interests. In any case, there is little or no evidence that defining terrorism as crime has done much to improve cooperation against it. At best, it may have allowed us to avoid the obstacle of debates about legitimacy, but where this has happened, self-interest would probably have done so anyway.

A more serious problem with defining terrorism by reference to the legal is that it does not allow us to distinguish between legitimate and illegitimate political violence. The legal definition, just like the intelligence community definition, accepts the authority of established governments. They are the ones who pass the laws. To say that terrorism is unlawful would mean that political violence should not be used even against a tyrannical government, since such a government would presumably not pass a law making opposition to itself legal. Even if it did, such violent opposition could not be said to be right or just or somehow morally superior to the violence of the government opposed because in this view there is no such thing as right or justice; there is only the law, and the law is merely the expression of the will of those who hold power. Whether or not such a view is consistent (at a minimum, it is an understanding of law that encourages unlawfulness),[12] it clearly contradicts the argument of the Declaration and, therefore, of our entire political tradition, which, from Jefferson to Lincoln to Martin Luther King, looks beyond the law of any government to a standard that prevails universally or by nature. It is by that standard that one can distinguish legitimate from illegitimate political violence. As we noted when discussing the Declaration of Independence, it is the legitimacy of the government making the laws, not the laws themselves, that determines whether violence contrary to the laws is or is not legitimate and is or is not terrorism. Because the FBI, Joint Staff, and Title 18 definitions, like the intelligence community definition, do not take the legitimacy of an established government as the determining factor in defining the legitimacy of political violence, they are not adequate definitions of terrorism.

Defenders of these definitions may insist that the FBI and Joint Staff work effectively against terrorism and so, by the standard of usefulness and practicality we raised at the beginning of this chapter, their definitions should not be discounted simply because of a minor theoretical problem such as obscuring the difference between just and unjust government. This may appear to some to be a good, practical, hard-headed argument, but it is not. The point at issue is not merely theoretical. As we have seen, it was a significant factor in the effort to assess Soviet involvement in terrorism. More important, for Americans the issue of what constitutes legitimate government is of immense practical significance because of the character of our government. According to the best authority, Abraham Lincoln, representative government in general and the government of the United States in particular rest on the opinion of the people. Terrorism, as the experts agree and as we have noted, is essentially a battle for the opinion of an audience. To combat terrorism with an understanding of terrorism that repudiates the Declaration of Independence, that corrupts our opinion on the issue of whether and for what reason our government and democratic way of life is just, concedes victory to the terrorists. Surely this is not an effective way to combat them. Second, speaking practically and beyond the narrow realm of combating terrorism, politics or at least international politics is the business of helping friends and hurting enemies no more than is necessary. To do this, we must be able to distinguish our friends, who share our principles and objectives, from allies of convenience or enemies, who do not. If we confuse ourselves about our principles and objectives, we will not be able to do this and will be less likely to serve our interests.

There is another practical reason not to insist that terrorism is criminal. This is a weak approach rhetorically. Those who support terrorism have habitually responded to the accusation that terrorism is criminal by raising the issue of legitimacy. For example, the 1990 edition of *Patterns of Global Terrorism* reported that Syria's Foreign Minister had publicly "condemned all forms of terrorism, including hijacking and hostage taking" but noted that "Syria continues to draw a distinction between 'legitimate struggle against the occupation troops' and acts of terrorism."[13] In effect, when we insist that terrorism is criminal we allow its supporters to take the moral high ground that is ours historically and by right. We should not cede this ground, especially since we have less reason to fear discussions of legitimacy in the post–Cold War world, and ignoring it has not led to international consensus for action against terrorism.

We may sum up what we have so far uncovered about the U.S. government definitions of terrorism by saying that the legal and intelligence community definitions are inadequate because they do not allow us to distinguish between legitimate and illegitimate political violence, while a definition based on the argument of the Declaration of Independence allows us to make this distinction but does not provide a basis for our sense of the limits to political violence, even when used against an illegitimate regime. We can see a resolution to this problem if we recall that a persistent theme in the U.S. government's discussions of terrorism has been that it is illegitimate violence because it is aimed at civilians or innocents. For example, in 1972, the State Department's legal advisor said that the United States sought to condemn acts of terrorism because of the interference they caused to the machinery of international life but also "because of their grave and inhuman effect on innocent persons." When Gerry Adams, the leader of Sinn Fein, the political front for the Irish Republican Army, visited the United States in 1994, a "senior official said that Adams's remarks during the visit were not 'optimal' but that he had at least 'opposed taking innocent lives.' . . . The State Department forewarned Clinton that Adams had not met customary U.S. conditions for a visa by renouncing violence unambiguously. During an interview with a consular official in Belfast, Adams made general comments opposing attacks on innocents, but department officials regarded the statement as vague."[14] The Title 22 definition of terrorism captures the U.S. government's long-standing concern with violence against innocents by discriminating among kinds of political violence not by the end this violence serves (attacks on legitimate or illegitimate governments) but by its means, how the violence is used. To the core definition, Title 22 adds the principle that terrorism is violence against noncombatants for political reasons.

According to Title 22, then, someone who resists tyrannical government would be a terrorist only if he targeted noncombatants, and a violent act to coerce another state would be terrorism only if it killed or injured noncombatants. In effect, Title 22 classifies those who use political violence in three ways. Freedom fighters use it to oppose tyrannical government, criminals to resist legitimate government, and terrorists to target noncombatants. The advantage of the Title 22 definition over other U.S. government definitions of terrorism is that it, like our political tradition, does not classify all political violence as terrorism, but provides, as the Declaration does not, a limit to political violence, even that which is legitimate. By focusing on a moral standard, on the abnormal violence perpetrated by terrorists, it avoids the contentious political issue of legitimacy, which in some cases we may not want raised, yet does not contradict it, which would repudiate our own political tradition.

The Title 22 definition represents a compromise, then, among a prudent respect for the dangers of talking about legitimacy, respect for our political tradition (which requires that we do so) and our sense that some kinds of violence, no matter what end they serve, are not acceptable. All compromises are somewhat unsatisfactory and this one is too, primarily because respect for our political tradition seems to suffer. Title 22 does not contain any statement of what constitutes legitimate government, although it does not contradict the Declaration's understanding of legitimacy. Given the importance to our political tradition of distinguishing between legitimate and illegitimate government, we may find Title 22's failure to do so unacceptable. We may find it particularly unacceptable now, when we no longer need to avoid the issue of legitimacy in our foreign relations to the degree we once did. Even during the Cold War, it was debatable whether avoiding this issue was the proper strategy in the long run. It seems even less defensible now. Still, we should probably accept the Title 22 definition, at least as a bureaucratic measure, because it focuses on something (targeting noncombatants) that is more easily determined than whether or not a government is legitimate. In addition, the Title 22 definition offers a rhetorical advantage. Discussions of terrorism based on this definition could address issues of legitimacy, if appropriate, but could do so within the context of a moral or humanitarian appeal. For example, we could stigmatize as terrorism violent acts that take the lives of noncombatants for political purposes and point out that illegitimate governments or revolutionary groups, those not respecting the rights of the governed, are prone to such acts. This would be a rhetorical strategy very close to the one Secretary Shultz employed to good effect in his terrorism speeches of 1984–1985. If we chose not to raise the issue of legitimacy, the Title 22 definition would still support a humanitarian appeal that should be rhetorically powerful and, unlike an appeal to our laws, universally applicable.

The rhetorical advantage of the Title 22 definition is admittedly open to question, at least in one respect. While useful, the rhetorical effect of identifying terrorists as killers of innocents might be blunted because the moral principle that killing innocents is never justified is open to question. One authority, even though he is intent on limiting the use of political violence as much as possible and evinces great skepticism toward the rationalizations of statesmen, nevertheless ultimately concedes, with great reluctance, that there are some "supreme emergencies" that override the rights of innocents.[15] Terrorists, therefore, might try to avail themselves of the argument that some "supreme emergency" justified their actions. From a rhetorical viewpoint, however, this will be a difficult argument for terrorists to win, since the cases in which there is truly no other recourse than killing innocents are rare. One might want to go further and argue that even when there is no other recourse, terrorism is not justified because we can be reasonably sure that terrorism will be futile ("Not a single government has been overthrown as a result of terrorist action"[16]) and violent acts likely to be futile are not justifiable. Even though as an instrument of coercive diplomacy terrorism has allowed its perpetrators and their sponsors to achieve some of their goals, from a rhetorical point of view, it will still be hard to claim that these gains justify the slaughter of innocents. Terrorists, of course, are not likely to be deterred or even bothered by rhetoric about killing innocents. But, in keeping with the indirect nature of terrorism, rhetoric to combat terrorists is directed not at them but at broader public opinion, which is also their chief target. That is where the battle is fought. From this viewpoint, the Title 22 definition, despite some ambiguity on the legitimacy of killing innocents, is superior to any other used by the U.S. government.

It may be, however, that what we say about terrorism is less important than the way we say it. During certain periods in the 1980s, U.S. government officials spoke often and vehemently about terrorism. Looking back, some of them feel that this was counterproductive.[17] By showing that we were taking the terrorists seriously, that they were getting to us, these officials argue, we only encouraged them to come at us again. This was particularly true in the early and mid-1980s, when we had not developed an effective counterterrorism capability or, at least, one that was as effective as our rhetoric was vociferous. In the future, it might be better to keep a lower rhetorical profile or, at any rate, to calibrate our counterterrorism rhetoric and capabilities.

Part of the rhetorical campaign against terrorism in the 1980s was to call it war. This claim, that terrorism is warfare, is the second issue that tests how our understanding of terrorism affects our ability to combat it. U.S. officials who claimed that terrorism was war or a kind of warfare or surrogate warfare never supplied a detailed analysis to support this contention. Such an analysis has been provided now, however. Basing his argument on Clausewitz's contention that war is the continuation of policy by other means, Donald Hanle asserts that war is the use of force to affect an enemy's will to resist. Terrorism is war, according to this analysis, because terrorism intends to affect the will of an audience to resist terrorists' demands. "Both terrorism and the more classical forms of warfare function in the same manner. Both employ lethal force against a victim to affect the morale of the much larger target or targets. Force is employed not so much for its physical but its psychological capabilities—that is, its ability to affect the target's morale and thereby influence its decisions and actions directly, or those of its superiors indirectly. Thus the only significant difference between terrorism and the more classical forms of warfare is the aforementioned selection of abnormal means by the terrorists."[18]

This analysis raises an immediate problem. We have used and continue to use lethal force, in strikes or raids, for example, to affect the morale, the will to resist of an opponent, without considering these efforts to be war. No one thought the raid on Libya in 1986 was war. Hanle's definition of war as the use of force to affect an opponent's morale is, then, too broad. It may be true that war aims to affect the will to resist, but it must do this in a way that is unique to those situations we call war, since we distinguish war from other forms of violence that are intended to affect the morale of our opponents. Hanle points to the distinguishing characteristic of war early in his discussion, by differentiating between total war and limited war: "in a total war you erode your enemy's power base so that he becomes *unable* to fight, and in a limited war you maximize his cost(s) until he becomes *unwilling* to continue to fight."[19] What

Hanle tries to bring together here as the targets of *war*, modified as total and limited, are really two different things: ability and will. Clearly, one can will to do something but be unable to do it or be able to do something and not will to do it. For example, in a conflict between states or other actors, a state or other actor may be able to resist but may decide not to either because it deems the object of the conflict not worth the effort or because, although the object is worth further effort, the state or actor is in a strategic position that makes this effort futile or too costly compared to what it might gain. We undertake all sorts of actions, from such measures short of war as strikes, shows of force and sanctions, to grand strategic initiatives, such as the opening to China, in order to affect the will to resist of our opponents by making them see that the price for resistance will be higher than any gain they can make or that such resistance from a strategic perspective will be futile. We call none of these actions war or even limited war. We reserve the designation *war* for our efforts to destroy the ability of our opponents to resist. What this requires depends on the objective at issue. If it is to expel an invader from some territory, it will require the destruction of the invader's ability to resist in that territory. Attaining this objective may require that we extend our destructive efforts beyond the territory immediately at issue (for example, to external lines of communications) but it does not necessarily require that we take our opponent's capital or that we destroy all his forces. Such efforts may be necessary, as they were in World War II, when our objective was the destruction of a nation's way of life. In either case, we call such efforts war because we seek to attain our objective not through persuasion or influence but through destruction. It is true that our effort to destroy the ability of our opponent to resist may persuade the opponent to give up before that destruction is complete, but in going to war it was not our intention to persuade. That is what coercive diplomacy and grand strategy try to do. The critical issue for a statesman is realizing when he must switch from coercive diplomacy to war. If the distinction between the two is lost or the choice between them put off, the consequences, as we learned in Vietnam, can be disastrous because these two ways of attaining our ends are distinct and impose different requirements. Coercive diplomacy attempts to persuade. The decision to go to war is the decision to destroy the ability of our opponent to resist. This is what distinguishes war from other uses of force.

Recognizing that a definition of war that emphasized destroying the ability to resist excludes terrorism from the category *war*, Hanle finds it necessary to use the term *total war* to denote this activity. This in turn allows him to use *limited war* to refer to those activities in which the purpose is not, as it is in total war, destroying the ability to resist but using force only to affect the will to resist. Again, however, the problem is that limited war so defined would include those activities mentioned previously (strikes or raids) that we do not think of as war or even as limited war. If we are not intent on finding some way to include terrorism in the category *war*, we can dispense with the term *total war* and refer simply to war, avoiding *limited war* entirely, since it refers to a category of activities that we do not normally consider war. By speaking only of war, we highlight the fact that war is a distinct, even peculiar, activity, different from both coercive diplomacy (the use of force to persuade an opponent) and grand strategy (the integrated use of all elements of national power in pursuit of national objectives). Both coercive diplomacy and grand strategy aim to make our enemies unwilling to resist us, but coercive diplomacy is not identical to war nor is grand strategy reducible to war.[20]

Having seen the distinguishing characteristic of war, we can also see the central problem in the effort to define terrorism as war. Terrorism, as all its students agree, focuses on the will, intentions or morale of a group. It is to influence or manipulate these that the terrorist commits his violent acts. War affects the will, intentions, or morale of an enemy too, we may concede, but it does so because it is or should be the continuation of politics by other means, and all politics is ultimately a matter of the wills, intentions, and morale of those involved. What distinguishes war among political activities is its focus on destroying the ability of an opponent to resist. Even though the opponent may want to fight on, he cannot. What distinguishes terrorism among political activities is its use of violence against innocents, or as Title 22 puts it, noncombatants to affect the will or intentions of a third party. Because he ignores this distinction—war targets ability, terrorism the will—Hanle must distort the definitions of both war and terrorism. For example, in addition to using the category *limited war*, he speaks of war, in the passage quoted at length previously, as if it were merely a matter of affecting morale, ignoring its principal target: the ability of an opponent to resist. When he is arguing that revolutionary terrorism is war, he asserts that it involves "armed engagements between contending political entities that are seeking to physically compel each other."[21] Students of revolutionary terrorism have insisted not that it is an effort physically to compel opponents but rather that it is a form of psychological warfare, that its violence is meant to affect will and morale, that it is a part of the political organizing that is necessary to prepare for the later stages of the revolution, where in fact, according to the theory, the contending forces aim at physical compulsion. The effort to define terrorism as war ends up obscuring both war and terrorism.

Having insisted so strongly on the distinction between war and terrorism, we must admit that there is a way in which efforts to combat terrorism may resemble war. It is possible to imagine a situation in which a state would respond to terrorist attacks by deciding to wipe out the terrorist group responsible for them and would proceed to destroy its bases, financial assets, and personnel. It would not undertake these actions to persuade either the members of the group to cease being terrorists or states not to sponsor their activities, although its actions might have this effect. The purpose would be simply to destroy the capabilities of this group to act in a way contrary to the interests of the government under attack. It may be that the Israeli response to the killing of its Olympic athletes in Munich was an action like this. The

Israelis sought to kill those responsible for the deaths of their athletes and to destroy the Black September terrorist organization. Such an approach to combating terrorism should be considered war, even though conventional usage restricts the term *war* to conflicts between states.

While in theory the idea of a state waging something that approximates war against a terrorist group is a possibility, in practice it is problematic both in itself and because of its consequences or lack thereof. Terrorist groups do not have the solidity of states. What are the criteria for success in destroying them? If intense pressure forces a group to cease its activities, it is likely that it will simply pass on expertise and personnel to another group. Killing all the members might be one way to destroy a group. But would this mean killing only those who pull the triggers or their supporters as well? If the terrorist group is a branch of a political and social organization like Hizbollah, will killing all the trigger-pullers get rid of the terrorist group or will the group simply regenerate itself from its political and social roots? Any intention to destroy the roots of the terrorist group leads to the central problem in treating combating terrorism as war against terrorists. The political cost to a state of such an approach would probably outweigh the benefit of destroying the terrorist group. For this reason, combating terrorism is primarily, at least for the United States, not a question of waging war but of using military force and other instruments of national power to persuade and coerce terrorist groups and their sponsors into giving up terrorism. Finally, since the most deadly groups have been state-sponsored, efforts to wipe them out would be a waste of time and resources. It is their sponsors that should be the target and, not so single-mindedly, the groups they sustain.

Supporters of the view that terrorism is war may believe that mentioning the state sponsors of this violence buttresses their claim. If a state uses this form of violence against another state, even if only through surrogates, does this not approximate the state-against-state model that conforms to our view of classical warfare more than does the use of terrorism in guerrilla war? Does this not make more plausible the claim that terrorism is a form of warfare? We have argued that there is a good reason to include in our definition of terrorism the notion that it aims to influence an audience. If we hold to this definition, then terrorism, even when sponsored by one state against another, would fall short of being war (the use of force to destroy the ability of an opponent to resist). The Syrians, for example, support the Kurdish Workers' Party as part of an effort to manage their relations with Turkey. There is no evidence that Syria intends with this support to destroy Turkey or its ability to resist Syrian demands. What Syria intends is to influence or manipulate Turkey's will to resist on several bilateral issues. Syrian support for terrorism, then, amounts to a form of coercive diplomacy, although using means that we consider abnormal and unacceptable. Certainly, a state could try to destroy another state by using surrogates. It could hire mercenaries or support indigenous forces and help them organize a coup d'état. We would appropriately call this surrogate warfare, but it would not be terrorism. Terrorism might be part of a surrogate war but would not be identical to it. War and terrorism are distinguishable and should be kept distinct.

Since terrorism and war are different, saying that the former is like the latter will only mislead us. Calling terrorism warfare may suggest the seriousness with which terrorism should be taken, but it will mislead if it suggests that our response to terrorism should be an effort to destroy the ability of terrorists to attack us. Terrorism is more a question of will than ability, it is more a political than a military issue. This does not mean that force or coercion cannot be used to respond to terrorist attacks. It means that the primary purpose for using them must be persuasion and not destruction. Whatever destruction we visit on terrorists or their state sponsors should be designed to influence their actions.

Our discussion of terrorism has brought us to the conclusion that it is more than crime and less than war, that it is violence against innocents or noncombatants intended to influence an audience for the sake of some political objective. With this understanding in mind, we are prepared to analyze the means that the United States has used to combat terrorism.

3

METHODS

Since the U.S. government spends so much time and energy responding to problems, it would be comforting to know that these responses do some good. Not surprisingly, a study sponsored by the government concluded that they did, at least as far as terrorism was concerned. The study, completed in 1985, concluded that the policy pronouncements and actions of the United States and other countries did influence the behavior of terrorists. The authors of the study pointed out, however, that there were a host of factors that influenced terrorists besides government policies and actions. They mentioned changes of government, inflation, death of terrorist leadership, and major international political events among the multitude of such factors. Because the influences on terrorists were so many, the authors warned that any study of the effectiveness of government policy must be put into a broader context. It must take account of what the researchers called "environmental factors." We have already noted two such factors, neither yet in play in the early 1980s when the researchers wrote their report: the collapse of the Soviet Union and the collapse of world oil prices. The researchers broadened and deepened their warning by pointing out that little or no theoretical guidance was available to help filter environmental factors to get a finer sense of the effectiveness of government policy and actions. In addition, their research had convinced them that terrorism, because of its complexity and the varied motivations that led to it, was particularly resistant to theoretical filtering. Finally, the complexity of terrorism was especially a problem when trying to assess the effectiveness of U.S. government policy because the United States and its citizens were involved in the world in so many ways and at so many levels.[1]

All of these warnings must be kept in mind during the following analysis of the ways in which the United States has responded to terrorism, because nothing relevant to them has changed. We still do not possess an understanding of terrorism, or of human or political interaction, for that matter, sufficient to allow us to filter all environmental factors so that we are left with the effects that are purely from government action. Terrorism remains remarkably complex and the involvement of the United States in the world still wonderfully varied. Nevertheless, we can develop a sense of which methods have worked against terrorism and which have not and what each of our methods has cost.

The United States has combated terrorism with nine different measures: international legal conventions, defensive measures, addressing the causes of terrorism, a policy of no concessions, economic sanctions, military retaliation, prosecution (after we have gotten hold of suspects by extradition, rendition or by seizing them overseas and returning them to the United States for trial), preemption, and disruption. Of these, "no concessions" is the most important. When attacked by terrorists, a country must first of all decide whether it will give in to the terrorists' demands. If it decides to, then its efforts against terrorism may well consist only of defensive measures designed to dissuade terrorists from attacking by making their most likely targets less vulnerable. Because it has decided to concede to demands, it will not emphasize developing other ways to respond. The decision about whether to concede or to what degree and in what situations is so fundamental to a country's orientation toward terrorism that it deserves to be called a policy decision, although conceding or not conceding to demands in a given case remains in itself one of the methods at a country's disposal for responding to terrorism. While U.S. government officials and others refer at times to counterterrorism efforts as policies (for example, our policy of using military force against terrorists) all of these are really methods of responding to terrorism, made more important by the U.S. policy of not conceding to the demands of terrorists.

These different methods of combating terrorism did not develop all at once or arbitrarily. As we have seen, the United States responded to modern terrorism's first wave, hijackings and kidnappings, by working to create an international consensus in support of treaties and conventions requiring, for example, that states prosecute or extradite hijackers. The United States supplemented its use of international conventions by acknowledging that the underlying causes of terrorism had to be treated as well. In addition, from the beginning, the United States sought to prevent terrorist attacks on its people and their property by developing defensive measures. As hostage-takings continued, it adopted a policy of not giving in to the demands of terrorists. A corollary of this policy of no concessions is a policy of rescuing hostages, since forcible rescue becomes more necessary as a way to get hostages back once concessions are ruled out. In the late 1970s, the United States began to develop its specialized counterterrorism forces for such rescues. In this same period, as state sponsorship became increasingly evident, the United States decided to impose sanctions on states that supported terrorism, eventually augmenting this economic retaliation with a policy of military retaliation. As a result of the Iran-

Contra scandal and the success of the Pan Am Flight 103 investigation, as well as a growing sense that the raid on Libya had had only limited effectiveness, the United States began to seize terrorists overseas for trial in the United States. Almost from the time of the first terrorist attack, a number of people talked of preempting such attacks.   For domestic terrorism, preemption or arresting terrorists before they committed their attacks proved difficult but feasible. Preempting attacks originating or taking place overseas proved more difficult but has occurred.   Finally, as U.S. capabilities grew and matured, efforts to disrupt terrorist organizations bore fruit, on one occasion at least.

Diplomacy is missing from this catalogue of ways we have combated terrorism. It is absent not because it is unimportant but because it accompanies all the others.   Typically, the first step we take when confronted by a state sponsor of terrorism is to make a diplomatic démarche. When this has failed to change behavior harmful to us, we have used economic sanctions to indicate that we are serious and to put pressure on the offending state. Finally, all else failing and the provocation being too great to ignore, we have resorted to military force. Throughout all these steps, however, we use diplomacy to make our case to our allies and directly or through intermediaries to our opponents. In the case of the judicial response to terrorism, diplomacy assists through negotiating agreements or persuading a country to turn over a suspect to us. Diplomacy may also support efforts to disrupt terrorist groups and discourage those who support them, as it did in the case of the campaign against the ANO. Occasionally, when intelligence is good enough, diplomacy may even be part of an effort to preempt a terrorist attack.   As we have seen, on at least one occasion, we warned the East Germans about possible Palestinian attacks on Americans, and they took steps to let their Palestinian allies know that such attacks would not be appreciated. As diplomacy supports each effort to counter terrorism, these efforts, in turn, support our diplomacy. Diplomats have been among the most consistent supporters of the raid on Libya, for example, because it gave their démarches a weight they would not have had otherwise.

Having provided this summary of our counterterrorism methods and explained how they and diplomacy depend on each other, we may now consider these methods in more detail.   We will consider first the policy of no concessions, then the judicial response (including international conventions and prosecution), economic sanctions, military retaliation, prevention (defensive measures and addressing causes), preemption, and disruption.[2]

NO CONCESSIONS

The principal argument offered in support of the policy of no concessions is that paying ransom or making other concessions to terrorists only encourages more terrorism. Because merely talking to terrorists may grant them standing or give them something in return for their terrorism, as was the case with the PLO's first contact with the United States, some argue that a policy of no concessions should exclude even talking with terrorists. The Reagan administration, for example, announced that it would honor the terms of the agreement the Carter administration reached with Iran but that it would not have negotiated with the Iranians in the first place.[3] Whether or not we understand the policy of no concessions to prohibit negotiations because they can be a tacit form of recognition and thus a concession, the argument against concessions is the same. Making them may save some lives now but will only endanger more later. If we make concessions, we allow terrorists to profit, ensuring that we will be paying them for years to come. Not only will a group once successful strike again, but other groups will follow its example and pick on the nationals of any government that gives in. A firm policy of no concessions will stop this contagion, its supporters claim. Another argument for no concessions is that making concessions to those who resort to terrorism will only undermine respect for the rule of law. If we negotiate with terrorists, we grant them and their methods at least some legitimacy. This diminishes respect for the proposition, upon which decent government rests, that not force but law should rule. To diminish respect for the rule of law ultimately undermines our liberal democratic way of life. By making concessions to terrorists, then, we are only helping them accomplish one of their goals.

The argument that making concessions encourages more terrorism has an intuitive appeal. If a given action produces a benefit, the actor is likely to repeat it. A survey concluded that experience in this regard has more or less confirmed intuition. Concessions by Germany and Japan in the 1970s "probably did contribute to their being repeatedly selected as targets. The same may to some extent apply to French and US concessions in the 1980s." Furthermore, terrorist groups may, in fact, learn from one another, even if they are not part of some organized international conspiracy. Concessions seem to "encourage a general and sometimes worldwide fashion or momentum in the selection of a particular type of target." Conversely, "a firm stand by a government or group of governments has . . . had a generally suppressive effect on terrorism."[4]

The lessons of experience, however, do not unequivocally support the policy of no concessions. The Austrian government made concessions on two occasions but was not hit by terrorists again. British firmness during the seizure of the Iranian embassy in London in 1980 and American firmness in the case of General Dozier in 1981 did not prevent the subsequent kidnapping of Americans and Britons in Lebanon. Finally, one study concluded, at least in a preliminary fashion, that when a government took a hard line with terrorists, made no concessions, and used force in response to their attacks, subsequently making concessions actually led to a decrease in terrorism. Other studies have also concluded that refusing to make concessions may not be as effective in limiting terrorism as the proponents of this policy claim.[5]

These diverse countervailing examples cast some doubt on the effectiveness of the policy of no concessions. It may have a deterrent effect, but the evidence is not conclusive. Not only are there examples to contradict the claim that a policy of no concessions deters terrorists but, more generally, given the complex circumstances in which such a policy is applied, it is virtually impossible to know if that policy or other actions, or unrelated developments, or all these in combination are the cause of a decline in a certain kind of terrorist incident. Indeed, one study has concluded that "government policies toward terrorism have much less of an impact on transnational attacks" than the general environment of world politics in which the attacks occur and the policies of the foreign governments "that directly bear on the issues that motivate transnational groups."[6]   Whether or not all the evidence this study presents supports this statement, it is at least clear that success in deterring terrorist acts cannot be attributed unambiguously or only to a policy of no concessions.

One important factor complicating an assessment of not making concessions to terrorists is the role played by effective hostage rescues. Using force is a natural corollary of a policy of no concessions. If we refuse to negotiate when confronted with a terrorist hostage taking or other terrorist attacks, then the initiative will rest with the terrorists, unless we use force. After such an incident, if terrorist attacks cease or decrease in frequency, is it the policy of no concessions that has succeeded or the willingness to use force? Since not making concessions and using force are so closely related, it may seem that this question need not be asked. Yet, government publications which tout the effectiveness of a policy of no concessions do so without mentioning the use of force. For example, *Patterns of Global Terrorism,* the State Department's annual report on terrorism, said in its 1995 edition that "US counterterrorism policy follows three general rules." The first of these is not to "make deals with terrorists or submit to blackmail" (the no concessions policy). The second is to apply the rule of law. The third is to put "maximum pressure" on the states that sponsor and support terrorism by "imposing economic, diplomatic, and political sanctions." This way of presenting a policy of no concessions and the use of force (sanctions) is misleading in that it makes the policy seem to be a deterrent by itself. In fact, the use of force to rescue hostages appears to be an important factor in making a policy of no concessions effective.[7]

One reason that a no concessions policy and the use of force may not deter terrorism is that the terrorists may not really seek immediate concessions, such as ransom, even though they demand them. Terrorists get benefits from their violent acts even if their targets do not immediately yield to their demands. Rather than immediate concessions, terrorists may seek publicity or the destruction of a society's sense of security and order. In this case and others, terrorists have motives to act independent of whether or not we grant them concessions.[8]

There are some reasons, then, to doubt that a policy of no concessions has deterred terrorism. There are also reasons to doubt that it has stopped its spread. It was feared that making concessions to one terrorist group would simply encourage others. This assumes, however, that disparate terrorist groups share the same motivations and operate in like circumstances. Of course, they do not.

Terrorists have different principles, purposes, motivations, tactics, and views on the sanctity of life. Contact between groups does not necessarily diminish these differences.[9] In addition, the domestic and international circumstances in which terrorists operate are different and, even if similar in some ways, may be perceived by the terrorists to be different because of their different beliefs and commitments. Such factors diminish both the danger that a weak response will encourage the spread of terrorism and the hope that a strong response will discourage it.

If there is reason to doubt that a no concessions policy is as effective as its proponents claim in deterring terrorism or stopping its spread, there is also reason to doubt that it is as important and relevant for combating terrorism as it once was. Not making concessions became the central element in our efforts against terrorism in response to the hostage taking of the late 1960s and early 1970s, when terrorist incidents usually involved some direct and simple quid pro quo, such as an exchange of hostages for imprisoned terrorists. While such incidents still occur and will probably continue to occur, terrorism now often happens without accompanying direct demands for concessions. Syria's support of the Kurdish Workers Party is not coupled with direct demands on the Turkish government for specific concessions but rather is one of a number of tools used to shape a complicated political situation in Syria's favor. This is also how the Iranians use the various terrorist groups they support. U.S. intelligence officials, at least when speaking anonymously, acknowledge this point. In a briefing to reporters, one of them noted that we now see less quid pro quo terrorist activity. "'We see relatively less of that [and] relatively more of inflicting pain for pain's sake,' the intelligence official said. 'No bargaining, no negotiations.'" The bombing of the World Trade Center would be an example of this kind of terrorism. To combat it, the policy of no concessions is less relevant than it was when hostage taking was the chief form of terrorism we confronted. In addition, in some situations when hostages are taken, such as Lebanon during the height of its Civil War, the policy may be less relevant than it first appears to be. The absence of government in Lebanon was at least part of the reason why Western and particularly American hostages were taken. In such anarchic situations foreigners held hostage may be most valuable not for the specific concessions that can be wrung directly from their governments but as bargaining chips when the hostage taking groups deal with competing internal forces or neighboring governments. Holding foreigners can get a group attention and give it clout that it would not otherwise have, even if it makes no demands on the governments whose nationals are held hostage. These situations may produce more hostage taking at the same time that they render our policy of not making concessions less relevant to the outcome. Finally, it is one thing to contemplate the deaths of several or even a hundred hostages as we adhere to a policy of no concessions. It will be something else to contemplate the possible deaths of thousands or tens of thousands of people should terrorists demonstrate the ability to use WMD. The pressures that would be at work in the threat of terrorism or other acts using WMD are evident in the policy of the United States and other nations toward North Korea, which is on the State Department's list of states that sponsor terrorism. North Korea has gained concessions from the international community in return for its agreement to abide by nonproliferation protocols it had earlier accepted and then reneged on.[10]

There is a final way in which the policy of no concessions may no longer be as relevant to combating terrorism as the U.S. government has claimed it is. When the policy was developed in the 1970s, terrorism was part of struggles for so-called national liberation. Although terrorism might occur outside the country where the struggle was taking place and thus be international terrorism, it was still understood to be part of a challenge to the legitimacy of a government. Palestinian terrorism is the archetype of this kind of terrorism. Negotiating with the terrorists in these cases was a form of tacit recognition—as we noted when recounting the first contacts between the United States and the PLO—which undermined the legitimacy of the government under attack by the terrorists and could not be allowed. In these circumstances policies of no concessions and no negotiations made sense, but these circumstances are much less prevalent now.

While in some cases the terrorism that affects us may still be part of an insurgent movement against an established government, the terrorism that has done most damage to us has not been this kind but the terrorism that is conducted as part of the foreign policy of other governments. In this case, the policy of no concessions must mean that we will not make concessions to these sponsoring states, since these are the real authors of the terrorist acts rather than the groups that carry them out. If the state is Libya, isolated, weak, and with little strategic position, making no concessions will not be very difficult. If the state is Syria, Iraq, or Iran, a key player in a region of great importance to us, or, for that matter, the Soviet Union during the Cold War, resolving not to make concessions will be less feasible. In such a case, we are likely to deal with the state even if it sponsors terrorism, since we would be unable to secure our regional or more general interests if we did not. We may stick to the line that we are not giving in to the specific demands of terrorists, but this will miss the point. The states in question sponsor and support acts of terrorism not so much to get concessions related to these specific acts but to further a broader strategy.[11] When we negotiate with them and make concessions, as both sides normally do in the process of a negotiation, even though we are not negotiating a specific terrorist demand, we are in effect negotiating with terrorists and giving in to their demands.

To the extent that the policy of no concessions claims to be a hard-headed deduction from experience about what furthers our interests, there should be no objection to setting it aside if our interests dictate. But a no concessions policy is also said to be necessary for moral reasons. To negotiate with terrorists grants them and their methods legitimacy and thus calls into question the legitimacy and value of a way of life like ours based on the rule of law. Thus, we should not negotiate with or make concessions to terrorists even if this requires sacrificing our short-term, narrow, material interests, or some of them at least, because in the long run the moral integrity of our way of life demands it. This argument has force but is self-limiting. What would it mean to say without qualification that terrorists have no legitimacy whatever? Does it mean that we would not extend to them or their sponsors any legal or humanitarian considerations of any sort?[12] This is what Islamist terrorists seem to mean when they call the United States the Great Satan. They are saying in effect that the United States and Americans are not part of the human race and thus not protected by the conventions that govern how human beings treat one another. Conversely, the fact that we do extend to terrorists both legal and humanitarian considerations, as we do to criminals and our enemies in war, indicates that we recognize their humanity no matter how terrible their deeds. But if we recognize their humanity, how can we say categorically that we would never negotiate or make concessions to them? The simple act of saying "cease your terrorism and we will talk to you" is both a negotiation with and a concession to terrorists. If we refused to make even this minimal concession and pursued terrorists only with unrelenting force (use of force being the corollary of no concessions), we would violate our own precepts. Thus, morality demands that we not adhere in an unqualified way to a policy of no concessions.

Expediency and morality, then, both argue for and against a policy of no concessions. This is why it has been impossible for the U.S. government to follow this policy consistently. There are practical and moral reasons to follow it and practical and moral reasons not to follow it. This means that a no concessions policy is in reality not an unbreakable principle but at most a guideline that must be applied in a variety of different circumstances. Its advantages and disadvantages must be weighed and then a judgment made. This is illustrated by the decision to publish a manuscript by the so-called Unabomber, "a serial mail bomber," who was responsible for sixteen attacks in seventeen years that killed three people and injured twenty-three. Federal officials persuaded the *Washington Post* and the *New York Times* to publish a 35,000-word manifesto from him because he said that if this were done, he would no longer target people. While the authorities would not comment on why they wanted the manifesto published, the newspapers involved cited public safety and the particular character of the bomber as reasons why the usual arguments about making concessions did not apply. They also suggested that publication of the manifesto might lead someone who read it to recall someone who had argued or written similarly and thus lead to a suspect. These explanations for why the manifesto was published probably reflect official views, since the papers' publishers cited advice from federal experts as the basis for their decision. According to newspaper reports, publication of the manifesto did, in fact, lead to a suspect. David Kaczynski thought he recognized in some of his brother's old letters ideas and language similar to the Unabomber's and contacted the FBI, who eventually arrested Theodore Kaczynski. This episode shows that as a practical matter exceptions to the policy of no concessions will be made. There are reasons to make these exceptions.[13]

That exceptions to the policy of no concessions are reasonable suggests that it should not be presented as an inviolable principle. Demoting "no concessions" will give our policy more flexibility. Some might argue that a more flexible policy will make us appear weaker. Yet, as one commentator has noted, "there is no logical reason to assume that a clearly stated but sporadically observed policy is any better than an ambiguous or flexible one."[14] We will violate an absolute policy of no concessions because there will be good reason to do so in certain circumstances. We tried to negotiate with the Iranians and did negotiate with the PLO, at least implicitly, because we felt that we would gain more than we would lose by making the concession of opening negotiations. In the future, a similar calculation may lead us to try another opening with Iran. While one might argue that in these particular cases we were or will be wrong to violate the policy of no concessions, it would be difficult to argue that there could not possibly be a time when it would be right for us to do so, especially since the deterrent effect of a policy of not making concessions is not absolutely clear. We should not enunciate an inviolable no concessions policy, therefore, since we can be reasonably sure that we will violate it at some point. A flexible policy, sensibly applied, can make us strong and appear strong, since it will allow us to protect our interests and principles.

Such a flexible policy on concessions would have two components. First, it would emphasize the complexity of terrorism, making clear that a no concessions policy is most useful only in those situations where terrorists make direct quid pro quo demands. It would explicitly exclude from the no concessions policy the minimal concession—stop terrorism and we will talk—and the contacts necessary to convey this point. In other words, it should make clear that "no concessions" does not mean "no contact" with terrorists and that we are prepared to talk to any group that gives up terrorism. This change would leave open the possibility of contact with terrorists or their sponsors without violating the no concessions policy. Second, a more flexible policy on no concessions would distinguish between negotiable and nonnegotiable demands. When police deal with a criminal hostage barricade episode, they often meet many of the criminal's demands, such as demands for food or to talk with particular people, in an effort to protect the hostages without giving in to demands for amnesty or free passage that would undermine fundamental notions of responsibility for criminal action. Distinguishing in this way between negotiable and nonnegotiable demands gives police greater flexibility in dealing with hostage situations. Similar techniques have been used when dealing with terrorist hostage barricade situations. Making this distinction an explicit part of the no concessions policy would make it compatible with normal practice in any negotiation, including those that U.S. diplomats and officials carry out everyday, and give us more flexibility in dealing with states that sponsor terrorism. A flexible policy on concessions is what we are currently using in our dealings with Syria in an effort to keep peace talks going in the Middle East. The Syrians still support terrorists but are limiting their actions; President Clinton has met with President Asad and Secretary of State Christopher was a frequent visitor to Damascus.[15]

A policy on negotiations and concessions more flexible than our declared policy has been could lead to weakness if, in avoiding the rigid policy, we rush to one that is spineless. One proponent of negotiating with terrorists seems to suggest that negotiations are always a possibility, that we can always find common ground. But this suggests that all issues can be compromised. There have been and will be conflicts over issues that cannot be compromised. If we sit down and negotiate with terrorists or their state sponsors, we may conclude that what we are being asked to concede cannot be given up. In this case, the resort to force, within the legal and moral limits we accept, may be inevitable. The only way to avoid this outcome would be to declare that avoiding the use of force is more important to us than anything else, a proposition we did not embrace even at the height of the Cold War, when the threat to our survival was greater by far than that posed by terrorism.[16]

In sum, then, the current policy of no concessions is most appropriate in the case of hostage taking, a terrorist method of declining importance, but even in this case will not necessarily diminish future terrorist attacks. A no concessions policy is least appropriate when dealing with state sponsored terrorism, the kind of terrorism that is most threatening to us, and in anarchic situations, when taking U.S. hostages may not be done to force concessions from us but to gain status in some local or regional drama. For these reasons, a policy of no concessions should be less central to our policy for combating terrorism than it has been in the past. A more explicitly flexible version of the policy will be more useful. Articulating it after years of public insistence on an absolute prohibition of concessions may be seen as a sign of weakness, as some officials fear,[17] but this need not be so if modifications to the current no concessions policy are made carefully and we attend carefully to how we use our other means of combating terrorism.

JUDICIAL RESPONSE

The judicial response to terrorism consists of establishing a regime of international law to control it and prosecuting those suspected of terrorism, who come before our courts through extradition, rendition, or arrest by U.S. officials, even outside our territory.

Arrest and trial has always been the required response to terrorist acts committed in the United States. For terrorist acts committed against Americans or their property outside the United States, we have come increasingly to rely on the same method. There are numerous reasons for this. Most important, such a response is compatible with our respect for the rule of law. It reinforces this vital principle. It does this in part by providing a counter to the emotional language that surrounds discussion of terrorism. The judicial response focuses on the facts and unfolds slowly, two factors that diffuse emotions and encourage a reasoned response. Beyond this moral and political effect, however, there are practical reasons for responding to terrorism with legal means. There is a broad consensus among those who have worked to combat terrorism that the apprehension of terrorists outside the United States deters terrorism or makes it more difficult for terrorists to carry out their plans. Arrest warrants and our ability to act on them outside the United States, with or without the help of other countries, inhibit the travel of terrorists. Since mobility is essential to the terrorists' trade, this is a significant means of disrupting their activities. Our ability to apprehend terrorists outside the United States and the network of extradition treaties we have established also have important political consequences for combating terrorism. In the past, according to a Justice Department official, other nations have been able to protect themselves from domestic criticism when they prosecute suspected terrorists by saying that unless they take action, the United States will. There have also been cases in which other countries, unable to arrest a terrorist for domestic political reasons, have agreed to let the United States do it, as long as it was done quietly. Our authority and ability to arrest terrorists overseas has thus permitted other states to increase indirectly their efforts against terrorism. The judicial approach also encourages cooperation among states or at least removes an impediment to cooperation by focusing on specific acts, such as killing, hijacking, or hostage taking and not the contentious political issues that surround these acts. In addition, the U.S. government's actions against terrorism have greater credibility than they otherwise might when the claims that the government makes about a terrorist act are based on the exacting standards of U.S. criminal procedure and on evidence that can be used in a public judicial process. Finally, when a terrorist only loosely affiliated with a group or state sponsor attacks Americans, arresting him and bringing him to trial may be the only response open to us, since the connection between the terrorist and a sponsoring state or group may not be sufficient to allow us to attack the state or group.[18]

The effectiveness of the judicial approach can be seen in the case of Pan Am Flight 103. After a three-year investigation, the U.S. and British governments indicted two Libyans for the bombing. The two governments then persuaded the UN Security Council to endorse a series of demands on Libya based on the indictments. When Libya failed to meet these UN demands, the United States and Great Britain persuaded the Security Council to impose sanctions on Libya. Although this legal process has unfolded slowly, it has kept pressure on Libya since 1991. During this time, apparently in response to the legal pressure and sanctions, Libya has ceased to sponsor international terrorist attacks. It continues to support terrorist groups, attacks Libyan dissidents, and retains its capacity to commit other terrorist acts, but the legal process has so far been an effective measure for combating Libyan terrorism directed at the United States and its allies. The judicial approach has also led to the arrest and prosecution of others accused of committing terrorist acts. For example, Ramzi Yousef, the man behind the bombing of the World Trade Center in New York City in 1993, was handed over to the United States for prosecution, as were two of his accomplices.[19]

Given the benefits of the judicial approach, we may well continue to favor it in our efforts to fight terrorism. As a nation, we have a presumption in favor of the rule of law and against the use of force, which, in the case of terrorism, is reinforced by the practical advantages of the judicial response. The result has been to make "the efforts of the United States and other nations to strengthen the rule of law and to apply the law to terrorists . . . the cornerstone of our policy" to combat terrorism.[20]

Despite the general enthusiasm for this approach, all supporters of the judicial response to international terrorism admit its limitations. First, there are practical ones. Criminal investigations outside the United States are possible only with the cooperation of another government. In addition, our powerful forensic abilities may not be applicable. If Pan Am Flight 103 had flown a few miles farther it would have been over deep ocean when the bomb exploded and there would have been no crime scene to investigate. The difficulties encountered investigating the explosion aboard TWA Flight 800 when its pieces fell into waters off Long Island highlight this problem. Supporters of the judicial method of combating terrorism also accept that there are political limitations to using it. Other nations may choose not to enforce the international conventions they have signed. The national interests and political issues that prevent some states from honoring their commitments have led some experts to describe international law as ineffective and the effort to use it as futile. Exercising our own extraterritorial legal authority may not be advisable because of the damage it would do to our relations with another country. From the perspective of our interests more generally, this damage could be worse for us than not "snatching" the terrorist suspect. Asserting our extraterritorial legal authority when not permitted to do so could also erode the international cooperation necessary to combat terrorism.[21]

Generally, the supporters of the judicial approach present these practical and political restrictions as only minor limitations on its effectiveness. In fact, however, its effectiveness is more limited than its supporters tend to acknowledge. To avoid political disputes over what may or may not be legitimate uses of force for political reasons, the judicial approach focuses on the individual and illegal terrorist act—a killing, a kidnapping, or a hijacking, for instance. By doing this, the judicial approach focuses our attention on individual terrorist actors. While apprehending and prosecuting them has the advantages outlined previously, it is not clear that the deterrence created is always worth the expense involved. As noted before, one FBI official has characterized the Fawaz Yunis arrest as undoubtedly the most expensive apprehension in law enforcement history.[22] It cost millions and required altering the activities of the sixth fleet. Even if a cost-benefit analysis of this arrest concluded that the time and money spent produced an appropriate level of deterrence, the fact would remain that this arrest and others like it address only the threat posed by individuals. They do not affect what has traditionally been the core of the terrorist threat: state-sponsorship. The cornerstone of our counterterrorism policy provides leverage, then, only against the margins of the terrorist threat.

Supporters of the judicial approach would respond that the effectiveness of their favored approach is greater than this. It provides a sound basis for the sanctions that have put such pressure on Libya, for example. But the sanctions against Libya and their effectiveness did not result from a judicial process. They resulted from a political process at the United Nations and foreign capitals. A host of factors besides the results of the criminal investigation determined the outcome of this process. This is evident if we consider whether a legal process would have led to sanctions against Syria or Iran. If sanctions had been adopted against Syria or Iran, would they have been as respected as have been those against Libya? It was difficult to get agreement to impose sanctions against Syria in 1986–1987 and there was continual pressure, even inside the U.S. government, to lift them. The source of these pressures is evident, as we have noted, in the remark of a German official, who defended German dealings with Iran on the basis of German national interests. For similar reasons, the UN has not been willing to impose meaningful sanctions on Sudan for its support of terrorism.[23] The judicial process, then, provides limited leverage against terrorism and is largely dependent on an international political process that it does little to shape.

In addition to being less effective than its proponents are inclined to claim, the judicial approach can also mislead us. First, the judicial approach emphasizes the criminality of terrorism. As we have seen, however, terrorism is not simply a crime. It has an irreducible political element. Emphasizing the judicial approach may cause us to forget this. For example, if we think of terrorism as a crime, we may insist that terrorists not "get away with it," even though in the normal course of diplomacy and international relations, for very good reasons, states and their agents are allowed to "get away with" all sorts of things. In other words, emphasizing the judicial response to terrorism may make us less able to respond flexibly—some might say cynically—to this form of political violence. Second, in adopting the judicial approach, we make the standard for action abroad as high as the standard for domestic judicial action. No nation has ever done this consistently, for the simple reason that it is an impractical standard, impossible to apply in many, if not most, cases. Proponents of the judicial response claim that we can, in effect, pick and choose when and where to use it. If it is workable in a case or up to a point, use it; if not, forget it. Unfortunately, given our attachment to the rule of law, the domestic judicial standard may become the only standard. Where it cannot be applied, we will feel we have no justification for action. Even before the legal response became so important in our counterterrorism efforts, there was pressure for political reasons to find a "smoking gun" before we responded with force to a terrorist attack. This is what the Reagan administration looked for leading up to the raid on Libya. With the increasing reliance on the judicial approach, this attitude may become more pronounced. For example, speaking of the Clinton administration's deliberations concerning the Iraqi attempt to assassinate former President Bush, the *Washington Post* reported that "intelligence analysis of this sort [based on circumstantial evidence] had been considered adequate proof of complicity in previous U.S. policy deliberations, but officials said senior Clinton administration policymakers—a group dominated by lawyers—indicated from the outset they wanted to act only on the basis of evidence that would be sufficient to produce a courtroom conviction." According to another press account of this affair, President Clinton asked the FBI and the Attorney General to take the lead in investigating the alleged assassination attempt, involving the State Department and the NSC only in the very final stages of the decision-making process.[24] The problem with such an approach is that it can breed hesitancy or indecisiveness. If it is true that a detailed forensic investigation gives credibility to U.S. government responses to terrorist acts, it would make sense that the absence of such an investigation or its inconclusive results would detract from State Department credibility and make officials hesitant to act. This makes the judicial approach a dangerously double-edged sword. Given the limitations of this approach, if we adopt its standard of evidence, we may restrict our scope of action to a point that is impractical in international affairs, to the detriment of the interests we are trying to protect by combating terrorism.

We can see another problem with using international law to fight terrorism if we consider what such an approach implies if pressed to its logical conclusion. Some have argued that we should continue to try to use international law, despite the difficulties involved, in hopes of someday making it effective, since an effective regime of international law would be a powerful tool in the struggle against terrorism and, more generally, international conflict. There are at least two reasons to reject this counsel. First, it is utopian in intent. Ultimately, to make an international rule of law effective would require an international legislature, executive, and judiciary, including an international police force with coercive powers. Apart from the practical difficulties involved in establishing such institutions, it seems likely that such a world government would have to be a despotic government, given the profound differences of principle among the earth's inhabitants. These differences are likely to make a world government by consent, the alternative to despotic government, unlikely. Encouragement to accept an effective regime of international law is really, therefore, encouragement to accept despotism as the price of a world without conflict. Such a bargain makes sense—assuming that a despotic world would be without conflict, a questionable assumption of course—only if peace is a greater good than freedom. Some might argue that the forces of economic and technological progress are homogenizing all people into a common humanity, making such a trade-off between peace and freedom unnecessary. This is a highly speculative matter, however, and such a consummation of our supposed progress would be many years in the future, if it ever occurred. Our decisions about a regime of international law, whatever they may be, are likely to be guided, therefore, by a more apparent fact. Working for an effective system of international law will bring us face to face, as international life already has, with situations in which international law will be accepted as prohibiting actions we deem and have deemed to be legitimate and in our national interest. For example, the International Court decided against us in the case of the harbor mining in Nicaragua. This second objection to supporting an effective regime of international law is likely to become more compelling as American influence in the international system declines relatively in the years ahead.[25]

Finally, a difficulty with the extraterritorial approach that its proponents have not sufficiently noted is that it establishes a precedent we may not want to live with. The Iranian threat to kill the novelist Salman Rushdie is, for example, an assertion of extraterritorial jurisdiction.[26] Some will object that there is no moral equivalence between the United States applying the law to terrorists and Iran condemning Rushdie for exercising his right to free speech. Indeed, any right-thinking democrat rejects such an equivalence. But this only highlights the problem with extraterritorial jurisdiction: if we assert it, we can deny the right of other nations to do so only by arguing that their law is inferior to ours. Inevitably, making this case will require that we insist on moral and political distinctions between nations that, for the sake of diminishing the causes of war, have been excluded from legitimate international discourse for more than 300 years. In other words, asserting our right to extraterritorial jurisdiction but denying it to nations like Iran suggests a willingness to engage in the modern equivalent of wars of religion. It is hard to see how this will enhance the rule of law among nations.

We can sum up the rule-of-law approach to combating terrorism, then, by saying that when based on international law, it is currently of limited use and, if made completely effective, would be incompatible with free government; that when based on extraterritoriality, it is of limited application, may undermine the international cooperation necessary to combat terrorism, and set pernicious precedents; and that in either case it may mislead us into responding to terrorism as if it were only criminal activity.

ECONOMIC SANCTIONS

Economic sanctions are the deliberate curtailment or cessation by a government of customary economic or financial relations in order to coerce another government. Conventional wisdom holds that such sanctions are not effective, especially if imposed unilaterally. They do not cause the states sanctioned to change their behavior and may in fact cause the sanctioned state or its population to become more recalcitrant. Their only effect is to cost the sanctioning state economically, by cutting off valuable foreign trade or irritating friendly or allied countries, which are pressured to comply with sanctions or whose companies are included in an extraterritorial application of sanctions. Recently, with the experiences of Iraq and Haiti in mind, conventional wisdom also holds that sanctions only hurt the little people and not the leaders, who are the real targets of the sanctions. This conventional wisdom holds as well in the case of sanctions used to combat international terrorism. As David Flores put it with regard to export controls directed at Libya in response to its support for international terrorism, "in terms of costs and benefits, export controls seemingly make no sense as instruments to combat international terrorism. The United States loses exports . . . ; the reliability of U.S. businesses as exporters is reduced; the supply of oil from Libya may be endangered; and controls may gain only the enmity of the countries against which the controls are directed." Congressman Tom Lantos, according to *U.S. News & World Report,* "says the U. N. sanctions imposed on Libya [for the bombing of Pan Am Flight 103] have thoroughly failed to achieve their stated purpose."[27]

David A. Baldwin has offered a spirited challenge to this conventional wisdom, criticizing it for faulty analysis of both the utility and effectiveness of sanctions and other economic measures of influence. He begins his defense by noting that the economic means of influencing other actors are various and can be both positive and negative. Promoting free trade, for example, is a means of influencing others; granting most favored nation trading status is a positive means of influence, economic sanctions, a negative one. All such economic means of influence represent a middle ground between démarches and the use of military force. Generally speaking, according to Baldwin, as means to influence other actors, economic measures are more effective and more costly than démarches but less effective and less costly than military force. He notes that although economic measures are usually less effective and less costly than military force, they are not necessarily less useful. "For the rational statesman," he argues, the cost-benefit analysis "is not between [the effect of sanctions on] his country and [their effect on] the target but rather between *his* costs and *his* benefits with respect to his alternatives." Even though economic measures of influence have costs and may be less effective than military force, they could be the most useful response if, for example, more effective military measures are too costly financially, morally, or politically. The cost-benefit analysis of economic measures may be in their favor financially, for example, once we take into account "the other policy goals that could have been promoted with the resources saved by not using expensive military measures," which are often the only coercive alternative to sanctions. Faced with starving mothers and children, the moral and political costs of sanctions may appear high, until we remember the same costs that even discriminate military force can generate. There is also a moral cost in not opposing terrorism, even if only with sanctions, that could lead to additional political costs if our failure to oppose terrorism encouraged others to accommodate themselves to it. Flores acknowledges this and offers it to balance his argument that from the viewpoint of cost-benefit analysis sanctions make no sense. Economic measures, then, can be the most useful, most cost-effective way to pursue our objectives, even if they are less likely to attain our goals than other means.[28]

Baldwin contends, however, that critics of economic measures have underestimated their effectiveness. They are inclined to say that sanctions either succeed or fail, "more often the latter," as if attempts at influencing the behavior of others were ever that clear cut. Baldwin argues that efforts to influence others, with political, military, or economic means, are rarely either wholly successful or complete failures. They generally fall between these extremes on a scale of effectiveness. After making this general point, Baldwin argues that to evaluate fairly our efforts at influencing, we must remember that publicly stated objectives are not usually the only ones in play. Implicit and unstated goals, as well as secondary goals and hoped-for effects on third parties, may all be in the minds of policymakers or form part of their secret discussions. If economic sanctions fail to achieve a publicly stated goal, they may still be effective because they attain or help attain other goals that were not publicly stated or emphasized. For example, sanctions imposed in an effort to stop the building of the gas pipeline from the Soviet Union to Europe did not stop the gas pipeline, but their political and economic cost to us did provide both the Soviets and our European allies with a demonstration of our seriousness in opposing the Soviets. As Baldwin notes, "economic sanctions may be effective not because of their economic impact, which may be nil, but rather because of the signal they send about the intentions of the state imposing the sanctions." Baldwin further argues that if the publicly stated goal of a sanction is to get country X to change its policy, the sanctions cannot be judged a complete failure, even if no policy change occurs, as long as the sanctions impose a cost on the target country. The cost may not be sufficient to cause a change in policy, but it will degrade the ability of the country to carry out this policy and may adversely affect its ability to carry out other policies as well. Our sanctions against Cuba have not toppled Castro but have limited the power of his government to carry out its policies. In this light, we can also judge these sanctions effective because they required the Soviet Union to spend resources it could not afford to support Cuba. Baldwin concludes his defense of the effectiveness of economic means of influence by referring to two factors peculiar to them. First, unlike military force, economic means of influence work silently and slowly; their effects are cumulative, rather than sudden. Analysts may tend, therefore, to underestimate their effectiveness. Second, sanctions may work with market forces in a way that will disguise their impact because the power of the market is often not noticeable. "To the extent that statesmen work through the market in making influence attempts, the effects of their efforts may be difficult to identify."[29]

In general, Baldwin defends economic statecraft by distinguishing utility and effectiveness and then showing that we must be more careful in analyzing both when assessing economic means of influencing other actors. His arguments about utility (cost-benefit) are more cogent than his arguments about effectiveness (achieving results), however, probably because in evaluating the latter there is always a greater element of judgment or prudence required than in evaluating the former, which yield to more mathematical analysis. The use of economic statecraft as a signaling device, for instance, exemplified by the case of the pipeline sanctions, which imposed self-inflicted costs on us to show that we were serious in opposing the Soviets, might be likened to a man lighting a match to his finger to show that he is tough. Such a demonstration may send the intended signal or may undercut it by revealing its sender to be an idiot. On the other hand, idiocy and toughness combined may scare more people than either one alone. In any case, judging the effectiveness of the signal requires viewing it in a broader context of the sender's and receiver's actions and reactions. Only then would we be able to make a judgment about the act. In effect, this is the argument of Michael Malloy, who offers an improvement on Baldwin's argument. Malloy distinguishes what he calls instrumental objectives, at which sanctions aim, from broader objectives, at which foreign policy as a whole aims. In this analysis, it makes no sense to say, for example, that "sanctions are ineffective because they did not end apartheid." Sanctions can attain the instrumental objective of restricting access to international capital markets but could not, in themselves, attain the broader objective of ending apartheid. The supporters of apartheid could have chosen greater poverty and repression over reform. By insisting on this distinction between instrumental objectives and the broader goals of policy, Malloy sets a realistic standard for judging the effectiveness of sanctions, while compelling us to examine the broader policy of which they are a part. "Sanctions themselves," he writes, "are instruments that may be used in a variety of contexts, but they are not the embodiment of policy. Sanctions will have whatever instrumental 'effect' the circumstances of their use will allow, but it is overarching policy—domestic and foreign—that should be judged in terms of its effectiveness, not sanctions."[30] We might caricature Malloy's argument as saying that there are no bad sanctions, only bad policy. More accurately stated, Malloy's argument is that when sanctions fail, it is really policy that has failed, because sanctions can never be more effective than the policy they support. Keeping this broader context of policy in mind best supports Baldwin's defense of sanctions as serving a variety of policy objectives that may be explicit, implicit, or only assumed.

The U.S. experience using sanctions against terrorism provides several case studies to test the arguments of Baldwin and Malloy. The United States has imposed sanctions to combat terrorism on eight countries: Cuba (1982, 1986), Iran (1980, 1984), Iraq (1979; lifted 1982; reimposed 1990), Libya (1973, 1979, 1985; with the UN, 1992, 1993), North Korea (1988), Syria (1979, 1986), Sudan (1993) and South Yemen (1979; lifted in 1990 because South Yemen ceased to exist upon its merger with the Yemen Arab Republic).[31] As we have noted, the U.S. government had a variety of reasons for imposing these sanctions. Congress forced a reluctant administration to impose sanctions in

1979 in an effort to make those countries that supported terrorism stop doing so. Sanctions on North Korea and Cuba were imposed later for the same reason but also fit into the larger strategy of the Cold War. Sanctions on Iran were first imposed as part of the effort to get back the hostages from our Embassy; they later became a more general response to growing Iranian support for terrorism. Syria was sanctioned in 1979 to discourage it from supporting terrorism and again for the same reason in 1986. These latter sanctions were also imposed to show solidarity with Great Britain, which caught a Syrian attempting to bomb an El Al flight departing from London in April of that year. In the case of Libya, under the Reagan administration, sanctions for supporting terrorism were part of a strategy to overturn Qadaffi's regime, which was involved in several activities judged to be contrary to U.S. interests. In the case of Iran and Libya, in particular, sanctions were also intended to diminish the target country's ability to support terrorism and related military operations. Finally, one purpose served by all these sanctions was symbolic. They were a way of signaling the seriousness of our effort to combat terrorism.

What are we to make of all these sanctions imposed for all these reasons? As of 1992, Cuba was the target of approximately thirty sanctions. Sorting out the effects of the two imposed because of Cuban support for terrorism would be difficult. In general, however, as noted previously, it is clear that sanctions have imposed costs on Cuba, impeding its ability to prosecute its domestic and foreign policies, while also imposing significant costs on its principal supporter and our principal adversary, the Soviet Union. Moreover, the cost to us of imposing these sanctions was much less than the cost of war, not only in terms of lives lost and dollars spent but in terms of the political costs to our relations with other Latin American countries and our European allies. A similar analysis can be made of sanctions imposed on North Korea (over twelve in total, two for sponsoring terrorism). According to the State Department, North Korea "is not known to have sponsored any terrorist acts since 1987" and Cuba has not maintained its former support for terrorism, although it continues to provide a safehaven for some terrorists. In neither case can we say with assurance that the sanctions stopped or inhibited support for terrorism, but they did impose costs, contributed to our ends, cost us less than the alternatives available to us, and achieved more than simple démarches would have. The assessment of sanctions against Iraq (sixteen in total, one for terrorism) must be different. When first imposed, sanctions were kept in place for so little time that it is hard to say what, if any, effect they had. Those imposed through the UN since the Gulf War (most of the sixteen) have not been intended primarily to stop terrorism. Indeed, although they have cost the Iraqis dearly, they have not eliminated Iraqi sponsorship of terrorism. As far as we know, however, no Iraqi-sponsored attacks on U.S. citizens have occurred except for the foiled plot to assassinate President Bush.[32] Less costly than some alternatives, sanctions on Iraq to combat terrorism have probably been less effective than those imposed on Cuba and North Korea.

Cuba, North Korea, and Iraq do not present good tests of the effectiveness of sanctions for combating terrorism because in each case stopping their support for terrorism was a relatively minor part of our policy. This is not the case with Iran, Syria, and Libya. While with regard to Syria the demands of Middle East politics have taken preeminence over combating terrorism at least occasionally, for the most part, support for terrorism or related issues have been at the top of our agenda with each of these countries for more than a decade.

In the case of Iran, sanctions (twenty in total, two for sponsoring terrorism) have been effective. Because the commercial and financial ties between Iran and the United States were as strong as they were during the Shah's reign, the sanctions imposed after the embassy hostages were taken, especially the freezing of assets, did hurt the Iranians. The war with Iraq made the sanctions more effective by making the Iranian need for U.S. products, particularly military equipment, greater. In the end, they significantly contributed to the release of the hostages. As one analyst has remarked, "without the pool of blocked assets as a 'bargaining chip,' one can only wonder what leverage the United States would have had in the face of continuing Iranian government intransigence." Sanctions have been less effective, however, in curtailing Iranian support for terrorism than they were in getting the hostages released, although they cannot be said to have failed. They have imposed costs on the Iranians and were certainly more effective than démarches alone would have been and less costly than the use of military force. It is reasonable to suppose that without the imposition of sanctions, the Iranians would have felt freer than they do to use terrorism. In this sense, at least, sanctions have been effective. They have worked as well with Syria (ten in total, three for supporting terrorism). The last sanctions for terrorism were imposed on Syria in 1986 following a particularly vicious terrorist attempt. Since then, according to the State Department, Syria has not sponsored any terrorist attacks, although it continues to provide safehaven and training facilities for terrorists. Sanctions alone cannot explain this change in Syrian behavior. The collapse of the Soviet Union and changes in Middle East politics were important factors. But for a country like Syria, with a weak economy and little in the way of valuable resources, sanctions can be a significant threat, especially when they are multilateral, as were those imposed in 1986. In the view of diplomats who have dealt with the Syrians on terrorism, sanctions played a significant part in stopping Syrian-sponsored attacks.[33]

Libya has the distinction of being the first country singled out for sanctions by the United States because of its sponsorship of international terrorism. Since then, three more of the twenty-two sanctions on Libya have been imposed for its support of terrorism. Slowly, in combination with economic mismanagement and corruption, the sanctions have had an effect. According to one expert, Qadaffi is desperate to get out from under them.[34] Their effect, while economic, has also been symbolic or psychological, making clear to Qadaffi his almost complete isolation. This is especially true since the unprecedented imposition of

UN sanctions in response to the bombing of Pan Am Flight 103 (December 1988) and UTA Flight 772 (September 1989). Sanctions have had this effect even though they have not touched the core of Libya's economy: its ability to export oil. Although various internal factors unrelated to sanctions have deepened Libya's problems, sanctions have over time played a significant role at relatively little cost to the United States. They may even yet contribute to overthrowing Qadaffi's regime.

This assessment of the effectiveness and utility of sanctions has been rather impressionistic. It would be useful, particularly for the policymaker considering their imposition, if more precise estimates of effectiveness and utility were available. This is unlikely to be the case. As our knowledge of trade flows and economics increases and we become better able to manipulate information, we may increase the precision with which we can predict or assess what Malloy calls the instrumental effect of a sanction. We may be able to predict that a given sanction will diminish trade, for example, between the imposing and the receiving country or countries by such a percentage. We may then be able to forecast, in general terms, the economic consequences of such diminishing trade. But real precision is likely to continue to elude us, since economics deals with human beings. Even more so will precision elude us when we consider whether this instrumental effect will translate into the political effect we were seeking. Will the same economic effect produce the same political reaction in a Qadaffi, as in an Asad, or an Iranian mullah? Ultimately, if people are in some fundamental sense free, we will not get precision in the prediction or assessment of the effectiveness of economic sanctions. Imposing them, like the statecraft of which they form a part, will remain an art and never become a science.

The art of imposing sanctions as a response to terrorism may be improved, perhaps, if we gather from past experience some guidelines, a few general statements about what worked and why.[35] The first of these guidelines is one that applies to all of our foreign policy efforts. They will be most effective if they are coordinated as part of a more comprehensive strategy that takes advantage of circumstances. Libya's current restraint is the result not of sanctions alone but of relentless diplomatic pressure, information warfare, direct military action, and indirect military action (support to Qadaffi's opponents in Chad). This strategy took advantage of such circumstances as falling oil prices (Qadaffi kept supporting terrorism as oil revenues declined sharply in the mid-1980s, but his support was more circumscribed than it had been and deprived him of money for other purposes),[36] the disappearance of a powerful ally (the pre-Gorbachev Soviet Union), and the inefficiencies of Libya's domestic arrangements, which prevent it from adapting well to changing circumstances. Syria's role in Middle East peace negotiations has meant that opposing its use of terrorism has at times competed with other priorities in our foreign policy, undermining the effectiveness of sanctions to combat terrorism. Such policy incoherence does not always result from poor thinking or managing within an administration. It can result from a careful assessment of changing costs and benefits. In addition, Congress has mandated many of the sanctions we have imposed on other countries because of their support for terrorism. If it is true that sanctions are more likely to be effective when part of a general strategy, then those imposed by Congress without the support of an administration are likely to be ineffective. Congress has difficulty articulating and executing general strategies to deal with foreign problems.

Sanctions that are part of a general strategy will have a greater chance of effecting their intended economic damage if they cover a wide range of activities (e.g., financial transactions and trade)[37] and are imposed quickly against a country with which the sanctioner has well-established commercial or financial ties. This is the lesson of the sanctions imposed when Iran held hostages from our embassy. If sanctions are imposed broadly and quickly, the target country has little time to adjust. It may not be able to move its money to avoid a freeze of assets or stockpile essential materials or find alternate suppliers. That Iran had a lot of assets in American financial institutions meant we could get at them easily; that its military had American weapons meant that our sanctions hurt when Iran went to war with Iraq. Conversely, the slow, piecemeal application of sanctions allows a target to adjust and diminishes the overall effect of the sanctions. Broad, quickly imposed sanctions work best, not surprisingly, against weak countries. Syria is more vulnerable than Libya or Iran because unlike these two oil producers it has no valuable natural resources for which there is a ready market. Sanctions may also work better against countries like Syria that play by the rules, even in a particularly vicious way, than against countries like Libya and Iran that have revolutionary aspirations or particularly megalomaniacal rulers (Libya, Iraq, North Korea). Syria, we have noted, employs terrorism as part of the usual balance of power politics that has dominated Western international politics since the end of the Middle Ages, while Iran aspires, at least in part, to overturn these rules. Revolutionary fervor and megalomania may be more likely to withstand the pressure of sanctions and other tools of statecraft than the shrewdness of a player in the balance of power.

In some cases, multilateral sanctions may be effective. Although reluctantly given, international cooperation helped with Iran in the hostage case.[38] Such cooperation may not always be necessary and always comes with a price. Arranging it may make it impossible to impose sanctions quickly. The effort against Libya following the attacks at the Rome and Vienna airports in 1985 provides an illustration. After press reports appeared that the U.S. was considering imposing sanctions, Libya actively sought to influence the debate through its own consultations with the European states, primarily focusing on Italy, which has extensive investments in Libya. As the weeks went by, international outrage over the airport attacks faded, while the companies which had extensive business ties with Libya began to lobby against the imposition of tough sanctions. As the consultations process unfolded, the United States found itself increasingly isolated diplomatically on the sanctions issue. When sanctions were finally announced, in early 1986, they consisted of only unilateral U.S. measures.

As economic power spreads to states that have not been our traditional allies and do not share our principles, it may become increasingly difficult to organize multilateral sanctions. The multilateral effort against Iraq following the Gulf War may prove to be an exception in the post-Cold War world and even this venture is showing signs of fatigue. If we are willing to bear high costs for imposing sanctions, we may still be able to organize others to support them but not if other states see significant advantages in dealing with the targeted state. This is the problem with our effort to organize sanctions against Iran in 1995 for its support of terrorism and opposition to Israeli-PLO peace talks. In such cases, we will have to rely on unilateral sanctions. These can still be effective, especially if the United States can use its clout in international financial organizations and groups to supplement them. According to press reports, we used this clout quietly and effectively against Iran in 1994. The relative decline of American economic power suggests, however, that unilateral sanctions will be less effective in the future than they have been in the past. Indeed, they have become less effective as our economic power has declined relatively. The sanctions we imposed on Iran in 1995 would have been more effective in 1970, when 60 percent of non-Soviet bloc oil production was controlled by seven large Western oil firms, five of which were American, and the international oil market was less well developed than it is today. To compensate for this decline in effectiveness, we must base our use of sanctions "on a careful analysis of the vulnerabilities of the target country." Although not normally considered an economic sanction, the issuance of a travel advisory against Greece in 1985 following a terrorist hijacking from Athens airport ultimately had an economic impact because it scared away many tourists and their dollars. It also appears to have helped produce the desired political objective of getting the Greeks to improve security.[39] It may be that such a careful analysis of vulnerabilities will reveal that we need the help of only a few countries to accomplish our purpose or that we can accomplish it by mixing precisely targeted unilateral sanctions with the discreet use of military force. In either case, we will need to keep in mind the fundamental guidelines for using sanctions that we have discussed and the possible ways of combining sanctions with all the different tools of statecraft. Finally, no matter how we go about it, our sanctions are more likely to succeed if we act in accordance with a comprehensive strategy.

MILITARY RETALIATION

As we have seen in recounting the history of the U.S. government's efforts to counter terrorism, the use of force in counterterrorism has been controversial. The controversy has arisen in part because of the fear that in using force we too might kill innocents and somehow validate terrorism. But the use of force against terrorism has also been controversial because of the prevailing view in the U.S.

military that force should be used decisively and overwhelmingly. Because it is difficult to do this against terrorism, the military has tended to argue against the use of force in counterterrorism. The *National Military Strategy* makes this point by declaring that any application of force will be made in a "decisive manner," while listing counterterrorism among noncombat activities.[40]

While we could find little good to say for the claim that terrorism is warfare, there are some good arguments to be made for the prevailing U.S. military view that any application of force should be overwhelming and decisive. In war, certainly, decisive or overwhelming force is appropriate because destroying enemy capabilities is the most immediate objective. In military operations other than war, overwhelming force (e.g., a larger than necessary deployment) can also be appropriate, providing some flexibility when things go wrong, as they inevitably will at some point, and helping compel an opponent to accept your preference.[41] It is also true, however, that overwhelming force will not always be appropriate or decisive outside of war. Some security threats cannot be removed by sheer power because those who pose them have neither conventional forces we can destroy nor capitals we can seize. When using force against states that support terrorism, decisive force will not always be appropriate because the capital we could bomb may be connected to the terrorism we want to stop only indirectly. Furthermore, overwhelming force in operations other than war may even be counterproductive to our larger political purpose if it arouses nationalist sentiments or otherwise increases resentment of the United States or of the presence of our troops, identifies us too closely with an outcome whose worth or durability we cannot guarantee, or creates a greater obligation for continued or deeper involvement. The effort to use decisive force in Somalia may well illustrate all of these difficulties. Using overwhelming force against the Somali leader Muhammad Farrah Aideed made him a sympathetic figure to Somalis and made us the guarantors of an outcome that we could guarantee only with a permanent presence. Finally, what constitutes decisive force depends on the commitment our opponents make to achieving their objectives and what they believe we are willing to commit to achieve ours. If their commitment is weak or they believe that ours is stronger than theirs, a small amount of force can be decisive. Flying U.S. jets over Manila stopped a coup attempt against President Aquino, for example. When discussing military operations other than war, including combating terrorism, whether it be a retaliatory raid or a use of force as part of a multifaceted coercion campaign, it would probably be better to speak not of the need to use decisive or overwhelming force but of the need to use appropriate force.

A powerful illustration of the difference between overwhelming and appropriate force comes from *The Village*, an account of a Marine Combined Action Platoon (a platoon made up of villagers and Marines) in Vietnam.[42] In their battle with Vietcong and North Vietnamese forces, the Marines in the village learn that they are better off without the heavy firepower that artillery or helicopter gunships can provide. The damage these instruments of war cause undermines efforts to win the support of the villagers. What the Marines need to prevail is the intelligence they can only get from the villagers. Without it, they are overrun. When they get it, because they have won the support of the villagers, they are able to secure the village by setting up an ambush that uses little force to achieve its objective. The point here is that a small application of force can be a decisive or, we might even say, an overwhelming use of force in a given situation. Whether it is depends on our objectives and the circumstances in which we are trying to achieve them, including the intentions and commitment of our opponents. In the initial days of our involvement in Somalia, something as subtle as an evidently well-prepared ambush would probably not have allowed us to achieve our objectives. The appearance of a few Abrams battle tanks on the streets was appropriate in these circumstances and proved to be an overwhelming or, at least, overawing use of force. It is through reflecting on our objectives in light of our circumstances and what we know of our opponents that we can determine what kind of force is appropriate.

The arguments and suggestions about the use of force that we have offered have probably not shaken the conviction among those who hold it that force must be used decisively and overwhelmingly. The strength of this conviction was forged in the experience of Vietnam, where limited war theories led us to pursue a policy of gradualism "in an attempt to balance military requirements, which argued for escalation, and [domestic and foreign] political concerns, which argued for restraint." The objection to this approach is that "gradualism or incrementalism makes little military sense."[43] Gradualism allows an enemy time to recover and robs from the use of force the element of intimidation and menace that is essential to its effectiveness. Thus, this argument concludes, force should be used decisively, to force the decision in our favor, rather than gradually, in an effort to signal our intentions.

It is true that gradualism makes no sense militarily, but this objection has no force when we are discussing military activities outside of war because these engagements are not essentially military in character. As we have argued, war is constituted by the effort to destroy the ability of our enemy to resist. In war, military force is the key to achieving our objectives. In this case, what makes sense militarily should take precedence. Therefore, in war, force should be used decisively and overwhelmingly. In operations other than war, where military force is not the key, its use and the manner of its use must be weighed against a number of other considerations. What makes sense militarily may not make sense for other reasons. Since the key to success in these situations is not the military, what makes sense militarily should not necessarily take precedence over all other factors. Applying force gradually to signal our intentions may work in these situations, even if this use of force does not make sense in strictly military terms. It did not work in Vietnam, because our enemy there was fighting a war, while we refused to make that commitment and continued to conduct coercive diplomacy, although on an increasingly massive scale. Vietnam proves, therefore, not that gradualism or signaling leads inevitably to defeat but that we must understand the difference between war and other forms of human endeavor.[44] This difference requires that we use military force in different ways in war and peace, if we are to succeed. The issue, then, is not whether using force to signal or to force a decision in our favor is the right way to use force. Each use of force may work, depending on when and how it is used.

The raid on Libya illustrates many of the points we have just discussed and illuminates the dilemmas the United States faces in using force against terrorism. On April 15, 1986, the U.S. Air Force and Navy bombed targets in Libya in response to the bombing of a discotheque in Berlin on April 5, which killed two and injured sixty-four Americans, and other Libyan actions. This was the first use of military force by the United States to combat terrorism. The primary purpose of this raid was to deter future acts of Libyan-sponsored terrorism. It was also intended to indicate to the world the intensity of U.S. resolve to deal with this kind of violence. Generally speaking, the raid achieved its secondary more than its primary purpose.

After an initial outburst of revenge attacks, Qadaffi did not sponsor an attack on Americans for roughly twelve months following the raid. Table 1 shows the number of Libyan-sponsored attacks by year (1979 to May 1992) in toto and against Americans.[45]

Table 1
Libyan Terrorist Attacks

Year	Total	Americans	Year	Total	Americans
1979	1	1	1980	3	0
1981	0	0	1982	0	0
1983	2	1	1984	3	0
1985	5	2	1986	11	7
1987	12	2	1988	9	5
1989	1	0	1990	3	1
1991	1	0	1992	2	0

Source: Defense Intelligence Agency

Of the seven Libyan terrorist attacks against Americans in 1986, one occurred before the April 15 raid, four following the raid in the month of April, one in July, and the last in September. Of the two against Americans in 1987, the first occurred in August, the second in December. These figures suggest that Qadaffi did restrict his support for terrorism against the United States for about a year following September 1986. Following this hiatus, and excluding the spate of anniversary attacks in 1988, five of which took place in April and one of which allegedly was the bombing of Pan Am Flight 103 in December, Libyan attacks against Americans returned to their typical level of one or two a year. Sanctions and political pressure following the investigation into the bombing of the Pan Am flight probably explain, at least in part, the absence of Libyan-sponsored attacks on Americans since 1990. An intelligence official has also claimed that the raid has played a part. He cites intelligence indicating that fear of another raid or worse is part of the calculus that has led Qadaffi to refrain from sponsoring terrorism in the aftermath of Pan Am Flight 103.[46]

This analysis rests on statistics that can be challenged. Different figures might result if different definitions of *terrorism*, or *sponsorship*, or *against Americans* were used. Again, since it is commonly accepted that the April 1986 raid made Qadaffi more secretive in his support for terrorism, it is possible that Libyan-sponsored attacks occurred after it that we do not know about. However, although broader definitions of key terms or an omniscient view of Libyan activity might change the statistics, it is unlikely that the changed statistics would show an alteration in the general pattern. Various governmental and nongovernmental counts of Libyan-sponsored terrorism incidents produce the same pattern: few Libyan-sponsored attacks against Americans before the raid, several in response, a quiet period of roughly twelve months, renewed activity culminating in Pan Am Flight 103, and then another quiet period. It is also unlikely that the Libyans have succeeded in hiding from us a lot of terrorist attacks that they have sponsored. With the exception of attacks associated with the Gulf War, in which there is no evidence that Libya participated, there has been a general worldwide decline in terrorist incidents over the past several years.[47] This suggests that there was not over this same period an upsurge in Libyan terrorist activity unknown to the United States.

The effect of the raid, then, was to reduce the number of Libyan-sponsored terrorism attacks against Americans for twelve months. On the other hand, counting immediate retaliatory attacks but not counting Pan Am Flight 103, Libyan-sponsored terrorism killed and injured more Americans after the raid than before. If the primary purpose of the raid was to deter Qadaffi from killing Americans, it did not achieve its purpose.

To reach a more complete view of whether the use of military force was effective in this case, we must consider the secondary purpose of the raid: signaling our resolve to deal with terrorism. The raid did have this effect. According to the diplomats in charge of our counterterrorism policy at the time, it got the attention of the Europeans and made them more willing to cooperate in efforts to combat Libyan-sponsored terrorism.[48] An immediate result of this greater cooperation was agreement on sanctions against Libya and the expulsion of Libyan diplomats and students from Europe. Since Libyan diplomats play an important role in Libyan terrorist attacks, these expulsions probably disrupted Libyan support for terrorism. The raid also made our European allies more willing to cooperate with us on other terrorist issues. For example, following the raid they were more helpful in limiting Syrian sponsorship of terrorist acts. This cooperation and the effect of the raid on Syria itself helped persuade the Syrians to curtail the activities of the terrorist groups they supported. Since until that time Syria had supported some of the most deadly terrorist groups known to attack Americans (e.g., the ANO), this indirect effect of the raid probably saved some American lives. After considering the secondary purpose of the raid, we must adjust our conclusion that the raid did not achieve its primary purpose. To a degree that is not evident at first glance, the raid probably did help reduce the number of American casualties from terrorism generally, if not from Libyan-sponsored terrorism specifically.

Calculating how many terrorist attacks did not occur and how many Americans did not die because of the raid is obviously a speculative undertaking. It would be difficult to say how the raid alone affected terrorists and their sponsors, but the raid was not the only factor working on the governments of Libya and Syria. As we have noted, declining oil prices, for example, diminished Libyan resources and, although not initially, by the late 1980s were probably curbing Libyan support for terrorist groups. Qadaffi's defeat in Chad, for which the United States was partly responsible, apparently chastened him, while the decline and eventual collapse of the Soviet Union changed Syria's strategic position, a fact that Syrian President Asad realized early on. We may conclude, however, considering its effects on all sponsors of terrorism, that the raid at least contributed to a decline in attacks on Americans and to American deaths caused by terrorism, especially if we do not count the deaths from Pan Am Flight 103.

Unfortunately, and not only for the sake of this analysis, we must count these deaths. If this incident was Qadaffi's revenge for the raid, it should make us wonder whether using military force to combat terrorism is worthwhile. After all, what seems finally to have stopped Qadaffi's attacks on Americans was not a military reprisal for this attack but the economic and political pressure that Great Britain, the United States and France were able to organize through the UN in response to the mid-air bombing of Pan Am Flight 103 and UTA Flight 772 over Niger in 1989. Even if the intelligence official cited earlier is correct and the raid is part of what is now restraining Qadaffi, we still must wonder whether the use of military force is worthwhile.

Generally stated, the problem with using military force to combat terrorism is that there will always be an asymmetry between the United States and countries that sponsor terrorism when it comes to using force. For one thing, the activities of the United States and its citizens around the world present many more lucrative targets to the terrorists than they or their sponsors present to us. More important, the fact that terrorists and their sponsors accept the killing of innocents indicates that they are much more unrestrained in the use of violence than we are. Our military activity may kill civilians, as it did in the raid on Libya, but we do not deliberately target them. Nor is this the only constraint upon our use of force. A raid on Libya's oil production capabilities would have been a devastating blow to Qadaffi but was ruled out in favor of attacks on targets associated with terrorism, since this would fit within the international legal understanding of self-defense.[49] Finally, coercing good behavior, which is what we are trying to do when we combat terrorism, may require applying the coercion again and again. The repetitive use of violence for this purpose is difficult for the United States given our attitudes toward the use of force. When Qadaffi launched his attacks on the second anniversary of the raid, we did not respond with military force. These constraints indicate why, in any violent confrontation outside of a conventional military engagement, we are likely to be at a disadvantage. Because of this disadvantage, it might be better when the United States combats terrorism if it emphasized diplomatic and economic pressure, where it can trump state sponsors of terrorism, rather than military force. Such an approach will not necessarily stop the use of terrorist violence against us, but it will prevent us getting involved in a tit-for-tat exchange that we are likely to lose.

This analysis of the raid on Libya suggests, finally, that if force is used to combat terrorism, it is unlikely to be used in an overwhelming fashion. Force may still be effective against terrorists and their sponsors but it must be used appropriately and as part of a larger strategy that supports, with all the elements of our national power, what will inevitably be an indecisive and restrained use of force.

PREVENTION

Preventing terrorism means dealing with the causes of terrorism. Prevention combats terrorism by focusing not on the symptoms of terrorism—bombings, assassinations, kidnappings, and hijackings—but on the reasons why individuals and groups use these tactics. To prevent terrorism, then, we must remove its causes: we must see to it that no individual or group has a reason to use terrorism.

We can prevent terrorism if its causes can be addressed by human action. To determine if they can be, we must first understand what causes terrorism. Those most commonly cited are socioeconomic, psychological, ethnic, religious, and political causes. Examples would be limited economic opportunities, the suppression of certain religious practices or of schools run by an ethnic or religious group, or the denial of local autonomy. All of these grievances might be reasons why people resort to political violence, including terrorism.

It is obviously a big leap, however, to go from a grievance to terrorism. Grievances are universal, while terrorism is not. A recent study of ethnopolitical conflict reports that of the 233 groups it examined, only 35 resorted to terrorism alone, while another 79 fought guerrilla and civil wars. Although the study does not say whether terrorism was used in these wars, it is likely that in some cases it was. Even so, terrorism is a small part of the violence in these kinds of conflicts. There must be a number of steps, therefore, between the common causes of political unrest or violence and this uncommon response. We might think of these steps as forming a pyramid. At the base would be a broad range of grievances. The next narrower step would be mobilization, in which a group organizes its resources to rectify the problem it faces. Above the step of mobilization would be the still narrower step of armed rebellion, and above this the even narrower step of terrorism.[50] To prevent terrorism, then, we should in principle be able to intervene at any of the lines dividing each step.

There are three reasons why such intervention is not possible. First, many of the causes of terrorism cannot be removed. The disputes can be intractable. Experts who have studied ethnic conflict deny that it is necessarily so; yet what they mean is that in some cases the conflict can be channeled away from rebellion and violence by political structures. This is, of course, an important consideration, but it does not mean that a final resolution is always possible. Various political structures and devices held ethnic conflict in Lebanon in abeyance for several decades but eventually broke down, with terrorism one of the consequences. Furthermore, removing some causes of conflict can actually give rise to others. Economic growth can remove such causes of conflict as limited economic opportunities, but economic growth can also threaten traditional ways of life and thus generate conflict. Much of the fundamentalist religious rebellion around the world exemplifies this dynamic. Pluralism is offered as one way to ease some political conflicts, but several writers have noted that terrorism is more prevalent in democratic societies.[51] The Soviet Union did not have a problem with terrorism; Russia does. Spain's terrorist problem got worse as Spain democratized. Encouraging economic growth and democracy may help resolve some conflicts only to generate new ones or create new opportunities for the violent expression of old ones.

In general, then, the counsel to remove the causes of terrorism should be treated with caution because the causes may be irremovable or, if successfully removed, may simply make way for others. A further reason to hesitate before attempting to prevent terrorism is that even if its causes are removable, we will not have the resources to remove them. For example, consider the broad base of grievances in the pyramid of protest that we have constructed. Obviously, we do not have the resources to try to address all the grievances that exist in the world. As we move farther up the pyramid, of course, the number of cases to be dealt with declines, but this would not appreciably alter the problem we face. We would not have had the resources to address the thirty-five cases of terrorism identified in the previously mentioned study of ethnopolitical conflict, let alone the other seventy-nine cases that produced violence. Indeed, numbers a fraction of these would have been beyond our means. We invested more than ten years and billions of dollars in El Salvador alone. What would it take to address similar problems in the Middle East?

Supporters of preventing terrorism might respond that our limited resources simply mean that we should focus on those cases most likely to produce conflict. But no one has yet been able to produce a theory, model, or computer program that would permit us to pick those situations most likely to result in conflict, let alone in that peculiar form of conflict that we call terrorism. Income inequality, for example, to pick one typical grievance, does not always produce conflict or violence. There is an unavoidable element of indeterminateness in the development of rebellion and terrorism that will frustrate our efforts at prevention. As one expert has noted, "the processes by which grievances and the potential for mobilization are translated into protest and rebellion are too complex and contextually specific to be summarized in general propositions. . . . Most ethnopolitical conflicts, including all sustained campaigns of protest and rebellion, are shaped by the strategic assessments and tactical decisions of the leaders and activists of communal groups."[52] Even if we assume that ultimately all elements of such leadership decisions are predictable, we would have to admit that we are not yet at the point where we can predict them. We are not able, then, to focus our limited resources on those cases that might develop into terrorism.

This emphasis on the importance of individual leaders opens up one final possibility for those intent on finding some way to prevent terrorism. If leadership is as critical in the development of rebellion and terrorism as the experts claim, then psychology might be the key to preventing terrorism. If somehow we could understand the leaders' psyches and learn to manipulate them so that terrorism became an unacceptable or unnecessary tactic, then we could prevent terrorism in this way. Unfortunately, the study of terrorist psychology has not uncovered anything like a terrorist psyche or personality.[53] This means that it is not possible to identify the psychological causes of terrorism or to prevent terrorism psychologically.

If economic, social, ethnic, or psychological factors by themselves do not explain terrorism, some combination of them might. One expert, basing his analyses on interviews with imprisoned terrorists, has outlined an explanation of terrorism that combines social, psychological, and economic factors to describe youths alienated from the social and economic life of their larger community. A similar combination of factors seems to explain the attraction of Islamism and Islamic fundamentalism to the young in Muslim societies. A small percentage of such alienated youths are drawn to illegal and ultimately violent actions, including terrorism, as compensation for their disaffection from society. This analysis, developed with some subtlety, is a persuasive account of how terrorists develop but does not make preventing terrorism more easily done. Reintegrating these individuals into society "by providing the terrorist (and the potential terrorist) with opportunities for gainful employment and with that, upward economic and social mobility"[54] might work, at least in some cases, but, in those countries where it is needed, is far beyond the economic and political means of the United States.

We must conclude, therefore, that a specific effort to prevent terrorism is not advisable because we lack both the knowledge and resources to do it. This does not mean, however, that we can do nothing more about terrorism than respond once it occurs. The effort to identify the causes of conflict and terrorism has identified a middle ground between grievances and terrorism. If we do not know how or why some of the former lead to the latter, we do know that the former, even if they are economic, ethnic, or religious, manifest themselves politically before they turn into political terrorism. We can use our influence, therefore, to press for political solutions—autonomy, assimilation, pluralism, and power sharing, for example, in the case of ethnic conflict—in hopes that we may thereby limit the number of situations that give rise to conflict and terrorism. This might help reduce terrorism by removing causes of disaffection and by demonstrating respect for the disaffected, a suggested way to deal with the alienated who sometimes become terrorists.[55] Similarly, we might be able to reduce terrorism in a few cases by encouraging countries to implement economic policies that encourage growth and more equal distribution of income (two goals, we should remember, that are not always compatible). This will be difficult work, however, for any government that needs encouragement to pursue such policies is probably in the grip of interests that we will not have the leverage to dislodge. Since our influence is a limited resource or, at least, requires our limited human and financial resources to be established and maintained, we will have to be selective in determining where we try to encourage such political solutions. This, of course, is what an effective foreign policy or national strategy always tries to do: to direct limited resources at critical problems. We may conclude, therefore, as we did when discussing sanctions, that an effective national strategy is a prerequisite for success in the limited efforts we can reasonably take to prevent terrorism.

Before leaving the subject of prevention, we should note that the U.S. government has in fact found a way to prevent terrorism, not by treating its causes but by defending against its symptoms. For more than twenty-five years, it has undertaken steps to make its personnel and facilities overseas harder targets for terrorists to hit. It has provided training and briefings on how personnel can make themselves difficult or unappealing targets and it has increased security at facilities by fortifying them and by providing them with concentric perimeters of security. The effects of these defensive measures, collectively called antiterrorism, have been notable. As long as proper procedures are followed and they are taken with appropriate seriousness, personnel and facilities are demonstrably more secure now than they were before these programs began. In 1980, there were 177 attacks on U.S. diplomats, military personnel, and other U.S. government officials. In 1995, there were ten. Terrorists have not given up targeting Americans, of course, and greater security measures for official Americans overseas may have only deflected some of their attacks to easier targets, such as American businessmen or other civilians, or compelled terrorists to devise more sophisticated or lethal means of attack, as the bombings of U.S. military facilities in Saudi Arabia in 1995 and 1996 indicate. Still, it is a gain that America now conducts its official business overseas with more security from terrorist attack than it did.[56] This success has come at a price, of course, in dollars and manpower, costs that will increase in response to the Saudi bombings. Imposing these costs is a success for terrorists and their sponsors because the United States has had to shift resources from other endeavors to antiterrorism.

PREEMPTION AND DISRUPTION

Preempting terrorist attacks means taking measures to stop a planned attack from being carried out. While prevention as a strategy to combat terrorism takes place, if at all, in the long term and aims at the conditions that promote terrorism, preemption is short term and aims to stop a specific terrorist act. Preemption is often taken to mean the use of lethal force or even to be a euphemism for assassination. While preempting a terrorist attack might require lethal force, it could also require nothing more than a warning to another country that a terrorist group was planning to use its territory, such as the warning that the United States gave to East Germany in 1986 about the attacks planned by Palestinian terrorists that it supported, or a police raid that arrests suspects before they can carry out a terrorist action.[57]

As we have noted, to the extent that it is possible, prevention presupposes an effective national strategy. Preemption does as well. It is only when we have thought through in a comprehensive manner what we must do to maintain our security that we can accurately weigh the contribution that risky and controversial preemptive acts might make. In addition, more than any other method of combating terrorism, preemption requires specific, accurate, and timely intelligence. While general trend analysis may suffice for prevention, it does not for preemption. A warning to the wrong country or the arrest of the wrong suspects will not stop a terrorist attack. Its reliance on intelligence is the great weakness of preemption. This is particularly true if preemption requires lethal force. We can apologize to another country for a false warning and free mistakenly arrested suspects, but we cannot raise the dead. It is possible to imagine one intelligence report or the coincidence of several presenting overwhelming evidence that an attack was about to take place. But such instances will be rare. Warnings of terrorist attacks are as frequent as they are uncorroborated. For the most part, then, any decision to use lethal force requires balancing the harm that may come to Americans with the harm that we may do to innocents. Because of the opprobrium and political damage that would result from a preemptive strike killing innocents, the United States has, at least tacitly, decided that it is better to risk the harm to Americans than to risk killing innocents. An important consideration for the future, however, is whether terrorist acquisition of WMD will change this balancing of risk and so make preemption using lethal force a more acceptable option. Until then, preemption is likely to mean only warnings to other countries and police raids.

The effort to find an offensive means of dealing with terrorism appears to be suspended, then, between prevention, which is of only limited effectiveness, and preemption, which is of only limited feasibility. Disruption, however, is a middle ground between prevention and preemption. Disrupting terrorist activity means targeting a terrorist organization and taking measures, not to stop one of its particular operations, but to render all its activities more difficult. The ultimate goal is to make the organization ineffective. Unlike prevention, disruption assumes that the terrorist activities have begun and, in fact, that we have been targeted and hit already. Therefore, a strategy of disruption allows us to focus our resources on targeting a specific group. Unlike preemption, disruption does not require that we act before a specific attack takes place and so allows for the gradual build-up of intelligence that permits accurate targeting.

The United States has already pursued at least one effective campaign of disruption against a terrorist group: the campaign in the late 1980s against the ANO, previously described. Intelligence officials involved in this operation believe it was highly effective. One high-ranking intelligence official not directly involved in the operation cited it as one of the most effective counterterrorism efforts that the United States has ever undertaken, noting that it severely hampered ANO operations. In interviews, State Department officials who made the démarches to the foreign governments involved concurred with this judgment.[58]

The ways in which terrorist operations can be disrupted are as diverse as the ways in which terrorists operate and support their operations. In addition to démarches, arrests, and various intelligence operations designed to increase the group's paranoia or weaken its infrastructure, they might include legal actions to keep in port ships that have falsified their logs in order to hide participation in terrorist activities or the sabotage of facilities that support terrorist operations. Such operations might hinder a terrorist group's activities directly or, by sowing discord, indirectly. In addition, such operations could be used to send a signal to governments that support terrorism that we know they are providing this support and can take measures to counter it. The fact that these operations could be clandestine or even covert means the message could be received without the public humiliation that overt military actions or public demands bring. Qadaffi may have felt compelled to sponsor the attack on Pan Am Flight 103 because the raid on Libya was such a stinging public humiliation. If sabotage or other disruptive techniques had been used discreetly, we might have made our point in a way that would not have compelled Qadaffi to respond. Diplomatic representation, buttressed with evidence of the damage done, could have carried the message privately to others who needed to hear it. Such an approach, especially if coupled with carefully targeted economic sanctions, might not even require us to cause much damage to the population of a country that sponsored terrorism. This approach may prove more effective than steering a cruise missile into a nearly deserted office building late at night, which is how the United States responded to the Iraqi assassination plot against President Bush. Technological developments will offer soon, if they do not now, the ability to inflict damage on our enemies in a variety of ways and at minimum risk to U.S. personnel.

Disruption shares two disadvantages with preemption: a dependence on intelligence and a risk of harming innocents. To be effective, a campaign of disruption requires a very good understanding of the organization, personalities, and operations of a terrorist group. Even with a lucky break such as a defector, developing this kind of detailed information is difficult and time-consuming. This suggests that we focus our resources on one or two groups that are particularly dangerous to us. While this may make our disruption efforts more effective, it cannot guarantee that innocents will not be harmed inadvertently, especially if disruption includes sabotage. This is a risk in any use of force, however, which we can only avoid by never using military force when dealing with terrorism or any other threat.

SUMMARY

During the past twenty-five years, the U.S. government has combated terrorism with nine methods: international legal conventions, defensive measures, addressing the causes of terrorism, a policy of no concessions, economic sanctions, military retaliation, prosecution (after we have gotten hold of suspects by extradition, rendition or by seizing them overseas and returning them to the United States for trial), preemption, and disruption. In addition to the specific recommendations we have made for improving these methods, our twenty-five-year experience and the preceding analysis suggest two general guidelines for our efforts to combat terrorism.

None of the methods that we have used deserves to be called the pillar or cornerstone of our effort against terrorism because none is necessarily more important than any other. In any given situation, one or more might be the best way to respond. Focusing on one or two responses as the most important or the first to be used could inhibit the flexibility that combating terrorism requires. An effective rhetorical strategy could be fashioned out of emphasizing all the different tools at our disposal to combat terrorism, while stressing the moral outrage that killing innocents generates.

The second guideline that our experience suggests is that combating terrorism should be part of a larger effort. The ultimate purpose of combating terrorism, after all, is to further the interests of the United States. Our effort to combat terrorism, then, must be an integral part of our overall national security strategy. Decisions about when to use which method of combating terrorism and how to blend them together must be made in this context. For example, as we have seen, on one occasion the opportunity to seize a terrorist was not taken because of the repercussions grabbing him would have had on our relations with an important European country. Making such decisions implies a firm grasp of what America's security objectives are and what are the best means to achieve them. Relating means to objectives is, of course, the purpose of strategy, which is why efforts to combat terrorism should be firmly embedded in a well-considered national strategy.

While we need to remember to take a strategic view of terrorism, it is also worth asking, given the apparently changing character of international terrorism, if the experience we have painfully gained over the past twenty years has become irrelevant. As we have noted, the two new developments in international terrorism are an apparent increased tendency to use WMD and the appearance of so-called ad hoc or autonomous groups, such as the group that carried out the bombing of the World Trade Center. If the tendency toward using WMD continues, it will undoubtedly increase the urgency with which we prepare to combat terrorism and manage the consequences of a WMD incident, but it is unlikely to render useless the methods we have developed for carrying out this combat, with the possible exception, as noted, of the policy of no concessions. We have much experience dealing with states that support terrorism, all of which is applicable in the case of states that might support WMD terrorism either intentionally or indirectly through faulty control of WMD materials. Since the destruction that a WMD attack could cause is so great, the greater likelihood of such an attack may lead us to put renewed emphasis on disruption and preemption. Again, what we have learned about these methods over the past twenty-five years will be relevant.

Before considering whether these methods will also continue to be relevant against autonomous groups, we should put these groups in perspective. To begin with, we should note that organized groups tied to state sponsors continue to predominate among the world's terrorists. Autonomous groups may never become a dominant force, for while they may be capable of horrendous acts of violence, they do not have the strengths of the older terrorist organizations. Their ad hoc character means they lack skill in the clandestine and other arts necessary for successful terrorist operations and are more vulnerable, therefore, to penetration and police investigation. The group that bombed the World Trade Center was remarkably amateurish, a fact that allowed the police to round up its members. Because of the benefits that organization provides and the power and advantages that even a weak state sponsor offers, over the long-term organized, state-sponsored groups are likely to remain the greatest terrorist threat we face.[59]

Autonomous groups remain a problem, of course, but one to which we can apply what we have learned fighting more organized groups. Although the newer more loosely organized groups do not have one dominant state sponsor, they still receive support from certain states. We have experience dealing with states that support terrorism and can apply it in response to the activities of these new groups. Given the way these groups operate, the task will be more difficult than in the past but is not unprecedented. If states do not support these groups or the individuals who are their catalysts, they may still be home to the nongovernmental organizations or individuals that do. Again, we can put pressure on states to curtail the activities of these groups and individuals or, if we have objectives in common with these states, we can share intelligence with them about the activities of the nongovernmental organizations and the individuals they support. Cooperation with foreign governments can also enhance our ability to apprehend individuals and bring them to trial in this country. Again, we have relevant experience in this regard, as we noted when discussing the judicial approach to combating terrorism. Apprehension of key individuals may become more important as a way of dealing with ad hoc groups since their relative autonomy makes it harder to put pressure on them than on groups we have dealt with in the past. If the threat from such groups increases, we may need to become more willing to seize such people and attack the nongovernmental organizations and individuals that support them, even in cases where we do so without the cooperation of a host government. Here also our experience is relevant, reminding us that in such a case careful calculation of costs and benefits will be necessary. The need for such calculation returns us to what may well be the most important lesson of all drawn from our experience with combating terrorism: the need to base our efforts to combat terrorism on a national strategy.

4

ORGANIZATION

No matter what methods we employ to combat terrorism, they all must be implemented through the various departments, agencies and bureaus of the U.S. government. Apprehending a terrorist on the high seas or attacking the overseas support operations of a terrorist group requires the coordinated efforts of various parts of the executive branch. Those unfamiliar with the channels, tunnels, and blind alleys of this part of the federal government may be surprised to find out that cooperation in the struggle against such an evil as terrorism did not come automatically or easily. It may also come as a surprise that even after twenty-five years of effort, and significant improvement, interagency cooperation against terrorism is still not complete. According to a press report, for example, for over a year, between May 1993 and July 1994, the United States failed to comply with a German request for information needed to extradite a terrorist from Lebanon in part because of a lack of coordination between various U.S. government agencies.[1]

No doubt, we will suspect that turf-conscious, lazy bureaucrats are to blame for such problems. Indeed, one source for the press report just mentioned opined "there is plenty of blame to go around. [The request] moves from bureaucrat to bureaucrat, sitting on somebody's desk who places no particular importance on it." Yet even if all such bureaucrats were suddenly removed from their chairs and replaced by public-spirited, energetic colleagues, agencies would still not cooperate perfectly. Failure to cooperate in combating terrorism and other matters occurs for many reasons besides what we suppose are the perverse preferences of civil servants. First, the very processes of government make cooperation difficult. When these are avoided or overcome, other obstacles arise from the work that agencies are supposed to do, their mandates, and the attitudes that these mandates generate. Other obstacles to cooperation arise from the character of our government. To understand why cooperation in combating terrorism has been difficult to achieve and remains a problem, we must examine all these obstacles.

We should begin by noting a problem that is not specifically an interagency problem but affects the ability of agencies to cooperate with one another: their size and complexity. These attributes make it hard for agencies to cooperate with themselves, as it were, which in turn makes it hard for them to cooperate with other agencies. Many of the agencies involved in national security and combating terrorism are large (the Defense Department is immense) and complex, carrying out a remarkable number of different activities. Structured hierarchically, these organizations consist of offices and staff that may have no idea what other offices in the same organization are doing. When these different offices talk at interagency meetings, which draw participants from the different levels of agencies, they may say things that incompletely represent their agency's position or activities, giving rise to misunderstandings and contradictory or inconsistent efforts. Better intradepartmental organization can minimize but cannot eliminate failures to cooperate because the issues that bureaucracies face cannot all be neatly segregated into different boxes and parceled out to distinct offices and divisions. Responsibility for issues overlaps, as the issues themselves blur. For example, several bureaus and agencies in the State Department have responsibility for arms control or some aspect of this complex military, scientific, and political issue. Better intradepartmental communication can minimize but not eliminate failures to cooperate because such communication is likely to lag behind bureaucrats, who, contrary to their popular image, often aggressively pursue their agendas.

Perhaps the most important way in which agencies reflect the complexity of certain issues is the division within them between regional and functional offices. Terrorism, for example, is a functional issue. General statements can be made about what terrorists tend to do and how they can be foiled that do not depend on local circumstances. For this reason, the State Department has an office devoted to combating terrorism. The Department's traditional business, however, is managing our relations with other countries. This is a business critically dependent on local knowledge. Therefore, the regional bureaus have long been the centers of power in the Department. The perspectives of the regional offices and the functional offices do not always reveal the same problems or the same solutions, however. This is true also in the CIA, where the counterterrorism center and the regional divisions have not always agreed, and at the Defense Department, although the problem there is much less important because the regional office, International Security Affairs, has a clearly subordinate role in an organization devoted to applying the principles of war everywhere it is called on to do so.

The regional/functional dispute within agencies is complicated by a regional/global dispute also reflected in the structure of the agencies. In the State Department, for example, during the Cold War, there was at times a split between those with a global perspective, who concentrated on confronting the Soviet Union, and those with a regional perspective, who saw the Soviets as one of many problems to worry about or felt that the Soviets were best confronted through regional strategies.[2] Another regional/global dispute focuses on the proper role in our foreign policy of such issues as human rights and environmentalism.   The bureaus responsible for human rights and environmental issues argue with the regional bureaus about whether their issues or friendly relations with regional powers should take precedence. Such global issues became more prominent in the latter stages of the Cold War (when, for example, the Office of the Assistant Secretary of State for Human Rights was established). They now vie with regional problems for the time and attention of policymakers. Their ascent to prominence is indicated by the proposal made early in the Clinton administration to establish an Office of the Undersecretary for Global Affairs at the State Department. The companion development in the Defense Department was the ultimately unsuccessful effort to establish an Assistant Secretary's office for Democracy and Human Rights, elements of which still exist at lower levels in the Defense bureaucracy. Ironically, this global office was proposed as Defense, having lost its global enemy, was shifting from a global perspective to more regionally focused defense strategies.

If the Defense Department is not marked by regional/functional or regional/global disputes to the degree that other organizations are, it is nonetheless distinguished by its own intramural tensions. Defense actually consists of two separate organizations, the staff of the Office of the Secretary of Defense (OSD), which is civilian at its most senior levels and a mixture of military and civilian at others, and the Joint Staff, which is military at all levels of leadership and has few civilian employees. Although the Secretary of Defense's civilian and military staffs both work for him, they are in fact different organizations, with different agendas and attitudes. While informal channels open up between these two organizations, there is authoritative communication between them only at the highest levels of each bureaucracy. At interagency meetings below these levels there is not necessarily a Defense Department position, only the positions of OSD and the Joint Staff, although usually these are coordinated in advance. Relations between these staffs, the Joint Staff insists, should be guided by the notion that civilian control of the military means that the civilians lay out the policy goals and the military develops the strategy, operational art, and tactics to achieve them. The Joint Staff jealously guards its prerogatives in this matter, for fear that civilian amateurs will meddle with things properly left to military professionals. A similar friction exists in the Justice Department, between the FBI's investigators and the Department's prosecutors, who are, in a sense, respectively, the soldiers and policymakers of their organization.

All the departments, agencies, and bureaus of the executive branch operate in what is called the interagency process, which, given its importance, appears excessively haphazard and informal with regard to its standard operating procedures. Like grit in a gear box, the procedural problems of this process impede the machine of government. Sand is an appropriate metaphor here, for the problems are numerous and tiny, as well as hazardous to efficient functioning. They include the failure of agency crisis centers to coordinate their hours of operation, the absence of mechanisms that assure the communication to all interested parties of the results of high-level interagency meetings, the absence of convenient, secure communications between agencies, the failure to prepare meeting agendas or to distribute them and other relevant material sufficiently in advance of a meeting to allow preparation, and the absence of standard formats for interagency paperwork and reporting.

While such problems appear to be the result of a willful disregard of elementary management techniques, one of the most important procedural impediments to cooperation is unavoidable: the restrictions on the sharing of information between agencies. While it is true that some people refuse to share information for petty reasons—because they believe that knowledge is power and do not want to share it—information is not shared for important reasons as well. The Joint Staff and the CIA protect their information in order to maintain operational security, which they must do to protect the lives and well-being of those involved in their operations. The FBI protects its information because of the rules covering evidence that are part of the judicial process. When federal prosecutors indicted Manuel Noriega without informing the State Department, which was in the process of negotiating with him about his departure, it did so, according to Justice Department officials, because of the "secrecy of the grand jury." As for the information on the suspected terrorist that never got to the German government, "U.S. sources familiar with the case blamed the delay on rigid compartmentalization among law enforcement and intelligence agencies," among other factors.[3]

Where effective, well-established procedures are in place, they can be overwhelmed by events. The steady flow of daily work or the stunning demands of a crisis can break down even established routines of coordination. This is more likely to happen if those involved are incompetent or, as is more often the case, ignorant of what other agencies or elements of their own are supposed to do. Ignorance as an impediment to interagency cooperation increases every time a new administration takes office. While career personnel provide continuity, political appointees often fill places in bureau hierarchies critical for fostering or impeding cooperation among agencies. If these appointees do not know what to do or what others can and should do, cooperation suffers.

Nevertheless, such procedural problems, compared to all else that impedes cooperation between agencies, are relatively easy to fix. Indeed, as they appear and are recognized, they tend to get fixed, although the supply seems to be inexhaustible. But there are more fundamental and immovable obstacles to better cooperation. The Departments of State, Justice and Defense, and the CIA, to mention only those agencies most involved in combating terrorism, perform different tasks. The first principally uses persuasion in pursuit of our national objectives, the second force, the third litigation, and the fourth guile. While persuasion may use guile and force, and litigation both persuasion and guile, the skills of the diplomat, soldier, lawyer, and spy are not identical. There is no reason to believe that those who study and practice the use of force, for example, will know best how to use the arts of litigation or will work very hard to preserve them. Only those who use these arts will know and want to do this. This is the case for the skills particular to each agency. Accomplishing the tasks of the agency, therefore, requires that the agency control its budget, personnel, and prerogatives. These are the interests of the agencies, the individual turf each so notoriously defends.

The effect of such turf defense on interagency cooperation is easy to understand. Cooperation means that an agency must let down its fences, so to speak, and allow another agency to graze on its money or personnel. Consider the arrest of the terrorist Fawaz Yunis in international waters discussed in chapter one. The Justice Department had the lead in this matter, since it was an operation carried out with a legal mandate. The Defense Department and the CIA provided support. In doing so, they were using resources for a purpose other than the one for which they were created primarily. Ultimately, these agencies are judged not by their ability to provide support to the Justice Department but by their ability to defend the United States from military attack, in the case of Defense, and to provide intelligence of use to policymakers, in the case of the CIA. To the extent that they help other agencies carry out their tasks, they are not performing those peculiar to themselves and risk getting a "bad grade," in the form of public or congressional reprimands, in their own special area of expertise and interest. Therefore, these agencies rightly want to control their personnel and resources so they can devote them to their core missions.

It is true, of course, that the personnel and resources devoted to arresting one terrorist on the high seas are unlikely to prevent the Defense Department or the CIA from accomplishing their missions. It is also true that not cooperating, as the State Department did not when the FBI wanted to investigate the plane crash that killed Pakistani President Zia and the U.S. Ambassador to Pakistan, puts the supporting agencies at risk of a reprimand. But if the number of support missions increased, then it would begin to have an effect. This is exactly what Defense fears may happen, and believes has already happened to some degree, with its increased role in peacekeeping and other so-called non-traditional military missions. Absent the Soviet threat, policy and opinion makers feel freer to have the military involved in a host of activities in addition to its principal task of deterring aggression against and defending the United States. The Defense Department has resisted undertaking these activities because they prevent it from focusing on its special responsibility. This generates interagency friction. For example, from the viewpoint of the State Department, the Defense

Department is not helpful when the issue of who will fund peacekeeping missions comes up at interagency meetings.

There is another way to understand why agency mandates complicate interagency cooperation. According to James Q. Wilson,

An agency with a strong mission will give perfunctory attention, if any at all, to tasks that are not central to that mission. Diplomats in the State Department will have little interest in embassy security; intelligence officers in the CIA will not worry as much as they should about counterintelligence; narcotics agents in the [Drug Enforcement Agency] will minimize the importance of improper prescriptions written by physicians; power engineers in the [Tennessee Valley Authority] will not think as hard about environmental protection or conservation as about maximizing the efficiency of generating units; fighter pilots in the US [Air Force] will look at air transport as a homely stepchild; and Navy admirals who earned their flag serving on aircraft carriers will not press zealously to expand the role of minesweepers.[4]

When an agency concentrates on its core mission, it tends to neglect its peripheral missions. But these peripheral missions may be other agencies' core missions or close to their core missions. If they are, agencies will tend to ignore precisely those issues where cooperation is most likely to be necessary. That Foreign Service Officers do not take seriously enough the demands of security complicates the job of the CIA's Directorate of Operations. That the CIA does not take counterintelligence seriously enough complicates the job of the FBI. Or, to mention an example not cited by Wilson, that the Justice Department does not take our foreign relations seriously enough as it focuses on apprehending and prosecuting someone who breaks our laws, even if he is a head of state, complicates the job of the State Department. As the U.S. Attorney in Miami said, explaining why Manuel Noriega was investigated and indicted while the State Department was negotiating with him about how he would resign, "the investigation resulting in the Noriega indictment was initiated and pursued without any consideration whatsoever to factors extraneous to law enforcement." As a State Department officer put it, with typical diplomatic understatement, "the Justice Department did not have much perception of or sensitivity to the foreign policy implications of what it was doing."[5]

Defending mandates and focusing on core missions and the particular skills necessary to accomplish them impedes interagency cooperation, impediments reinforced by the interests that the different agencies represent. These interests are kept in the forefront of the minds of agency executives by various lobbying groups who work through Congress and in other ways to fortify agency devotion to mandate and protection of turf. The Commerce Department, for example, seeks to maximize U.S. overseas trade. For this reason, it has not been in favor of using sanctions as a way of handling foreign policy problems.[6] In interagency meetings, it defends trade and opposes the actions of other agencies that impinge on it.

Devotion to mandate and protecting turf produce a byproduct that further complicates and impedes cooperation between agencies. This byproduct is what some observers have called an agency's culture, a distinctive "persistent, patterned way of thinking about the central tasks of and human relationships within an organization."[7] In other words, cooperation between agencies falters not just because the agencies do different, sometimes conflicting things but also because the individuals who staff the agencies do these things in different, distinctive ways.

Consider the example of diplomats and soldiers. During deliberations on Lebanon in the early 1980s, a participant has noted that at one point the White House, OSD, and the Joint Chiefs of Staff wanted to "take firm measures" with a recalcitrant Prime Minister Begin. "State was a dissenter," the participant notes, "advocating flexibility in the American position until it was clear how Ambassador Habib's efforts [to deal with Begin] were proceeding. State's guiding principle was to keep U.S. options open by refraining from actions that could later complicate Habib's efforts with Begin." The State Department negotiates. That is its job, its bureaucratic mandate. To carry out this mandate, it encourages in its diplomats through various incentives a tolerance of ambiguity and the flexibility to deal with it, attributes that are necessary to keep options open and negotiations alive. The military, on the other hand, brings force to bear in service of our national interests. It carries out this mandate by seeking clear objectives against which it can plan, since it must select the proper personnel and equipment for the job and move them many miles. A diplomat summed up the difference between the two by saying that "the military is enamored of timelines, no-later-than dates and ultimatums. [Diplomats] on the other hand spend endless hours waiting and toiling for the slightest glimmer of hope in a situation unencumbered by deadlines and concrete results."[8]

Richard Holbrooke provided a particularly illuminating example of the diplomats' willingness to tolerate ambiguity and remain flexible in a comment he made as he shuttled among Balkan capitals trying to contrive peace. "If I can get a cease-fire, I'll take that. If I can get some constitutional principles, I'll take them. If I can get a corridor to Gorazde, I'll grab it. If I can settle Sarajevo, I'll do it. We're inventing peace as we go." Reading these words, we may wonder about the deeper issue of whether a sound house can be constructed of rooms designed without regard for the structure of the whole. For the moment, however, we should focus only on Holbrooke's remark as an illustration of the degree to which the diplomat thrives on ambiguity. As he negotiates, however, he often requests the soldier's support. The soldier, then, requests from the diplomat a clear objective. The diplomat cannot always give him one because the objective, what the negotiations might lead to, cannot be known with certainty before the negotiations conclude. As James Q. Wilson has noted and Holbrooke has demonstrated, "diplomacy is a process of suggesting, testing, considering, and reconsidering proposals and counterproposals. It would be difficult if not impossible to [specify in advance the objective] in each case, in large part because the government itself does not know; its preferences are formed by the process of negotiation." Faced with a situation in which his objective is not clear, in which, therefore, he cannot properly plan, which is tantamount in the military's view to a situation ripe for failure, the soldier withdraws. He does not offer "options" to the policymaker or, in effect, suggests that there are only two: do nothing or use massive force. The first option avoids the ambiguous situation, the second overwhelms it, destroying the ambiguity and the possibility of diplomacy. This drama of cultural misunderstanding is now a commonplace in our national security decision-making.[9]

Consider another, perhaps less evident, example of how devotion to mandate produces cultural differences that complicate cooperation between agencies. The operations officers of the CIA and the military's counterterrorism forces have not always gotten along well. For example, one result of the failed mission to rescue the hostages in Tehran was an effort by these forces to develop within their own organization some of the operational support capabilities they had needed for the mission but that the CIA had not been able to provide. Although the CIA has recently taken steps to improve its support to the military, it remains the case that for the rank and file in the Agency, support to military missions is not a priority. The primary purpose of the Agency's operators is the collection of intelligence from human sources and not covert or paramilitary operations. It is recognized excellence in the former and not the latter that leads to a successful career. Indeed, many CIA operations officers argue that covert or paramilitary operations should not be part of the Agency's mission because they use resources and bring blame that prevent the Agency from pursuing its mandate to collect human intelligence. This attitude of operations officers is less debilitating for our defense and national security than might first appear because operational support to the military of the sort that the CIA provides is relatively infrequent compared to the overall volume of the Agency's intelligence operations. Yet it is significant because it points to fundamental differences in attitude or culture that affect the degree to which the Agency's operators and the military's special forces can cooperate.

The cultural differences between those involved in direct action missions, such as counterterrorism, and those who recruit and handle human intelligence assets might be summed up by saying that the former are inclined to find the latter too cautious, while the latter are inclined to see the former as too reckless. This difference results from the different mandates of the two groups, which requires them to do different jobs, which in turn gives rise to different attitudes or cultures. For example, those who operate in an area continuously, as do the Agency's officers, have a different idea of what "high profile" means and thus a different sense of what is acceptable risk than do those who are there only for a short time to perform a specific mission. Beyond such particular causes, the essential difference between a human intelligence operation and a direct action mission is that the target of a human intelligence operation is a human being, which means that human intelligence operations are usually longer, more tedious, more uncertain and more ambiguous than direct action operations, which, whatever their target, are most concerned with overcoming material factors, such as time, distance and human reflexes. These material factors yield to daring and force in a way that the human psyche does not. Thus, those engaged in direct action missions emphasize daring in a way that human intelligence officers do not.

The differences in attitude and manner between diplomats and soldiers and between those involved in direct action and those involved in human intelligence collection persist because they are not accidental or the result of mere prejudice. Military operations *do* require systematic planning. Diplomatic negotiations *do* require flexibility. Clandestine operations *do* require concern for security. Direct action missions *do* require daring. Those who take on these different missions come to have different ways of thinking about and acting in the world, at least to the degree that they tend to emphasize different human characteristics. This results from what the various agencies must do to accomplish their missions. To begin with, they recruit different kinds of people and train them differently. These people then acquire different experiences as they go about doing their different jobs. The agencies also dispense awards, bonuses, and promotions to encourage certain characteristics and certain human capabilities among their employees. The end of this unavoidable process is that by the time agency representatives reach the level at which they are involved in interagency meetings, they see problems differently and different kinds of solutions make sense to them. A military officer and a diplomat are different because their jobs require different things from them.

The differences between a diplomat and a military officer are reinforced in the United States because of a characteristically American trait: the tendency to see peace and war as separate discontinuous states. A clear example of this tendency from the military viewpoint was provided by a Major General on the Joint Staff. Speaking of "the touchy issue of letting military commanders do their jobs without interference," the General said "if the [problem] has deteriorated to where you've got to take military action, then, by God, let the military guys do it, and as soon as the military thing is over, we immediately turn it back to the political guys." Operation JUST CAUSE, the invasion of Panama, provides an example of the practical effect of this attitude. In planning for the operation, the Defense Department focused on a set of military activities and did not coordinate with the State Department on how to handle their repercussions. Defense planned to take care of the military problem and then, as the General says, "immediately turn it back to the political guys." Not having been coordinated with, however, the "political guys" were not ready for the hand-off. The result was a post-intervention fiasco—widespread looting—that undermined the success of the operation. It might have been avoided had Defense and State cooperated better.[10]

This attitude toward war and peace is also evident in the State Department's activities. When the fighting started in the Gulf War, the "political guys" in the regional office at State reportedly turned the problem over to the Department's Office of Politico-Military Affairs, which handles those "military guys." When the fighting stopped, the regional office took charge of policy again. In another case, in Lebanon in the early 1980s, a former NSC official has argued that career officials in the State Department never integrated the threatened use of force into their negotiating strategies, with results that were less than optimal for the United States.[11]

Examples such as these suggest that diplomats and soldiers tend to see peace and war, persuasion and force, and thus the activities of the State and Defense Departments as discrete and discontinuous. Such attitudes do not foster interagency cooperation and would frustrate the desire of a chief executive to have at his disposal an integrated response to the problems he faces overseas.

Some might object that this characterization, at least of the State Department, is a caricature. State, they would contend, does not ignore force in pursuit of its objectives. On the contrary, to the consternation of the military and the surprise of many observers, it is often more bellicose than the Department of Defense. That "diplomacy is a very weak weapon if . . . not backed up by the credible threat of force" is a commonly held idea among diplomats. We have noted, for example, that diplomats were the officials most supportive of the raid on Libya. When it came to ousting General Noriega in Panama, "the diplomats wanted a muscular military policy."[12] The diplomats were also more eager than the military to get the military on the ground in Haiti. Yet these examples do not contradict the point that ambassadors and generals tend to see persuasion and force as distinct. Even when the State Department argues that force or, more often, the threat of force should be used, it tends to do so with the understanding that a negotiated solution is the preferred outcome. In other words, it sees force as a negotiating tool and is not inclined to see negotiations as a way to prepare for the more effective use of force. Diplomats praised the raid on Libya because it improved their negotiating position with the Europeans and the Syrians, but did Richard Holbrooke have in mind military requirements and their role in a larger strategy for the Balkans as he traveled about inventing peace? Although eager to get the military on the ground in Haiti so its negotiators would have more leverage, the State Department did not sufficiently involve the Defense Department in the negotiations that produced the Governor's Island Agreement, which was supposed to return Jean Bertrand Aristide to Haiti. At least partly as a result of this, Defense and State did not sufficiently coordinate the preconditions for the landing of U.S. military personnel on Haiti, one of the first crucial steps in the return of President Aristide. The result was that the troops did not land, an embarrassing failure for the U.S. government. In none of these cases were persuasion and force integrated. They remained as discrete and discontinuous as the activities of the State and Defense Departments.

This attitude toward persuasion and force has roots deep in the history of the United States. Founded to a significant degree in explicit opposition to Old World ways, the United States, as its great seal declares, was to be a new order of the ages. In foreign affairs, it was to avoid or at least de-emphasize raison d'état and the use of force as a way to resolve its problems with other nations in favor of an appeal to reason. This appeal and the inseparable appeal to human equality as the fundamental principle of our regime made the American founding revolutionary. Together they produced an ethos that emphasized peaceful intercourse among individuals and nations and sought to deny force any legitimate role in human affairs. Perhaps the most extreme expression of this ethos was Jefferson's private proposal to John Adams, then Ambassador to London, that the United States and the United Kingdom grant reciprocal rights of citizenship to each other's citizens and that this arrangement be established with other states until the circle of friendship, as Jefferson called it, spread around the world.[13] For such a view of the world, the resort to force was neither normal nor acceptable. It was an admission of failure.

Faith in the appeal to reason guided and distinguished the United States, even when, through choice or compulsion, it acted in ways that contradicted it. Remarkably, this modern aspiration was possible to an unprecedented degree because the United States was blessed with circumstances called for by ancient authors. In their writings, isolation from other cities or empires is a precondition for utopia because the presence of threatening enemies compels a nation to put foreign affairs ahead of domestic concerns, to emphasize the use of force, and to cultivate among its citizens a warlike or at least military character. If it does not, according to these writers, it will soon cease to exist. Protected by two oceans and eventually the British navy, the United States had the luxury of indulging its revolutionary aspiration. It could concentrate on its domestic affairs and, through a bloody civil war relatively free from outside interference, rid itself of the domestic institution—slavery—that was the epitome of unreason, inequality and force. Having done so, when it first strode onto the international stage, it did so as a democratic state and the enemy of the appalling tyrannies it confronted. It did so, whatever circumstances may have on occasion required, still inspired by its revolutionary or utopian ideals. Reinforced throughout our history by a Christian millenialism that operates still both in its original form and as the secular inertia of long-forgotten religious impulses, this idealism continues to shape our attitudes and beliefs. Congressman Ron V. Dellums, for example, while Chairman of the House Armed Services Committee, said, following the attack on the Iraqi intelligence headquarters in retaliation for the plot to assassinate former President Bush, that no nation, especially an unrivaled superpower, should presume to use unilateral force to seek to vindicate the rule of international law. "Had [President Clinton] sought my counsel, I would have urged him to take further diplomatic action. . . . We must move past the time in human affairs when violence is the first recourse of statecraft."[14] The spirit that moved Dellums to disparage the use of force and call for ascending to the next stage in human development is the same spirit that inspired Americans of the revolutionary generation to call the United States a New Order of the Ages, Woodrow Wilson to declare a "universal dominion of right" and to promote the League of Nations, Roosevelt to champion the United Nations, George Bush to invoke the New World Order, and Clinton to advocate aggressive multilateralism.[15]

Our principles and historical experience have combined to teach us, in the words of one student of strategy, "that war is episodic, is waged abroad, that progress is possible in human affairs—so one should not be fatalistic about the danger of war—and that there is not a constant, high level of menace in the external world." The result has been that we have never developed "a coherent national strategy for the consistent pursuit of political goals by diplomacy in combination with armed force."[16] The examples cited earlier are compelling illustrations of this point. There are exceptions, of course (among contemporaries, one thinks of Henry Kissinger and George Shultz), but generally speaking Americans and their diplomats and soldiers tend to see peace and war, persuasion and force, as discrete and discontinuous activities. If, as Winston Churchill wrote, "at the summit true politics and strategy are one," Americans have seldom, if ever, made it to the mountain top. Nor, to return to our prosaic theme, do they have key foreign policy agencies that cooperate easily. If the activities of diplomats and soldiers are considered not complementary, not activities that need to be combined to attain common objectives, but as contrary or antagonistic, then it should not be a surprise that the Departments of State and Defense do not cooperate easily. Both prefer to be left alone and to leave each other alone so that they can get on with what they think to be their proper work.

All the impediments to interagency cooperation that we have discussed—the size of bureaucracies, faulty procedures, commitment to mission, agency cultures, and American peculiarities—have another effect. They also inhibit the coordination of policy and operations. This coordination is the most important aspect of interagency cooperation because success in counterterrorism and anything else a government does depends on it. Policy establishes goals; operations try to achieve them. If these two activities are not coordinated, government will always miss the targets at which it aims. A most telling example of this occurred in Somalia, in the second phase of our involvement there, when the policy toward Mohamed Aideed changed from pursuit to reconciliation, but this change was not coordinated with operations, which continued to pursue him.[17] When the pursuit led to a pitched battle on October 3, 1993, there was no policy framework in place publicly or privately that could make sense of the loss of eighteen American lives. The result was the collapse of the U.S. government's efforts in Somalia.

At first glance, it may appear that interagency cooperation and policy-operations coordination are the same thing, particularly if this glance is in the direction of the State and Defense departments, the two most important agencies for policy and operations, respectively, overseas. If one agency does policy and the other operations, coordinating these two functions of government will require interagency cooperation. This is true, but while similar and overlapping, interagency cooperation and policy-operations coordination are not identical. Agencies coordinate on policy matters without regard to operations, as do Defense and State, or on operations without discussing policy, as do the CIA and Defense. In addition, policy-operations coordination takes place within agencies. For example, the policy making office in Defense must see that the Joint Staff, the Unified and Specified Commands, and Services follow the policies that it sets down. The lawyers in the Justice Department are in a similar position with regard to the FBI. State also must coordinate policy and operations, at least in the sense that it must see that its diplomats overseas carry out the policies set down in Washington. (This is not a pure case of policy-operations coordination, however, since diplomats overseas sometimes have a policymaking role in a way that soldiers, spies, and law enforcement officers do not.) In short, policy-operations coordination and interagency cooperation are not the same thing. The essential difference between the two is that interagency cooperation occurs horizontally, so to speak, between agencies or officeholders of more or less equal authority. Coordination of policy and operations takes place vertically, within or among agencies, between agencies or officeholders who are, at least in principle, in a relationship of superior to inferior. Policymaking and policymakers are supposed to lead, operations and operators to follow. Although not the same, policy-operations coordination and interagency cooperation should be considered together because the policy-operations coordination most vital for an effective foreign policy, that between the State and Defense Departments, is an interagency matter. Often, when people speak of a failure to coordinate policies between agencies, they are describing the similar but narrower problem of coordinating policy and operations.

The first point to be made in considering policy-operations coordination is that while true in general, the principle that policy leads and operations follow is subject to some qualifications depending on the situation in which we find ourselves. Exploring these qualifications will allow us to see why, although important in any governmental endeavor, the coordination of policy and operations is particularly important in counterterrorism and similar operations other than war. To understand the qualifications, we should begin with the two extreme situations of policy-operations coordination, war and peace, in which the nature of things is clearest. In war, operations are subordinate only to the highest policy considerations because it is the success of operations that ultimately determines what policy objectives are attainable. War, we have previously argued, is the effort to destroy the ability of our enemies to resist our will. Thus, in war, we give the greatest possible scope to operations, since this is the only way to achieve our policy objectives. Policy is still the superior, setting out war aims, but it is heavily dependent on operations and thus should defer to operations, limiting them only for the highest reasons of policy. In peacetime, in the absence of any open conflict, military operations are much less important than in war. They are subject sometimes even to the demands of petty policy considerations because military operations are not necessary to achieve policy goals. Between the extremes of war and peace, the relationship between policy and these operations is more complicated. Where there is conflict but not yet the decision to go to war, operations are more important than in peacetime but not as important as in war. In these cases, the emphasis is still on persuasion and not destruction, to use the terms we have previously used to distinguish peace and war. The context is still predominantly political, not military. Yet force or the threat of force will have a significant role to play. Operational necessity must be taken into account more than it would be in peacetime, but is still likely to be subject to a greater number of policy considerations than in war. In such situations, success requires that all operations, even at the tactical level, be informed by the policy goals the operation is meant to achieve. This is one reason the British refer to such operations as corporals' wars. Actions taken at the tactical level (the way noncombatants and their property are treated, for example) can have political consequences that determine the outcome. Success in such conflicts can be achieved only if there is the closest possible coordination of policy and operations.

Counterterrorism illustrates the point we are making. Terrorism, we have argued, is not war and combating terrorism not warfare. Terrorism focuses not on destruction but on persuasion through intimidation. Violence is employed primarily for political effect. Countering terrorism will, in most cases, employ violence for the same reason. This means that a variety of political or policy considerations must inform operations and tactics. For example, it may be feasible operationally to disrupt a terrorist group by seizing one of its members in a foreign country or by sabotaging there some of its equipment, facilities, or financial activities. But such operations might have political repercussions detrimental to our interests in the long term, such as diminishing cooperation with other countries. Whether such operations take place depends on policy decisions that weigh political consequences. This was true of the raid on Libya. It was not intended to destroy the ability of Libyans to sponsor terrorism. It was meant to discourage them from doing so. It was an act not of war but of coercive diplomacy. Therefore, the targets and the method of hitting them were chosen with a number of political considerations in mind, among them hitting targets related to terrorism but only those not near heavily populated areas. The assistance of the British also dictated some of these limitations on the operation. In this case, and in combating terrorism generally, as in all conflicts short of war, a number and variety of policy considerations had to be taken into account when planning operations, if the operations were to have any chance of success in the overall effort they were part of. These policy considerations are likely to be greater in operations other than war than during war. For this reason, such operations require the coordination of policy and operations in detail from the strategic to the tactical level.

Another illuminating example of the need to coordinate policy and operations carefully in conflicts short of war can be drawn from the British experience with counterinsurgency. When civil order broke down in the British empire and the military was called in, they were expected to take swift and decisive action to restore it. But, according to one historian of this experience, the process by which they did this was not straightforward. "To a military man, the task seemed crystal clear. . . . Any constraints imposed by the civil authorities were . . . counter-productive." The military believed that their operations, "swift, decisive and relatively cheap," should be conducted "with no constraints on the use of appropriate force." When these operations had restored order, then the civil authorities could resume control. While such an approach appealed to the military, "it was rarely allowed to develop" for three reasons. First, giving the military a free hand in what was still a civil setting contradicted the British tradition of civilian control of the military. Second, there was a concern that civil authority would be hard to reestablish once martial law had been declared. Third, the British generally recognized that behind any disturbance or rebellion there was probably a legitimate grievance. This meant that the conflict could only be handled in a definitive way if political considerations remained predominant. This meant, in turn, that the civil authority had to maintain control of the military and that policy considerations had to permeate and guide operations. Military force could be used to counter violence, but "such force had to be tempered by a desire to persuade the ordinary people to accept the promises of the government." This required, in turn, that civilians "aware of long-term policy aims" had to be in charge, rather than "heavy-handed and politically short-sighted" military men. While it is doubtful that civilians always think in the long term and their military colleagues never do, the British experience shows that the "imposition of civilian primacy in policy-making inevitably limited the role of the military and necessitated the acceptance of civilian control in policing actions." The lesson is that in all conflicts policy must predominate but that in conflicts short of war, policy and operations must be intertwined in a way that is not necessary in war. Failure to do so limits the chances for success.[18]

In theory, everyone agrees that policy and operations must be coordinated. The military agrees that policy should drive strategy and that tactics should accord with strategy. Diplomats want military means to contribute to the success of their policies. In practice, however, as we have noted, the same obstacles that impede interagency cooperation also impede the coordination of policy and operations. The American tendency to see war and peace as discrete and discontinuous states, reinforced by the cultural differences between diplomats and soldiers, which in turn contribute to failures of cooperation between agencies—all this affects directly the more specific problem of coordinating policy and operations. It does so by creating a sense that, as the

Major General from the Joint Staff put it, the "military guys" and the "political guys" should do their jobs seriatim rather than jointly. This is the antithesis of the attitude necessary to encourage coordination of policy and operations. This attitude, which is found among diplomats as well, is particularly crippling in conflicts short of war because of the vital importance of diplomacy in such situations. Since our survival is not at stake in any one of these conflicts, we have much room for maneuver. In such cases, it is appropriate that our goals change or emerge more clearly only as coercive diplomacy proceeds. In his playful consideration of the opportunities open to him, then, Holbrooke was not wrong. But policy and operations must be coordinated in such cases continually and modified as each has its effect. The possibilities and problems of operations must inform policymaking, just as the goals and restraints of policy must inform operational planning. Achieving such coordination requires awareness of the need for it and then good vertical communications, back and forth, between policymakers and operators within the framework of an overall strategy that both understand and accept. Something like this happened during the first phase of our involvement in Somalia. When it does not occur, it may be because policymakers and operators see problems differently or are caught up in a faulty process or because diplomats seek to preserve flexibility, operators try to preserve operational security, and some of all and sundry try to obscure their responsibility should the policy or operation fail.

Having detailed the reasons why agencies fail to cooperate and policy and operations lack coordination, our first impulse may be to deplore the mess and search for ways to clean it up. Before indulging this impulse, however, we ought to consider what might be lost in too thorough a housecleaning. Take that most reviled of problems, bureaucratic turf fighting. This grows out of the particular mandate and tasks that each agency has been given and the interests that it represents. If we condemn this fighting, we are saying in effect that one or more of these mandates or interests is not worth defending, that the particular skill that each agency represents is not necessary to preserve the security and prosperity of the United States, that one or more of the interests represented by these agencies is not part of the national interest. Conversely, if we think that these skills and interests are important, then we should not condemn the fighting. When agencies fight to protect their prerogatives, authority, and resources, they may make interagency cooperation more difficult but they also protect capabilities essential to our well-being that nobody else will protect because nobody else has a similar self-interested motive to do so. Likewise, while the cultural differences between soldiers and diplomats impair the ability of the U.S. government to handle complex problems such as counterterrorism, they cannot be removed without doing away with some of the capabilities essential to the successful pursuit of our national objectives. We need the different abilities and attitudes, the cultures of both military officers and diplomats. It might improve interagency coordination if one were indistinguishable from the other, but ultimately this would do us no good.

However painful and messy, interagency turf battles and cultural misunderstandings are a positive good.

Recognizing that even the most frustrating aspects of interagency conflict
serve some good purpose should moderate our impulse to charge in and clean
things up.   Additionally, we should remember that even given all the
impediments to interagency cooperation and the coordination of policy and
operations, the U.S. government does manage to get things done. The process is
seldom pretty even when it works, but on occasion agencies manage to blend
their various abilities and policymakers communicate their objectives to
operators in a way that allows them to organize their activities to achieve these
objectives. We have already mentioned the case of Somalia. Historians may
come to see as another example the period immediately leading to the
restoration of Aristide, after the U.S. government overcame the problems that
plagued its first efforts to implement the Governor's Island Accord. They will
probably also come to see, as did those who participated in them, that our efforts
to combat terrorism were another case in which agencies cooperated and policy
and operations were coordinated, resulting in an effective program. Alone these
efforts do not explain the decline of terrorism in the late 1980s and early 1990s
but they were part of the reason for this decline. At least, there is a consensus
that interagency cooperation and policy-operations coordination increased to the
point where their absence was no longer a major deficiency in our
counterterrorism efforts. That this was no small accomplishment is clear if we
consider our counternarcotics efforts. These are all but universally considered
to lack cooperation and coordination. Just before his nomination to be "Drug
Czar," General Barry McCaffrey said that "the Clinton administration's strategy
for stemming the flow of drugs from Latin America to the United States [had]
been hampered by poor interagency coordination."[19]

To explain the success of the U.S. government's counterterrorism program,
observers of and participants in this effort point to the small interagency group
that came in the mid-1980s to have the job of managing ongoing noncrisis
counterterrorism operations. Participants in this group cite several reasons for
its success. It was small, met frequently, generally consisted of specialists, had
a relatively stable membership, and had the support of the cabinet-level heads of
the departments or agencies represented in the group, as well as direct access to
them when necessary. These characteristics allowed the group to overcome or
avoid the obstacles to interagency cooperation and policy-operations
coordination that we have just discussed.

Perhaps the most important reason for the success of the interagency
counterterrorism group was the high-level support its members received.
Although high-ranking, the representatives at the interagency group's meetings
did not have enough authority to direct their agencies to cooperate with other
agencies, nor by themselves could they have overcome the problems of
bureaucratic complexity internal to these agencies. They could not, for
example, by themselves have overcome the opposition of regional offices or

other functional bureaus to initiatives they developed. They overcame such internal opposition and external coordination problems when they did because they had the support of their principals. William Casey and George Shultz were the most public in their emphasis on the danger of terrorism and the need to counter it, but members of the group from the Defense Department have commented that Secretary of Defense Caspar Weinberger helped them win bureaucratic battles in Defense as Casey and Shultz helped their subordinates in their own agencies. These men, particularly Casey and Shultz, agreed on the importance of combating terrorism, as they sometimes disagreed about appropriate methods. Supporting this cabinet-level concern was the President's interest and rising public anxiety at certain points. Together these factors helped establish fighting terrorism as a priority for the entire government. The painful lessons of non-cooperation (e.g., the kidnapping of General Dozier and the crash of President Zia's plane) encouraged cooperation, but high-level interest and support was critical in overcoming resistance to cooperation in and between agencies.

While the small size of the group was the result of a consensus view, based on long and frustrating experience, that large groups could not do anything, the quality, stability, and effectiveness of the group's membership was the result of high-level interest in counterterrorism. While there were eight different people in charge of terrorism at the State Department in the 1970s and five from 1989 to 1994, there were only three in this position from 1980 to 1988. As high-level interest in counterterrorism increased, the various counterterrorism offices became more influential. Being responsible for counterterrorism became more career enhancing, and the position attracted some of the best or at least most aggressive people in each of the agencies, all of whom had an interest in staying in such a highly visible position. Apart from the size of the group, then, its character and hence its success depended on the interest of a few powerful, high-level supporters.

As one would expect in a small, stable group that met often, its members got to know one another well. As they did, they developed trust in one another, especially as they saw that information from their meetings did not leak to the press. Several representatives from the operational agencies stressed the importance of this, saying that the trust and confidence that developed in the group allowed them to speak frankly and share information, as they would not have done in the much larger, more anonymous Interagency Working Group on terrorism. Frank sharing of information is obviously useful in promoting cooperation among agencies. It is also critical for coordinating policy and operations. As we have argued, coordinating policy and operations, especially in the gray area between peace and war, requires that operations derive from and aim to achieve the goals policymakers set forth and that policy goals be informed by operational difficulties and possibilities. This reciprocal sharing of information and judgments is impossible if policymakers and operators cannot be frank with one another. The level of trust and frankness that developed in the interagency group was particularly useful for ensuring coordination of policy and operations because originally the group consisted of representatives from the three policy agencies (State Department, OSD, and NSC) and the three operational agencies (Joint Staff, Defense Department, and FBI) that are involved in combating terrorism.

In a small, tight-knit group such as the interagency counterterrorism group, a danger exists that an orthodoxy or groupthink will develop, preventing the group from considering problems in an innovative way. At the level of policy, this happened. There was a consensus on what the U.S. government needed to do to combat terrorism and on the high rank that combating terrorism should hold among all of the government's priorities. In some cases, it seems that this consensus may have clouded the judgment of some members of the group. While from one perspective such a consensus might appear to be groupthink, from another it appears to be the sharing of assumptions and principles necessary for the agreement that interagency cooperation demands. There can be no such cooperation if there is not a minimum level of agreement. On the operational level, a stultifying orthodoxy does not appear to have been a problem, since innovative means were proposed to achieve the group's commonly shared policy goals.

So far, this account of why the interagency counterterrorism group was effective in overcoming impediments to interagency cooperation has focused on its relations with the rest of the bureaucracy. From their own accounts, however, it is clear that the participants in the interagency group did not forget what agencies they were representing when they attended the group's meetings. Clashes occurred. Mandates conflicted and the participants saw things as representatives of their agencies usually did. When compromise was not possible, they went to their superiors for support. The impression one gets from the participants, however, is that they cooperated and compromised with each other much more often than they did not and for the same reasons that their agencies did: high-level interest and public pressure to succeed, as well as learning through experience what non-cooperation cost.

Other factors also increased cooperation in the interagency group, although they are harder to analyze. The participants in the group were proud of what they were doing and to some extent developed an "us against them" attitude that made the success of the interagency group more important to them than the triumph of their home agency's agenda, at least to the extent that those agendas conflicted with the requirements of combating terrorism. Again, the pride the participants felt in their work and its high profile encouraged them to work things out among themselves. Finally, as they worked together, they learned about each other or, in the terms we have used, learned about each other's culture, the distinctive ways of thinking and acting that define each agency. This point should not be overemphasized. Familiarity can breed contempt. Getting to know someone does not necessarily mean getting to respect them or what they stand for. For example, even after several years' experience dealing with lawyers from the Justice Department as members of the group, some former members still did not think lawyers belonged and argued that they detracted from the group's effectiveness. Despite this example, however, one does get a sense in talking to participants that they did learn about the institutional peculiarities of their colleagues in a way that improved cooperation. This was most marked in the case of the CIA and the FBI, although what they learned did not completely overcome their history of mutual suspicion and antagonism.[20]

Once we see the importance of high-level interest in promoting interagency cooperation, including an effective counterterrorism program, we see that the argument in the first years of the Clinton administration over the reorganization of the State Department was largely irrelevant. The reorganization plan, reportedly first suggested during the Bush administration, called for placing the State Department's counterterrorism office under an Assistant Secretary, who would in turn work for the new Under Secretary for Global Affairs. If this reorganization had taken place, it would have interposed two levels of bureaucracy between the counterterrorism Coordinator and the Secretary of State, whereas now the Coordinator reports directly to the Secretary, at least in principle. Congress objected to this plan, its opponents arguing that "the status and influence of the terrorism unit . . . would appear diminished if it reported" through the Under Secretary. This argument is irrelevant because it assumes that organization creates status and influence. It does not. Status and influence follow from high-level interest. Organization eventually reflects this. The State Department's counterterrorism official became an Ambassador-at-Large under Secretary of State Shultz because counterterrorism was important to Shultz but reverted to a mere Coordinator under his successor James Baker because it was less important to Baker, appropriately so, we have argued. Title and position in the bureaucracy do imply relative status and influence, but ultimately all of these things depend on the priorities of those who run agencies. These priorities should change as circumstances change and organization should change accordingly. In this light, the proposal to reorganize State's counterterrorism office and the attendance of lower-ranking officials at interagency meetings in the Bush and early Clinton years was a rational response to the declining threat from terrorism.[21]

Granted, once the bureaucracy changes to reflect declining attention to counterterrorism, terrorist groups or their state sponsors may conclude that the U.S. government is no longer as well prepared to respond to terrorism as it once was. If such a problem arises, it is a self-correcting and inevitable one. If terrorist attacks on American citizens and property increase, as they surely may, or are connected to central issues in our foreign policy, as they surely are, top-level officials will pay more attention to terrorism. They will attend interagency meetings devoted to it and reorganize their agencies and departments accordingly. For example, in 1992, with the Cold War ending, the FBI transferred four hundred agents from foreign counterintelligence to violent crime.   In 1996, with terrorist attacks increasing, the FBI transferred five hundred agents to counterterrorism. In addition, over the objections of the CIA, it sent fifty-nine agents and twenty-five support personnel to staff twenty-three new offices overseas.[22]   Attention to and resources for domestic terrorism increased following the bombing of the federal building in Oklahoma City in April 1995. The same thing happened with regard to antiterrorism following the bombings of two U.S. military installations in Saudi Arabia in 1995 and 1996. In this sense, the "bureaucratization" of counterterrorism, if it is a problem, is a self-correcting one.   It may seem foolish or wasteful to de-emphasize and restructure, only to re-create in the future the structure and procedures that prevailed until recently, but this is unavoidable. All resources, including the time of senior officials, are limited. All top-level officials need to follow a greater number of issues than they can, in fact, follow effectively. By force of necessity, they must choose. The decreased attention to terrorism was, in this sense, inevitable and justifiable, because the threat had diminished.   While Congress can mandate organization, it cannot mandate bureaucratic status and influence.

The limits to establishing bureaucratic status and influence are one reason why, for all its success, the interagency counterterrorism group is a model for improving interagency cooperation and policy-operations coordination of only limited applicability. To the extent that this group's success depended on the interest and support of high-level officials, it cannot be duplicated by fiat. That level of interest and support was itself the result of a confluence of factors, foreign and domestic, over which no element of the U.S. government has control. The group is also a model of limited usefulness because it consisted of a group of experts who focused on a specific issue and did not, for the most part, formulate policy but implemented it. Few issues lend themselves to treatment by such a group. Where they do (for example, in the case of countering the proliferation of weapons of mass destruction), the counterterrorism interagency group may be a model to follow. Fundamentally, however, the counterterrorism group is not a model for improving the performance of the bureaucracy because it was implicitly designed to skirt the bureaucracy by its exclusivity and its direct connection to the highest levels of decisionmaking. This access made the group more efficient and effective. When they made decisions, the members were rather confident that higher-ups would not overturn them, causing them to have to revisit issues and proposed operations, many of which were time-sensitive and could not wait for extensive discussions and interagency staffing. The attraction, if not necessity, of such a mechanism will be apparent when we consider that, according to one count, approximately thirty agencies and organizations make up what is called the counterterrorism community, carrying out more than 150 specific activities to combat terrorism.[23]

The experience of the interagency counterterrorism group suggests that the interagency process works best when it is worked around. Although a study of economic policymaking in the Ford administration suggests that the small team approach may have broader applicability,[24] it is probably the case that ad hoc interagency groups to overcome bureaucratic inertia are not a cure-all. This may suggest to some, especially at a time of rationalizing and reinventing government, that some of the counterterrorism functions shared or spread across agencies could more rationally be combined in a single agency. This new agency could combat terrorism and use the techniques appropriate for such a fight for other similar missions as well, such as countering the proliferation of WMD or fighting organized crime. There is a precedent for such an approach. The Drug Enforcement Agency was established by combining two organizations that dealt with drugs. While such a structural fix would not solve all interagency problems associated with counterterrorism and did not solve all drug enforcement problems, this model might be helpful. Interagency cooperation problems would be minimized if one agency combined nearly all the skills necessary to take action against terrorism. These would include, for example, the direct action capability that now exists in the Defense Department, the intelligence and clandestine operational support capability that now exists in the CIA's Directorate of Operations, and other capabilities in both the FBI and Defense. Such an organization would amount to something like a new version of the Office of Strategic Services.

Even if bureaucratic objections to and budget problems with such an idea could be overcome, implementing it would not necessarily produce a more effective counterterrorism organization. The lack of understanding and cooperation that characterizes, for example, relations between direct action personnel and human intelligence collectors derives primarily not from the fact that they belong to different organizations but from the kind of people they are and become as they train for and undertake their specific activities. These differences would not be overcome even if both activities were housed in the same agency. Indeed, this difference in attitude we are discussing existed in the early years of the CIA, between those involved in human collection (the Office of Special Operations, OSO) and those involved in covert operations (the Office of Policy Coordination, OPC). As a historian of the Agency has commented, "OSO personnel regarded OPC's high-risk operations as a threat to the maintenance of OSO security and cover."[25] Far from solving the problem, combining direct action and human intelligence activities in the same agency would probably make matters worse, insofar as one capability would dominate the other, as collection dominates covert action in the Directorate of Operations, and either the direct action mission or the human collection and support mission would suffer. Similar problems would develop if the different hostage rescue capabilities that the U.S. government now has were combined. The FBI's team is best suited for domestic operations, the Defense Department's for operations overseas. That both can function in either environment does not change the differences between them, resulting from a difference in ethos that, in turn, derives from traditional American ideas about the separation of military and police powers.

This brief discussion of how the government has and might organize itself to combat terrorism suggests that the differences between agencies and the friction or problems these differences generate can only be managed, not resolved structurally or administratively. A small interagency group can help with this management, but its effectiveness ultimately depends on high-level support. Since this interagency group functions under the aegis of the NSC, this interagency organization might suggest itself as a way of overcoming interagency problems. But the NSC is ultimately the creature of the principals who make it up. To speak of management at their level is misleading because it underestimates the difficulty of what they must do. Their most important task is to discern both our national interests and those situations that threaten or help us secure them. It is this exercise of discernment that assigns combating terrorism its priority and enlivens or deadens the government organization that is, in the last analysis, only the tool of those with the authority to use it.

It is not impossible that the principals will have the necessary discernment to do their jobs. But this will not entirely solve the problem of interagency cooperation or policy-operations coordination. Even if they put the right emphasis in the right places, cooperation and coordination will depend on their subordinates in the various agencies. Cooperating and coordinating, however, does not come easily to aggressive professionals who have been rewarded for defending their agency's prerogatives and shaped in other ways during a career by the interests and culture of their agency. It is assumed that somehow, miraculously, as these professionals reach the executive or the general officer rank, they will develop some of the broader vision necessary to accommodate viewpoints and interests other than their own, so that the final result is something that approaches compatibility with the complex common interest of a country such as the United States. Training and education helps pull off this miracle and, ultimately, as we have noted, there is always the appeal to the highest levels, where priorities among competing interests are set. It is here, at the summit, where we hope true statesmanship lies. This hierarchical system was well suited for the Cold War, when we faced a predominant enemy and our primary concern was global war with this enemy. In this situation, the policy and strategic issues were widely known and had been weighed and evaluated over a period of years. The results then sifted down, becoming the sediment of military doctrine and the standard operating assumptions of various agencies. Such a system is less well suited to our current strategic environment, which is more complex and less well known and in which we face not one overriding security issue that acts as a thread we can follow from the labyrinth to safety but a variety of issues and problems that suggest no fixed course. In such a situation, it is more important than it was that discernment of some sort exist further down the chain of command. It must extend even to the corporals, if we are to have the cooperation and coordination necessary for success in the corporals' wars we will fight.

5

STRATEGY

In discussing the efforts of the U.S. government to combat terrorism, particularly the government's methods and organization, we arrived at one conclusion repeatedly: to be effective, counterterrorism must be part of a larger strategy. Economic sanctions, legal efforts, and diplomatic pressure were ineffective in getting Noriega out of Panama at least in part because they were not coordinated. The raid on Libya in April 1986 would have done little by itself to curb Libyan support for terrorism or the other activities of the Libyan government that were inimical to American interests. Combined with economic sanctions, bilateral and multilateral (UN) diplomacy, and military activities in Chad, the raid was part of a long-term strategy that has hurt Libya.[1] In addition to allowing the U.S. government to focus the activities of its various agencies, an overall strategy provides a scale with which we can weigh the risks and benefits of the various initiatives we undertake. For example, the apprehension of terrorists overseas has proven to be an effective way to combat terrorism, but it should be used only when an apprehension hurts us less than the terrorism it prevents or might deter. As we have already noted, an apprehension could harm our relations with an ally. Unless we have a good sense of why the ally is important to us, we will not be in a position to judge whether it is worth hurting this relationship to apprehend the terrorist. Making such a judgment requires not only some understanding and ranking of our interests but an understanding of how we are most likely to protect them. This is what a national strategy provides.

The need for such a strategy is particularly acute with regard to such threats as terrorism, for two reasons. First, countering terrorism is inherently reactive. As we have seen, our few efforts to be proactive, as the jargon has it, were not sustainable. As a reactive enterprise, the effort to combat terrorism cedes the initiative to the enemy. It puts us at a disadvantage, therefore. We can overcome this disadvantage only by combating terrorism as part of a comprehensive and effective strategy.   The Reagan administration, for example, placed its counterterrorism efforts within its larger effort to roll back the Soviet empire. This is clear from the remarks of then Secretary of State Haig upon taking office that the Soviet Union was supporting terrorism, a theme continued, although broadened and deepened, by his successor, Secretary Shultz. Much of the success of the Reagan administration's effort against terrorism was due to making the fight against terrorism part of a bigger battle. Second, threats like terrorism are hard to evaluate. If the United States were faced with imminent invasion, the danger would be apparent and our response evident. When survival is at issue, nothing can be held back. Generally speaking, the more imminent and evident the danger, the less free are we in choosing our response. Against methods such as terrorism, which are indirect and slow, attacking public opinion rather than organized forces, whose effects are cumulative and difficult to gauge, we have greater freedom to respond and must weigh a greater number of costs and benefits than when our survival is immediately at stake. We have used sanctions to punish Libya, Iraq, and Syria for their support of terrorism, for example, but how we have applied them and when has varied in each case, depending on a number of considerations, such as the status of our confrontations with the Soviet Union or Iran or the condition of Middle East politics. Depending on our assessment, we have decided what priority to assign the fight against these different sponsors of terrorism. We can make such decisions intelligently only within a broader context that allows us to consider relative costs and benefits. Without considering this strategic context, we risk doing more harm to ourselves than good, especially when we respond vigorously to indirect threats like terrorism.

Developing a strategic context for our counterterrorism efforts is particularly important now. While the Soviet Union existed, the terrorism used against us was compatible with its goals. Consequently, our efforts against terrorism, insurgency, and other forms of subversion were properly subject to the priorities of our struggle against the Soviet Union. Now that that struggle is over, we have no context ready to hand in which to place terrorism and other forms of subversion or, for that matter, in which to place any of the foreign policy or national security issues that we now confront. In this situation, the danger is that we will make too much of the unimportant and too little of the important, a danger to which the Clinton administration could be argued to have succumbed, when it focused on Somalia and Haiti at the expense of Europe.[2]

The current strategic vacuum is a danger, then, but also an opportunity. It is an occasion to rethink our strategy root and branch. This process began before the Soviet Union collapsed but was excited to a fever pitch by that collapse. Debate has arisen on such fundamental issues as the meaning of the terms *threat* and *interest* and the future relevance of war and national sovereignty. Such debates are important in themselves and as part of the process by which a national strategic framework will develop. How they are decided will determine the ranking of terrorism as a threat, helping us decide how we should respond. But these strategic debates also implicate terrorism and other forms of subversion in another way. They figure in the arguments of those who contend that we must think about our security in unaccustomed ways, who see in these forms of subversion another indication that our idealist approach to foreign affairs will be increasingly irrelevant as our relative power declines. Historically disdainful of raison d'état and power politics and relatively unpracticed in their use, the United States may in the future have to take its counterterrorism effort, properly understood, as a model for its response to a world of increasingly dispersed and competitive power. In such a world, success will depend more on the steady, patient, and purposeful application of power in all its forms than on the episodic conduct of a crusade with overwhelming force.

The following discussion of strategy, then, addresses the broader issues that make up the current debate over national security because doing so is necessary to evaluate both the threat that terrorism poses to us and an appropriate response. It will not address, at least directly, the purposes to which we might put our national power. Determining these ends is a political issue; strategy then determines the best means to achieve them. Explicit discussion of our ends is not necessary because at the highest level our goals and interests have never been much in dispute. Both Democratic and Republican administrations have described them in roughly the same way: the security of the United States and its people, a prosperous economy, and a world in which democracy and free trade are at home.[3] Disagreement exists, of course, over what these ends mean in detail, but most controversy centers on how to attain them and on what stands in our way, on what threatens us. We will begin our discussion of strategy by addressing this last issue, what threatens us, since it is in response to threats, those things that could prevent us achieving our goals, that we devise our strategy, our plan for using those means available to us to attain our goals. Having analyzed what threatens us, we will then consider how to respond. Broadly speaking, three strategic approaches are open to us: fortress America, global engagement, or selective engagement. We will defend selective engagement as the only strategy appropriate to the circumstances in which the United States finds itself. Having established in this chapter the framework necessary for evaluating terrorism, we will turn to that evaluation in the Conclusion.

WHAT THREATENS US?

This emphasis on threat may seem somewhat outdated. For forty years, the Soviet Union was the greatest threat we faced, indeed the greatest threat we had ever faced. When it disappeared, the notion of threat seemed, at least for a time, a less appropriate way to discuss our national security. As President Bush and others spoke of a New World Order of multilateral cooperation, official statements emphasized not just the threats that confronted us but the opportunities that lay before us. This new emphasis was understandable. The collapse of the Soviet Union gave us a strategic depth we had not enjoyed since the end of World War I.

Threats to the United States had receded both temporally and spatially. Soviet forces had withdrawn or were withdrawing from eastern Europe and their readiness for war collapsing, as the Soviet presence diminished in strategic positions around the world such as the horn of Africa, Cuba, and Vietnam. Even strategic nuclear weapons, which have done more than anything else to diminish the security offered by time and space, seemed less threatening. But as these official statements noted, problems remained.[4] In fact, the new opportunities and the remaining threats were inextricably linked. The demise of the Soviet empire ended one threat but created the space and freedom of action for others to develop, such as ethnic conflict in the Balkans, smuggling of fissionable material and increased jockeying for position in a multipolar world. Certainly, these threats were not as grave as that the Soviet Union had posed, nor were they all of equal weight. Still, the end of the Soviet Union has not meant an end to threats.

Some have argued not that the notion of threat is outdated but that it has changed fundamentally. They contend that the older notion of political-military threat, embodied most recently by the Soviet Union, is too narrow for the complex, interdependent world we now inhabit. In the immediate aftermath of the Cold War, for instance, a sentiment grew that "geo-economics" had replaced geopolitics, as "the methods of commerce" had displaced "military methods." This analysis is as true now as it was in the late nineteenth century, the last time economics appeared to have trumped politics as a determinant of international order. This notion will be disproved now as it was then by the rise of new military powers, a process we are already witnessing in Asia and, in an early stage, perhaps in Iran. Another argument about the changing nature of threats emerged before the end of the Cold War but was sucked into greater prominence by the post–Cold War strategic vacuum. In the early 1980s, prestigious foreign affairs and national security journals began publishing articles arguing that we should redefine national security to include more than just military threats. Defining a threat as an action or event that degrades the quality of life of the inhabitants of a state or limits the options of its policymakers, these articles argued that economic decline, environmental degradation, massive earthquakes in California, overpopulation, mass human migrations, the spread of AIDS, a deteriorating educational system, and resource scarcities should all be considered threats to our national security. Showing the influence of such thinking, President Bush's *National Security Strategy* mentioned as "new kinds of security issues . . . the strength and resilience of our economy," illegal drugs, and environmental depredations and remarked that "a security strategy that takes the Republic safely into the next century will tend to these as well as to more traditional threats to our security and well-being."[5]

What should we make of the claim that we need to expand our notion of threat? Clearly, an earthquake that devastated California would have an adverse effect on the U.S. economy and thus our national well-being. Similarly, declining educational standards or contagious and devastating diseases could harm us. Does it make sense, however, to speak of earthquakes in California or poorly educated teenagers as threats to our national security? Traditionally, the term *threat* in the context of national security meant the explicit or implicit intention to inflict harm. Most often, the ability to harm was directly related to the ability to use organized violence. While an earthquake in California would diminish our national well-being, it is not a threat in this sense. We could, of course, accept the attempted redefinition of security to include the earthquake, but this would merely obscure an important distinction. As traditionally understood, threats were the result of an enemy's decision. Natural disasters, on the other hand, simply happen, while bad economic or educational policies are self-inflicted wounds. Responses to these events are correspondingly different. Armed aggression, for example, can be deterred; earthquakes cannot be. Conflating all these events into a broader definition of *threat* obscures important differences between them. As one critic of expanding the definition of national security has put it, a point echoed in our discussion of the definition of terrorism, "if everything that causes a decline in human well-being is labeled a 'security' threat, the term loses any analytical usefulness and becomes a loose synonym for 'bad.'"[6] The next step, no doubt, will be to refer to earthquakes as "natural terrorism."

The issue of conceptual clarity is important because if the definition of *threat* becomes uselessly broad, it will become more difficult to respond appropriately to the threats and problems we face. While elements of the U.S. military may be able to help with the aftermath of an earthquake, for example, we should not forget that the military's primary purpose has always been to use organized violence to respond to threats of such violence, to deter attacks on the United States and to defeat our enemies should deterrence fail, in the now traditional formulation. In carrying out this task, the military has developed skills that can be used to deal with other problems. But to confuse these problems with threats as traditionally understood and to apply the military's specialized skills to dealing with them will only detract from its ability to carry out its primary mission. This will not be to our advantage. The use of organized violence on behalf of our interests may someday be unnecessary. But that day has not yet arrived, and acting as if it has will not enhance our national well-being.

The debate about "new security threats" can be read in another way. It can be read not as an argument about whether to expand the notion of threat but about what kinds of things fit into the old notion of threat. It can be read, that is, as an argument that we need to broaden our understanding of what can cause violent conflict or instability. Thus, while it may be improper to consider an earthquake or falling educational standards national security threats, it would not be improper to consider environmental degradation such a threat, if it increased conflict that impinged on our interests. Arguments like this achieved official sanction of sorts in 1990 when Senator Nunn and several of his colleagues called for spending Defense Department resources to address global environmental problems because they "were worsening and leading to tensions that could pose military problems, especially in the third world." This led to enactment of a $200 million strategic environmental research program that used Defense assets (laboratories, computers, etc.) to study environmental problems. In another example of this approach, spy satellites undertook environmental missions in 1995. One researcher at the American Federation of Scientists remarked that this use of spy satellites "reflects an expanding definition of national security" and defended the change, as did a congressman, by arguing that "environmental changes can be an important source of regional conflict." The growing influence of this argument is evident in official pronouncements and publications. Timothy Wirth, Under Secretary of State for Global Affairs, gave a speech in the summer of 1994 in which he claimed that "environmental degradation, poverty, disease and conflict-driven migration" were "the primary threats to human security." It is fitting, perhaps, that an Under Secretary for Global Affairs should speak of "human security" rather than "national security," but the effect of a broadened notion of threat is evident as well in President Clinton's *National Security Strategy* report. The 1996 version refers to "security risks that are not solely military in nature," such as "environmental degradation, natural resource depletion, rapid population growth and refugee flows," that disturb international stability and "present new challenges to U.S. strategy." This view of security attained popular and lurid expression in an article by Robert Kaplan, "The Coming Anarchy," published in February 1994, which has been widely influential. According to press reports, both President Clinton and Vice-President Gore studied and mentioned the article, their senior foreign policy advisors read it (perhaps explaining Wirth's pronouncement), and it was circulated throughout the White House and the National Security and National Economic Councils. In addition, it became part of the curriculum at several senior war colleges.[7]

Proponents of this broader definition of national security threat point to a variety of problems to support their case. Lack of water, they contend, is a major source of tension in Central Asia and in the Middle East, explaining Syrian support of Kurdish terrorist attacks on Turkey, while deforestation has contributed significantly to the economic and political problems of Haiti, driving Haitians to become refugees and producing a national security problem for the United States. India and Bangladesh are involved in disputes, also involving China, about deforestation in the Himalayas, which causes flooding in Bangladesh. Conflict has also arisen in the India-Bangladesh border region because of the migration of Bangladeshis seeking a better life in India. Other examples they point to include land use policies in the Philippines, which put people on unproductive land, keeping them impoverished, and leading them to support the New People's Army, a Maoist organization that has assassinated ten Americans since 1987; El Salvador's overpopulation and subsequent impoverishment, which led to support for the Farabundo Marti National Liberation Front, a Marxist terrorist group; and higher population growth rates in nonindustrialized countries, which will make all of today's industrial democracies, except the United States, "little" countries by 2025, creating a world more threatening to our interests. Finally, proponents of a new understanding of "security threat" point to the need to include in our understanding of threat the economic difficulties we face. U.S. economic decline will undermine our authority in the world, diminishing our security from traditional threats.[8]

At first glance this new analysis of national security threats diminishes the significance of terrorism by greatly increasing the number of threats competing for our attention. Yet in Kaplan's version of the argument, terrorism or subversive violence becomes a more salient threat. Part of the coming anarchy he foresees is a shift from large-scale, state-sponsored war to communal, low-intensity conflict, including terrorism. Perhaps the most efficient way to assess this new understanding of what threatens us and its affect on our assessment of terrorism is to begin by examining Kaplan's influential article. The ingredient list of its witches' brew contains every one of the new security threats, especially environmental problems. In breathless tones, in fact, Kaplan insists that "it is time to understand 'the environment' for what it is: *the* national security issue of the early twenty-first century. . . . The environment . . . is part of a terrifying array of problems that will define a new threat to our security . . . allowing a post-Cold War foreign policy to emerge inexorably by need rather than by design." Environmental decay will produce scarcity as population growth booms, according to Kaplan, prompting mass migrations that will engender conflicts between groups, which, held together by the intensity of their ethnic or religious self-identity, will replace collapsing nation-states as the major instigators of violent conflict. "Future wars," Kaplan warns, "will be those of communal survival, aggravated or, in many cases, caused by environmental scarcity."[9] If this future is what is unfolding before us, certainly our national strategy should address it, in hopes of taking the Republic safely into the next century, as President Bush's national strategy put it. But is it true, to begin where Kaplan says we must, that environmental degradation causes violent conflict, including terrorism?

Kaplan and other proponents of the environmental explanation of conflict delineate two processes: that by which environmental factors produce conflict *between* states and that by which such factors produce conflict *within* states. In both cases, they use the term *environment* broadly to include, for example, demography, human migrations, scarcity-induced economic decline, and resource availability. To determine whether environmental problems cause conflict, let us begin with the question of whether it causes conflict between states.

Those seeking to prove that environmental problems produce conflict between states cite the supposed historical examples of states fighting with one another to decide control over resources (e.g., Iraq and Kuwait or, through proxies, Syria and Turkey). Given that resources will become scarcer, according to this argument, one may conclude that such wars will become more frequent. Since these wars will endanger U.S. citizens and affect U.S. access to resources, proponents of this view conclude that the U.S. government ought to devote national security resources to environmental problems. This argument is not persuasive, however. Even if we grant that environmental scarcities have caused conflicts in the past, such causes need not operate in the future. A critic of the argument that environmental scarcities cause conflict cites three reasons why scarcity of resources may become less important as a cause of interstate conflict: the world trade system allocates resources in such a manner that states can satisfy their resource needs without occupying territory; the balance of military power around the world is such that it is now more difficult for developed countries to seize territory from undeveloped countries than it was earlier in the 20th century; and industrial societies are increasingly capable of making what they need out of basic materials (iron, aluminum, silicon, hydrocarbons) that are ubiquitous and plentiful. To take a specific case, water, it is not at all clear that it will be so scarce in the future. New technologies and irrigation methods, as well as the marketing of water at a price that reflects its value as a commodity, may deprive water of the role in conflict that many foresee it assuming.[10]

Decreasing scarcities should decrease concern over scarcity wars between states. But a more fundamental problem with scarcity as a security threat is that it demands that we address the environmental causes of conflict without being precise about the connection between environmental problems and the conflicts they supposedly cause. As even Thomas Homer-Dixon, the man that Kaplan anoints as the prophet of environmental threats to security, has admitted, it is impossible to find a pure example of a "resource war." There is little historical evidence that environmentally induced scarcities have caused wars between states. Was World War II a "resource war," as one expert has claimed? Was the Gulf War fought only over oil? Can tensions between Turkey and Syria, let alone Israel and its Arab neighbors, be explained only in terms of water scarcity? Clearly not. Nor would anyone seriously maintain that World War II or the various Arab-Israeli wars would not have been fought if only men had been farsighted enough to address environmental problems. This line of argument, rather than persuading us that environmental problems cause conflict, merely shows how such problems become occasions for it. For example, Homer-Dixon cites an environmental problem in the Senegal River Valley to show that such problems can lead to ethnic violence involving two states, in this case, Senegal and Mauritania. But as his own account makes clear, the root cause of the violence was ethnic conflict, not the environmental problem.[11] If environmental problems are not the cause of conflict, we are not likely to enhance our security by devoting a lot of attention to solving them. In any given case (for example, talks between the Israeli government and the Palestinian Authority), a resource issue (in this case, water rights) may be one of the issues that need to be resolved but this would not warrant a reorientation of our strategic thinking or even a greater emphasis on environmental issues. As the Israeli/Palestinian Authority example illustrates, to the extent that environmental issues enter into conflicts, they can be addressed by traditional diplomatic methods.

The difficulty of connecting environmental problems to conflict recurs when we look at the issue of intrastate conflict. Indeed, the problem is clearer in this case, since the argument linking environmental problems and intrastate conflict has been made in more detail. Proponents of the view that environmental problems cause conflict within states make a complicated argument, linking two sets of causes and effects. They argue first that environmental problems (for example, population growth, deforestation) cause economic decline or, more vaguely, a diminished quality of life. Then they argue that economic decline or diminished growth causes conflict.

This argument is vulnerable at each intersection of cause and effect. Consider the connections between environmental problems and poverty. One demographer has pointed out, for example, after reviewing a study of thirty-two countries, including China, Brazil, India, Indonesia, Bangladesh, Pakistan, and Mexico, that "rapid population growth has not prevented major improvements in productivity in many of the societies most directly transformed by it." Per-capita economic growth accelerated even after the post–1950 population explosion. More generally, societies without any resources have prospered (for example, Hong Kong) because economic development results primarily not from an abundance of resources or a well-maintained ecosystem but from dispositions to save and innovate within a political environment and an economic system that encourages both. Deforestation has no doubt contributed to poverty in Haiti and the Philippines, but given the other problems in these countries they would be little better off even with full forests. Indeed, pointing to the environment as a sort of fundamental problem, as Kaplan does, gets the cause and effect backward. Deforestation, at least in the Philippines, has been caused in part by corruption and by bad development and land-use policies. In general, poverty is more likely to be caused by bad policies than by environmental degradation. The Ivory Coast, one of the countries that Kaplan visited and which he offers as an example of our anarchic and violent future, has recently seen economic growth, in part because prices for its primary commodities have risen but also because it corrected earlier errors in economic policy, by devaluing its currency and introducing some deregulation.[12]

The first intersection of cause and effect in the argument that environmental problems produce conflict—environmental problems produce poverty—is difficult to map. The second—poverty produces conflict—is equally hard to document. Students of rebellion have not been able to establish a simple connection between poverty and conflict or between relative deprivation and conflict. Conflict may take place in the presence of poverty or in its absence. Similarly, economic inequality may have no effect on the level of conflict. Besides economic factors, several others, such as the legitimacy of the established order, the presence or absence of social mobility, repression, the existence of dissident organizations and leadership cadre, and the influence of ethnicity and religion, must be taken into account when considering why conflict occurs.[13]

We may conclude, then, that environmental problems are of limited importance when considering causes of conflict, whether intrastate or interstate. The most we can say is that in some cases they may be a factor. The threat posed by these problems, therefore, does not justify a reorientation of our national security strategy. Another way to see the limited significance of environmental factors as a threat is to consider their connection to migration. Kaplan argues that environmentally induced scarcity will induce mass migrations, which will in turn generate violent conflict between ethnic or religious groups. Homer-Dixon offers a similar argument but does so in a way that undercuts the urgency with which Kaplan discusses this issue. Unlike Kaplan, Homer-Dixon notes the many cases in which migration has occurred without conflict (e.g., Canada, Thailand, Malawi). He also notes that migration produces some good effects. It can act as a safety valve, thus diminishing conflict in the state from which the migrants come, or relieve labor shortages and thus be an economic boon in the state to which migrants go. Homer-Dixon also emphasizes, as Kaplan does not, that "contextual factors" are decisive in determining whether migration produces violent conflict. For example, "migrants often need the backing of a single state (either of the receiving society or an external one) before they have sufficient power to cause conflict, and this backing depends on the region's politics." Finally, Homer-Dixon offers only one example of migration induced by scarcity producing violent conflict: the movement of people from Bangladesh to India because of population growth.[14] In most other cases where migration has produced or coincided with conflict (for example, Pakistan and India), there has been a previous political or ethnic problem that the migration has aggravated (in the case of India and Pakistan, Hindu-Muslim differences and political separation). Homer-Dixon's discussion of environmentally caused migration undermines the notion that it is a significant cause of conflict.

This is not to deny that migration is a significant factor in world politics. Balkan politics were roiled by migrant problems even when the Austro-Hungarian empire existed. The return of Jews to Israel since the end of World War II has fundamentally altered Middle East politics and precipitated a good deal of violence. In the 1980s, both Haiti and East Germany used emigration to get leverage on the United States and West Germany, respectively. The Haitians restricted emigration of their citizens when the United States increased its aid, and the East Germans controlled the emigration of Tamils to West Germany once aid from that country was increased. Castro has similarly played the refugee card in an effort to influence U.S. policy. But in these later cases, the central issue was a political one. If the migration issue were not at hand, the conflict would be waged with other means. Political disputes and not migration itself are the problem. When such disputes do not already exist between sending and receiving countries, migration, whether caused by scarcity or other reasons, does not necessarily create them. Additionally, in all these and other cases, recognizing the political issues at the base of the conflict, states have used traditional political/military means to handle these problems. This was so even for the latest twist in the political use of migrants—by Iraq, which used migrants as human shields for military and industrial targets and as bargaining chips to pressure certain nations to break UN-imposed sanctions.[15]

On balance, to return to the immediate issue before us, one can refer to environmental problems as "*the* national security issue of the early twenty-first century" only by making a number of questionable assumptions about the connection between environmental problems and poverty, on the one hand, and poverty or scarcity and conflict, on the other. Moreover, even if we found a case in which environmental problems were clearly a cause of violence, it might be more efficient and effective to deal with what Homer-Dixon calls the "contextual factors" (for example, political and economic organization, or land-use policies) that determine whether these environmental problems will cause conflict than with the environmental factors themselves. In the vastly complex and little understood realm of the environment, the law of unintended consequences will operate with full force. Arguably, therefore, we may avoid more problems if we avoid environmental solutions. After all, it was the unintended consequences of and irrigation scheme in the Senegal River Valley that, by increasing the value of farm land, provided the occasion for some of the ethnic conflict that Homer-Dixon discusses.[16]

While criticizing the claim that environmental problems are as critical as Kaplan and others have claimed and that our security strategy must accord them a prominent place, we have touched upon another threat many have claimed deserves more attention than it received in our Cold War security strategy. Ethnicity, we noted in discussing Homer-Dixon's case study of Senegal and Mauritania, is one of the contextual factors involved in conflict. Kaplan weaves ethnicity into his vision of future anarchy by focusing on ethnic groups as the participants in future conflict. He also sees Islam's clash with the Westernized world as a significant contributor to future endemic violence. Kaplan, of course, is not alone in noting the importance of ethnic conflict. With the collapse of the Soviet Union, ethnic and religious conflict have come to prominence, as repressed ethno-religious conflicts have sprung back to life. "Worldwide," President Clinton's *National Security Strategy* tells us, "there is a resurgence of militant nationalism as well as ethnic and religious conflict." Ethnic or religious conflict has an immediate relevance for a discussion of the United States and terrorism, since so much of the most deadly terrorism directed at us has been connected with Islam.[17]

In this regard, we may have reason to be more optimistic about the future than Kaplan and others think. A leading scholar of ethnic conflict has offered what he describes as view of such conflict that is less pessimistic than the one commonly heard, which foresees a world of political fragmentation "in which "tribal wars of independence and vengeance will lead to a mounting toll of humanitarian disasters and refugees in need of international assistance." His extensive study and analysis of ethnic conflict has led him to the conclusion that it has been rising since the 1960s in the aftermath of decolonization but that its rate of increase has actually decelerated from the 1960s–1970s to the 1980s–1990s. Secessionist conflicts have also declined since the 1980s, except in the former Soviet Union and Yugoslavia. "There is no evidence to date," he concludes, "that civilizational or religious cleavages are becoming more important as a source of ethnopolitical conflicts," nor are "material inequalities" a strong factor in these conflicts. For the most part, these ethnopolitical conflicts are restricted to "a few world regions," such as Africa. Another scholar, whose focus is the central Asian countries of the former

Soviet Union, has reached a similar conclusion. "It is generally true that there is pressure against 19th century boundaries . . . but since 1991 there has been no net upsurge of ethnic conflict except in the [former] Soviet Union and Yugoslavia, because those countries manipulated ethnicity to justify a repressive state."[18] This analysis suggests that Kaplan and others have exaggerated the threat posed by ethnic conflict.

Militant Islam is a more difficult case. Assessments of the threat to the United States and the West posed by segments of the Muslim world tend to divide into two camps, with journalists and terrorism experts on one side and scholars of Islam on the other. The former are inclined to think that the threat is great. One journalist and self-described specialist on terrorism and the Middle East has described Islamic fundamentalism as

the most important, captivating and wrenching dramatic political story, not just of the present but of the next century . . . a true life drama being played out throughout the world with life-and-death consequences for entire nations and peoples . . . a duel-to-the-death challenge over mankind's most primal competition, to determine whose god will reign supreme, which is really only a guise for the competition of whose state will reign supreme.[19]

Scholars, on the other hand, are somewhat less apocalyptic. Surveying the breadth and complexity of Islam, they see those Muslims that threaten the West with violence as a small minority, one that never had much political power and is losing what it had. Generally speaking, those burdened with protecting the security of their countries have tended to agree with the terrorism experts, although in less colorful language. Former Secretary of Defense Perry identified what he called "Islamic extremism" as one of the three major threats we face, remarking that it threatened to capture "more nations than it has now captured," including Algeria, Egypt, and Pakistan. The Secretary General of NATO had earlier expressed a similar view, contending that "[Islamic] fundamentalism is at least as dangerous as communism was. Please do not underestimate this risk." Indeed, in their talk of ideology, revolution and war, their emphasis on the party, and their suppression of civil liberties, Islamic extremists do seem to be like the Marxist-Leninists of old.[20]

It is difficult to determine which of these evaluations of Islamic extremism is the more accurate. For example, the efforts of scholars to place Islamic extremism in perspective are not always reassuring. In his explication of Islam, one notes in different places that "the mission of the Islamic community is to spread the rule or abode of Islam globally," that Islam "found its central expression in law," and that "Islamic law stipulates that it is a Muslim's duty to wage war against polytheists, apostates, and People of the Book who refuse Muslim rule, and those who attack Muslim territory." Taken together these statements mean that waging war for Islam throughout the world is part of Islam's central expression, a view confirmed by the words of Muslim extremists themselves. Sheik Omar Abdel-Rahman, the leader of a group drawn from a number of different Muslim countries, four of whose members were found guilty of bombing New York's World Trade Center in

1993 and himself convicted of a conspiracy to wage a bombing campaign against America, was videotaped saying that "we must be terrorists and we must terrorize the enemies of Islam." In speaking this way, he was consistent with the views of other Islamic extremists, who maintain, in the words of a scholar of Islam, that "Jihad against all unbelievers is a religious duty." It may be true that this is not the traditional Islamic view. Indeed, Islam is in a certain sense more tolerant than Christianity. Since Islam's focus is the law, non-Muslims can live in even the most strictly observant Islamic society as long as they publicly obey Islamic law. Christianity, on the other hand, emphasizes belief. Therefore, when it has sought conformity, it has not rested with outward compliance alone but has sought inward agreement. This has often made it more intrusive and demanding than traditional Islam. At the same time, because its focus is belief and theology, Christianity has been more open than Islam to reason, and this openness in time has contributed to its tolerance. In any case, no matter how traditional or untraditional, current Islamic extremism is defined in a sense by its emphasis on war against non-Muslims. The West and the United States in particular are its enemies because, in the view of one scholar, it interprets Islam, again contrary to tradition, as calling for society to duplicate the oneness of God in uniform social and political practices. This is the antithesis of the modern Western view, a view that is integral to our way of life and implicit in the Western culture that, at least superficially, is spreading around the globe. Nothing better captures this antithesis than the respective attitudes of Thomas Jefferson and Ayatollah Khomeini toward Plato's *Republic*, a book dominated, we might say, by oneness and unblinking in its acceptance of the consequences. This is the only book of Western philosophy Jefferson is known to have despised and the only such book Khomeini approved. He reportedly felt that it anticipated his thoughts about the rule of Islamic clerics. This disagreement is at the heart of the struggle now ongoing between Western culture and those who take seriously the obligation to spread Islam around the world and who have an untraditional view of the role of Jihad in that effort. This contrast is what leads some to speak of "a duel-to-the-death challenge over mankind's most primal competition, to determine whose god will reign supreme." There is an element of truth in this view.[21]

This element is confined, however, almost entirely to the sphere of exhortation. As a practical matter, Islamic extremism has not had great political success. The Revolution in Iran has not been duplicated and has lost its way. What influence Iran has in regional or world politics comes from its location, oil wealth, commercial possibilities, and use of terrorism, not its example as a militant Islamic state. Its appeal in this regard is generally restricted to some segments of the Shia population, a minority among Muslims. Extremists are threatening governments in other Islamic countries, but even if they come to power, it is far from clear that they will be able to act on their principles over the long term. Typically, these Islamic groups lack the personnel, plans, and experience to govern. More critically, one scholar has concluded that as they become mass political movements, the militant Islamic groups become indistinguishable from those they hope to replace—the Islamic Salvation Front in Algeria had much in common with the ruling National Liberation Front—and face similar crippling problems. In addition to contending with the inevitable withering of revolutionary enthusiasm, a process already underway and turning political Islamic movements into more personal channels, having gained power, Islamists must either liberalize the economy, which diminishes their power and contradicts their program of oneness, or stick with some version of state socialism, which impoverishes them and encourages corruption, thus ultimately also reducing their power. Not even Iran with its oil wealth has escaped this dilemma. In their relations with other states, geopolitical and national interest, as well as ethnic and religious differences, determine policies, not Islamic solidarity. This means that if other Islamic parties come to power, they might seek the help of the United States, for example, to counter Iran's pretensions to regional dominance, pretensions that are based not on some vision of Islamic unity but on traditional Iranian imperial objectives. Finally, contrary to the assertions of NATO's Secretary General, Islamic fundamentalism is not like communism because Islam does not have communism's universal appeal and because no Islamic state approaches Russia in potential for empire.[22]

The threat that Islamic extremism poses to the United States, then, is not geopolitical in the sense that an empire of Islamic extremist states or even a federation of such like-minded states might arise comparable to the Soviet empire that has just disintegrated. As one scholar notes, "Islam will remain a civilization without an empire or even a core state to carry out a civilizational foreign policy. This means that the clash between the West and Islam is not likely to take place at the level of conventional or even nuclear wars between Western and Islamic states." It is more likely to consist of "a long series of terrorist actions, border skirmishes, and ethnic wars." Traditional methods of statecraft can be used to control this violence because Islamic state support for terrorism is based on calculations that combine an understanding of what both national interest and Jihad require. By putting pressure on the states that support them, these methods can also be used against the autonomous or ad hoc terrorist groups that have emerged recently. These groups can also be countered directly with police and intelligence work aimed at arresting individuals and disrupting the activities of the groups and their various sponsors. As far as militant Islam is concerned, then, the task for the United States is to counter the violence it gives rise to with the traditional means of statecraft and the methods we have learned to use against terrorism over the past twenty years, while letting the internal dynamics of this movement work themselves out in the midst of the pressures of international politics.

Certainly, given our past experience, the point here is not that Islamic fundamentalism could never lead to terrorism against the United States. Nor is it, to return to our larger theme, that under no circumstances could environmental degradation produce scarcity as population growth boomed, prompting mass migrations that engendered conflicts between ethnic or religious groups. But for the reasons we have given, these various seeds are unlikely to blossom into a poisonous anti-Eden of violent anarchy. The path of cause and effect from seed to bloom is not as simple or as straightforward as Kaplan's and similar arguments suppose, nor are the blooms, such as migration, necessarily all evil. Moreover, ethnic assertiveness is becoming less frequently fractious and violent as the age of decolonization recedes. This pattern is likely to continue as the last stage of decolonization, the break up of the Soviet empire and the reorganization of its former elements, proceeds. Finally, a point we mentioned when discussing scarcity and interstate conflict: technology may remove or alleviate some of the problems that Kaplan and others fear will complicate or occasion future intrastate violence.[23]

Our analysis to this point suggests that the threats we face in the future, including terrorism, will have pretty much the same character that they do now. The new threats have been exaggerated or, in the case of conflict associated with migration, are problems familiar to international politics. This optimistic conclusion, if we may call it optimistic, rests, critics might say, on a failure to see the larger significance of environmental degradation, mass migration, ethnic conflict and terrorism, and other forms of subversion. These are not just possible threats to our security, but part of a broader, possibly revolutionary development: the decline of sovereignty. For more than 300 years, the sovereignty of individual states, the exclusive, recognized control of territory by a state, has been the cornerstone of the international system. Migration and ethnic conflict, in this view, are slowly eroding the foundations of sovereignty by destroying homogeneous populations or undermining heterogeneous loyalty to the state. When this conflict takes the form of low-intensity conflict, like insurgency or terrorism, the state is essentially defenseless, which further undermines it. At the same time, environmental problems require that states work together and so give up some of their sovereignty. These pressures on sovereignty are increased by global technology and economic integration, which diminish the authority that states have over their own economies (their economic policies must take into account global market forces) and the need to limit the spread and development of WMD, which requires states to submit to international control regimes. Another supranational force operating in the world is concern for human rights, which leads states and private organizations to object to the ways that some governments treat their citizens, an issue previously considered solely the business of those governments. Finally, organized crime and other more benign nonstate activities and organizations, from the Internet to various private voluntary organizations, are said to be weakening the authority and cohesion of sovereign states. Taken together, these developments indicate, according to some analysts, that state sovereignty is eroding.[24]

Generally speaking, there are two ways to assess this purported erosion of sovereignty. If you are an optimist, you see emerging the long-hoped-for international order of peace and democracy. This seems to be the view of President Clinton. During an interview in the Oval Office, the President accepted some of the arguments we have just sketched, remarking that the more I stay here and the more time I spend on foreign policy . . . the more I become convinced that there is no longer a clear distinction between what is foreign and [what is] domestic. . . . The longer I stay here, the more convinced I become that all my successors in the 21st century will have to find different words for domestic and foreign. . . . People will be discussing things that happened within our borders and beyond our borders in general categories, rather than foreign and domestic, because they are tending to flow together in the global economy.[25]

The President continued by admitting that in this future integrated world without sovereign states subversion and terrorism might be more prevalent. Where "everybody can move around with relative freedom . . . and you can move money around and all that . . . organized groups basically have the capacity to reap destruction everywhere." He emphasized, however, the hopeful view that "there's a chance that the world will not involve the potential of great-nation conflicts." In the pessimist's view, the erosion of sovereignty will bring what Kaplan calls "the coming anarchy," in which perhaps otherwise tractable problems become intractable as the international system of states collapses into a fractious collection of besieged wealthy enclaves, ill-defined regions, noxious urban sprawls and shantytown states, many populated by hardened warriors. The administrator of the Agency for International Development claimed in 1994, for example, that "'disintegrating societies and failed states . . . have emerged as the greatest menace to global stability'" and should be seen as a "strategic threat."[26]

We need to consider this argument about sovereignty because, if true, it means that we are heading for a world fundamentally different from what we have known, in which the meaning and relevance of a national security strategy will be called into question. We also need to consider the argument about sovereignty because it bears directly on terrorism. Those who argue that sovereignty is eroding see terrorism and similar forms of subversion both contributing to the wearing away of sovereignty and increasing as sovereignty erodes.

To assess the claim that sovereignty is declining, we must first distinguish between the power of a state, its ability to do what it wants at home and abroad, and its sovereignty, its recognized control over a given territory. Sovereignty means, in part, that a state is recognized by the international community as having the authority to organize its internal affairs as it sees fit. Yet it may have only a limited ability to do so. For any number of reasons, a state may not be able to control its border areas, for example. It may enter into negotiations with neighboring states to control migration or crime in these areas, but it may not be able to persuade or compel the neighboring state to do what it wants. Such a weak state, however, can still be a sovereign state. Even during a civil war, one government may be recognized as sovereign even though it does not effectively control all its territory and has a rival claimant. If the fortunes of war go against the recognized sovereign, the rival may at some future date receive the crown. Even in an area where a state has all but ceased to function, such as Liberia following the civil war that began in 1989, there may be some entity that other states recognize as sovereign or such an entity may slowly emerge from the fighting and assert control over the territory of the previous sovereign, or what is left of it. Sovereignty, then, is different from power. Simply put, sovereignty is the recognized authority to act; power is the ability to do so. As the examples of civil war or state collapse suggest, power can diminish to the point that sovereignty is not a practical possibility, but this does not mean that power and sovereignty are identical. States have long conducted themselves toward one another as equals in sovereignty, and continue to do so, even though they are very unequal in power.

If there were some global trend of state power diminishing to the point that sovereignty became a practical impossibility, then it might be true to say that we were witnessing the erosion of state sovereignty. This presumably is what those who speak and write about the erosion of sovereignty mean. The trends they cite, however, do not point toward the null point of state power. First, it is important to bring some historical perspective to the discussion of the withering away of sovereignty. The Treaty of Westphalia (1648) "is taken to mark the beginning of the modern international system as a universe composed of sovereign states, each with exclusive authority within its own geographic boundaries." But, as Stephen Krasner has argued, the Westpahalian system of sovereignty is best understood not as an "empirical regularity" but as a convention or reference point or model that international practice regularly has ignored and that every treaty from Westphalia itself to Helsinki has violated. In other words, sovereignty was never as solid as some have supposed. What appears to be erosion is just a recognition of the way things have always been. As for the various forces supposedly rendering the model obsolete, historical perspective gives them a different appearance as well. The current level of economic "globalization" is frequently cited as corrosive of sovereignty but, as Vincent Cable has pointed out, "the process of globalization has generally been longer and slower than much contemporary conceit will admit. It has also been cyclical and subject to major reversals." The economic miracle following World War II has only returned us to a level of globalization close to that which prevailed in 1913. In addition, many aspects of the global market and even some of its transnational companies are not unprecedented. The United States was an emerging market in the 19th century, in which Great Britain invested heavily; transnational companies have "recognizable forebears in the trading companies of centuries past." Many renaissance kings depended on international finance; finance ministers have always been limited by international financial markets. "The gold exchange standard operated by Britain in the late nineteenth century arguably imposed more rigid constraints on the domestic monetary autonomy of states than do contemporary financial flows and agreements." As for such supposed sappers of sovereignty as migration, ethnic conflict, and the fear of war, these predate the nation-state, yet the nation-state came to dominate the international system in their company. Immigration and, as Bruce Porter points out, conflict can help build a nation-state. At least some of the ethnic conflict we see around the world (for example, in the former Yugoslavia) is the unavoidable process of nations making or remaking themselves. Some of these nations may develop sovereign state structures that survive, while others may not for a variety of different reasons. In neither case does the outcome necessarily tell us anything about the status or fate of sovereignty. States have resisted and continue to resist powerful ethnic or religious forces. The surge of Islamist and Islamic fundamentalist groups with international branches has not altered the fact that in the Muslim world "the nation-state framework continues to be the determining one." The stateless Kurds, whom Kaplan mentions, continue to be of significance in international politics not because the sovereignty of the states in which they live is eroding but because these states continue to use the Kurds, or various Kurdish factions, against each other.[27]

Putting the issue of sovereignty in historical perspective is unlikely to persuade those who believe it is eroding. They point to several factors that they believe are undermining sovereignty as never before: global financial integration, technological developments, concern for human rights, and the rise of international organized crime. We should consider these in turn. Increasing global financial integration has led to much comment on the decline of sovereignty, but this increased integration has not strengthened the constraints under which governments function, it has only "changed the timing and the severity of the consequences if those constraints are ignored." We also need to remember that the current international financial system depends on institutions established by states. Indeed, as Ethan Kapstein has noted, rather than demonstrating "how the expansion of markets is a product of eroding state power, the historical record shows that concerted state action has made possible the sustained growth of international finance."[28] For example, following a financial crisis in the early 1970s caused by two bank failures, governments of industrialized countries set up regulatory institutions and established minimum standards for capital adequacy, helping to stabilize global finance. States retain the power to change the institutional structure and policies that undergird the worldwide integration of finance. Some changes would be more costly than others, of course, but there is no reason to suppose, for example, that a free trade regime will necessarily prevail. Policy decisions could drastically curtail it, increasing the role of the state in economies.

Technological developments are also affecting sovereignty and state power but not necessarily eroding it. Dealing with environmental problems and the proliferation of weapons of mass destruction does not necessarily require sacrificing sovereignty. States have long dealt with threats to their security and well-being by forming alliances or negotiating treaties. They can do the same to handle technological problems. This may require a temporary sacrifice of sovereignty, but is probably best seen as a device to preserve sovereignty rather than as evidence of its erosion. While technological developments may limit sovereignty by promoting globalization, they also moderate globalization. As labor becomes a smaller portion of the cost of a final product, for example, there is less reason to move production to countries where labor is cheap. As computerized manufacturing allows for the accommodation of a greater number of local tastes at competitive prices, world products and the economic integration they imply become less appealing. We should also remember that states need not remain passive recipients of the changes technology effects; they can turn technology to their own advantage. Technology provides states with new ways to protect their power and defend their prerogatives. This is particularly true of the new information technologies that are supposedly doing so much to integrate the world and undermine sovereignty. Law enforcement agencies, for example, used the Internet to track down a hacker and arrest him as he worked at his computer.[29] Democratic states may limit their use of the power technology provides them, but this power is still available to them.

Concern for human rights is said to undermine sovereignty because it leads some states or nongovernmental organizations to disregard the sovereign right of a state to organize its internal affairs as it sees fit. Such interference occurs most readily and effectively, however, with weak states. The susceptibility of a state or many states to this interference, then, tells us more about the importance of power than it does about the status of sovereignty. China has resisted external pressures generated in response to its human rights record. Even weak states can triumph over the power of governmental and nongovernmental organizations. Zaire has been bordering on chaos or slipping into it for years now and is certainly not highly regarded for its human rights record but has retained the trappings of sovereignty, including its seat in the UN.

International organized crime poses a serious threat to the fair and efficient functioning of governments and economies in several states. It has done so in Colombia and in Italy for decades, yet during this time Italy contrived to become a modern, successful economy and Colombia to manage its economy better than most Latin American countries. Neither country is without its problems, like all countries. But in these instances as well as in Russia and some other members of the former Soviet Union, organized crime has developed its power only through the collusion of corrupt politicians. In Italy, the prosecution of corrupt politicians and businessmen and the related fight against the Mafia will indicate whether the power of organized crime will decline once the corruption is exposed and steps are taken to sever organized crime from its state support.[30] Whether or not it does, it is clear that organized crime has not produced by itself a generalized crisis of governability. In all the cases we know about, it has taken advantage of state weakness, not caused it by itself. Organized crime got its hold in Italy after World War II as the Italian government struggled to recover from the war and defeat an internal communist threat. Colombia was plagued by internal violence long before cocaine trafficking became a multi-billion-dollar enterprise.

None of the factors most commonly cited as erosive of sovereignty provides compelling evidence that sovereignty is now more vulnerable than it once was. We should also remember that states are not just passive actors when their sovereignty is challenged by violence. They are not, for example, at the mercy of low-intensity conflict or subversion, as Martin Van Creveld has maintained. He argues that states are defenseless against political-military subversion and that its increasing prevalence means the end of the nation-state. In making this argument, Van

Creveld does not take into account the help that insurgents got from the Soviet Union and the United States, both of which in different ways supported the end of colonialism and created opportunities that insurgents exploited. More fundamentally, he simply ignores the numerous cases in which terrorism and insurgency have failed to topple a government, including Malaysia, Vietnam, the Philippines, South Africa, El Salvador, and more recently—so far—Algeria, Egypt, and Israel. Although the United States has been the principal target of international terrorism, this political violence has not called into question either the power or the sovereignty of the United States. Even such a weak state as Peru has been able to inflict severe losses on an indigenous terrorist group, Sendero Luminoso. Colombia has survived almost fifty years of insurgency and internal political violence. In the mid-1990s, it had significant success against the Cali Cartel. In addition, Van Creveld ignores the fact that insurgents do not fight to put an end to sovereignty but to see that it changes hands. Thabo Mbeki, a leading member of the African National Congress, struggled to overthrow the government of South Africa for years. Now that he is Vice-President of South Africa, he has become an ardent defender of its sovereignty. In the midst of a disagreement with the United States, he declared "we have been prepared to negotiate everything but we cannot compromise the sovereignty of South Africa. As a state we are mandated to protect the sovereignty of the country." Finally, sovereign states have an interest in protecting sovereignty, which means they tend to support each other's sovereignty, even the sovereignty of weaker states. As Olivier Roy has noted, "the great powers and the United Nations guarantee the world map, thus the borders, thus the territories, and thus, ultimately, the states that incarnate them." This guarantee is not absolute, of course, but is nevertheless an important support for sovereignty.[31]

While states defend their sovereignty from external and internal threats, they also respond to domestic problems. Michael Mann has pointed out that states are extending the reach of their sovereign power over these problems with the consent of those they govern. They are extending their control into previously private family and health matters, as "national education systems, mass media, and consumer markets are still subverting localism and homogenizing social and cultural life into" a national life. While economic integration, free trade, and technological progress may increase pressure on state autonomy, they will also increase wealth and thus give states more power to act in other areas. Indeed, since 1980 average public spending in the "big economies" has increased from 36 percent of gross domestic product to 40 percent. "After 15 years of accelerating [global] integration [governments] are tending to control more not fewer" resources.[32]

In sum, then, we may conclude that we are not witnessing some global trend toward the diminution of state power to the point at which sovereignty for most states becomes a practical impossibility and nation-states are replaced by an assortment of brutal empires, sordid mega-cities, and anarchic outlying territories, all marked by vicious low-intensity conflict and terrorism. The power of states and to some extent their sovereignty is limited now as it has been in the past. No state, for example, has ever had absolute control over its borders. But over the past several hundred years the power and sovereignty of states has increased and could increase more in some areas. Sovereign states, therefore, are likely to remain the most important actors in world affairs, despite current predictions to the contrary. Such predictions first emerged in the 1950s, as analysts ruminated on the possible consequences of nuclear weapons and concluded that they would make territorial states obsolete or cause them to wither away. As nongovernmental international organizations became active in the 1960s, similar predictions about the sovereign state again were announced.[33] Sovereignty has proven these reports of its death premature and will probably do so as well with the latest round.

One might object that the analysis of the sovereignty debate outlined here is too narrow and retrospective. While it is possible to address seriatim, as we have done, a host of challenges to the notion of sovereignty and counter them separately, this does not address the feeling in many observers, including President Clinton, that something unprecedented is happening, even if conventional analysis does not demonstrate it. Freed from Cold War preoccupations, observers are noticing not just ethnic conflict but global economic integration, mass migrations, environmental problems, information, and other technological revolutions and are arguing that if not individually and actually, then collectively and potentially, these developments are undermining national sovereignty and the 300-year-old international order based on it.[34] In a sense, of course, this argument is true. But the sovereignty of states has been under attack at least since the adoption of the American constitution. This document declares that the people, not the state, are sovereign; its most authoritative interpreter, in *Federalist 10*, explained that this people could and should be heterogeneous. The constitution and this interpretation rest, in turn, on the Declaration of Independence and *The Wealth of Nations*. The former expressed the philosophical basis of popular sovereignty; the latter explained how a sovereign people might live a free, orderly, and prosperous life by curtailing the power of the state and exploiting the power of technology and economic competition. From this perspective, calling revolutionary those developments usually mentioned as eroding sovereignty, which have come to the fore only since the 1950s, seems rather myopic. Indeed, the developments most often noted as cracking the traditional order are mere epiphenomena of the epochal change that first took political form in the American founding. For example, financial markets are said to impinge on sovereignty. But the limits that the international financial markets currently place on central banks are the consequence of the revolution represented by Thomas Jefferson and Adam Smith, for the market is in fact the result of the decisions of millions of individuals. It is an expression of popular sovereignty. Just as the sovereignty of the American state has survived and adapted to the sovereignty of the American people, so is the sovereignty of nation-states likely to survive and adapt to the market.

We should be happy it will. While not all nation-states have been democratic, democracy has blossomed within the world of nation-states. We should not assume that it or human happiness will thrive amidst alternative arrangements. As we noted when discussing the judicial approach to combating terrorism, world government is likely to be despotic, since the fundamental differences among the various peoples of the world would make government by consent impossible. If the forces of globalization wear away these differences, we are likely to be bored to death, homogenized Last Men staring blankly at 500 channels of video programming. A world of regional blocs or tribal satrapies might be more interesting but would not necessarily be more free and would almost certainly be more violent. More important, as several commentators have pointed out, states have provided the order that has allowed justice and the other virtues to develop.[35]

This recognition of the worth of the state is critical to the debate over the future of sovereignty because sovereignty is not a brute fact completely at the mercy of technological or economic trends. It is essentially a political and moral idea, crafted in response to the wars of religion in the sixteenth and seventeenth centuries. By declaring each state the supreme authority over religion within its borders, states removed a significant cause of conflict from their affairs. The idea of sovereignty gained currency and continued to receive support because it was held to promote this good—peace between nations. If we come to believe that sovereignty does more harm than good, that, for example, respect for the right of a state to order its internal affairs as it sees fit leads to unacceptable risk of nuclear war, environmental degradation, or abuse of human rights, then we will no longer support the idea of sovereignty.

This balance of benefit and cost is now in play, with some academics and politicians for the first time speaking favorably of restrictions on sovereignty. The invasion of Haiti was noteworthy in this regard, setting a precedent for the international community to suspend the rights of a state because of a sense among some powerful members of that community that the way a government came into existence and acted, although in keeping with local traditions, was not in keeping with their understanding of justice. As the case of Haiti makes clear, human rights are the critical issue in moral and political arguments about sovereignty. States have long dealt with threats to their security and well-being by forming alliances or negotiating treaties that do not lessen their sovereignty. As we have noted, these same techniques can be applied to the proliferation of WMD and to environmental problems that involve more than one state. Violations of human rights might be treated in a similar way; the Helsinki process exemplifies such an attempt. Yet human rights touch more fundamental issues than either WMD or environmental problems. They are the modern counterparts of the religious issues that once inflamed international relations. If adherence to one or another version of these rights becomes the criterion for acceptance as a legitimate member of the international community, whose rights and prerogatives other nations are bound to respect, then our notion of sovereignty will have changed fundamentally and we will have set a course toward the deeply problematic alternatives to sovereign states.

Our effort to assess the threats we face, as preparation for devising an appropriate strategy in which we could properly place counterterrorism, has led us down some speculative paths but has brought us back to a world familiar to us. This is not to say that our emerging circumstances are identical to what we have known. Henry Kissinger has nicely summarized the difference in a remark that ties together the diffusion and development of power with the technological advances that are bringing parochialism to an end. "No previous international order has contained major centers of power distributed around the entire globe. Nor [have] statesmen ever been obliged to conduct diplomacy in an environment where events can be experienced instantaneously and simultaneously by leaders and their publics."[36] In deciding to press ahead with its nuclear testing on its Pacific territory, France had to consider, as it would not have a few decades ago, the reactions of countries in the Pacific and around the globe, as well the effect of pictures of rioting Tahitians broadcast world-wide. There is a World Wide Web page that keeps track of the Indonesian government's activities in East Timor. As we have argued, however, these changed circumstances, while significant, do not alter the fundamental fact of international relations. For the foreseeable future, states will continue to be the principal international actors. Some may be weak, others may grow stronger; some may disintegrate as others come into existence, but the nation-state will remain as an organizing principle of international politics.

This means we will address the problems we confront, from the environment to terrorism and WMD, within some version of the state-centric political-military ethos that has dominated international life for the past 300 years. It is possible, of course, that we may as a matter of policy decide to act as if the sovereign state is eroding or should erode. But, as we noted earlier when discussing the need to maintain our ability to use organized violence to serve our interests, it will not be to our advantage to act as if a revolution in human affairs has occurred before it has in fact occurred.

Having sketched the dominant characteristics of the world we are entering, we can now consider the likely status in this world of terrorism and other forms of subversion. The persistence in some form of the state-centric system we have known does not mean that we will always confront and have to respond only to conventional military forces in pitched battles, as we did in World War II and the Gulf War. For several reasons, low-intensity conflict, including terrorism, is likely to loom large in our future. First of all, it has loomed large in our past, as it has in the pasts of all nations and societies. Indirect conflict has always been more common than war. Several factors are likely to ensure that this is the case in the future as well. WMD are a disincentive to direct violent conflict that can escalate toward their use, putting both massed troops and civilian population centers at risk. The spread of these weapons means that such disincentives are now or soon will be generalized. This is part of the reason that major war is becoming obsolete or is occurring less frequently. In industrialized democratic societies, it is politically and economically unprofitable.[37] This does not mean that it will not occur, but it does suggest that violent conflict will tend to take more indirect forms. For those opposed to the United States in particular, in the aftermath of the Gulf War, attacking our interests with conventionally organized and operating forces will seem an unprofitable way to do business. Our military-technological superiority will discourage direct confrontations with us. Moreover, if our opponents reflect on our history, they will see that the United States has tended to have difficulty dealing with indirect, protracted conflicts. Iran has had greater success with terrorism than Iraq did with maneuver warfare. To repeat, this does not mean that we will have to contend only with indirect violent threats. With the obvious exception of the Gulf War itself, all of the conditions mentioned here as encouraging indirect attacks on our interests applied when Saddam Hussein sent his armored divisions into Kuwait. Such a direct attack could happen again. People make mistakes. They get themselves into situations where they do not have time to wait for an indirect, protracted strategy of political pressure and violence to work against a stronger opponent, or they are blinded by megalomania, or they believe that our difficulties in situations like Lebanon in the 1980s mean that we cannot muster the will to respond decisively and forcefully when our interests are at stake, or they misunderstand what we think our interests are. All of this happens. Yet it does not alter the fact that there have always been disincentives to direct military challenges and that these disincentives operate now with enhanced power. By and large, therefore, in the future as in the past, when the competition between states takes a violent turn, it is likely to be into the byways and alleys of protracted and indirect conflict, where terrorism and subversion lurk.

HOW SHOULD WE RESPOND?

What is an appropriate strategy for such a world? How should we respond to such threats as terrorism and subversion? During the Cold War, our strategy was containment. Containing Soviet power and influence was the means we used to maintain our independence and preserve our way of life. Whatever the merits of this strategy, its immediate cause is no more. The Soviet Union has collapsed and Russia does not now have the ability to project its power and influence in a way that makes it the preeminent threat to our security that it was. With the collapse of the Soviet empire, two general strategic possibilities present themselves to the United States. One is a fortress America approach, the other, an ongoing engagement with the world and its problems. The fortress America approach should not be confused with an isolationism that did not exist historically and would not be possible now. America has always had foreign contacts and trade. At the height of what some presume was our isolation from the world in the nineteenth century, for example, the United States, even after it stopped participating in the slave trade, had more trade with Africa than any other country in the world did.[38] In a fortress America approach, the United States would not isolate itself but would reduce its military forces abroad even further than it has already, withdrawing them entirely from Europe, leaving, in addition, a reduced naval presence outside its borders. It would also withdraw from its alliances with

NATO and Japan and from participation in most multinational organizations and avoid other entangling alliances. It would maintain diplomatic missions abroad but a significantly smaller number than it now does. It would tend to be protectionist and avoid trying to promote democracy and human rights or relieve the suffering of others through humanitarian assistance. Recognizing that we no longer face immediate threats to our vital interests, in this strategy, the United States would conserve its strength and sally forth only when a threat to its vital interests emerged, meeting it with decisive, overwhelming, technologically superior military force before retreating once again to its fortress. Its list of vital interests would be quite short.[39]

Having in effect fought three world wars this century, it would be understandable if the United States now wished to turn away from the world's problems. Such disengagement, however, would not be in our interest. While no one can guarantee that our involvement overseas will produce a more peaceful, secure, and prosperous world, it is unlikely that the international problems we face will diminish if we ignore them. Our sallies will become more and more lonely and, therefore, less and less likely to succeed, if we do not tend to possible allies before and after we need them. As has become evident, foreign terrorists can attack within the United States. Our ability to prevent and respond to such attacks depends, in large measure, on the cooperation of countries around the world. Winning such cooperation requires that we engage with these countries on a daily basis, managing an array of bilateral and multilateral issues. Similarly, our fortress will be more and more vulnerable if we do not cooperate with other nations to prevent the spread of weapons of mass destruction. Our economy will be less productive and we less well off if we deprive ourselves of the competition that foreign goods provide. To isolate ourselves from the world except when our vital interests are at stake would only put us in the position of having to make a more desperate defense of those interests when they were threatened. A fortress America was imprudent when our primary concern was global war. It is equally imprudent now that our primary concern is the gradual erosion of our security in a world that has returned to the disorder, violence, and complexity that is the normal burden of humanity.

Terrorism has provided us some useful lessons in this burden and in the way that our security can be eroded gradually. Terrorism has killed many Americans, of course, but its effects go beyond that. By sponsoring terrorism against the United States as part of a general struggle to save Islam, Iran has gained power in the Middle East, which has complicated our efforts to maintain a favorable balance of power there. The same can be said of the efforts of Syria, Iraq, and the PLO. Even outside the Middle East (for example, in the Balkans), the threat of Iranian-sponsored terrorism shadowed American troops.[40] Disputes about how best to respond to this terrorist activity and to Iran in particular have complicated our alliance relationships. As an element in a strategy of erosion, then, terrorism has been effective.

Terrorism's effectiveness derives at least in part from the fact that its benefits have accrued over time in such a way that the United States never felt compelled to respond with more than a fraction of its power. Even in the mid-1980s, when U.S. efforts to combat terrorism were at their peak, terrorism was subordinate to a number of other issues. Terrorists never felt the full force of America's power in part because of the shield provided by the Soviet Union. The very nature of terrorism also helped shield it. Like other indirect techniques, terrorism, whether used as a tool of diplomacy or as the forerunner of an insurgency, seeks to gain its ends not through a single decisive stroke but by slow and steady pressure that achieves its objectives gradually, in almost imperceptible stages. An individual terrorist event can be dramatic, but none has posed a danger as evident as that posed by the North Korean invasion of the South or the Iraqi invasion of Kuwait. Over time, however, the terrorist campaigns of the last twenty-years in the Middle East have achieved at least some of their objectives, unlike Saddam's invasion of Kuwait. The PLO became the recognized representative of the Palestinian people; Syria and Iran gained influence in Lebanon at the expense of the United States. The cumulative effect of lower-level threats, therefore, can erode our security in the long-run more effectively than more obvious, direct threats. The "Report of the National Bipartisan Commission on Central America" (1984) made this point with regard to the Soviet use of Cuba.

The problem has been that [our security] was eroded incrementally. This often made it difficult to see the erosion clearly, and, as a practical matter, made it even more difficult to halt at any given point. The increases in the Cuban threat were always so gradual that to stop them would have required making a major issue of what was, at the time, only a small change. The total effect of such small changes, however, has been—over five Administrations of both political parties—an enormously increased military power and capacity for aggression concentrated on the island of Cuba, and the projection of that threat into Central America (as well as into Africa and the Middle East).[41]

The Soviet Union and Cuba no longer pose the threat they once did, of course, but the lesson remains valid. Skirmishes can help shape the battlefield and affect the disposition of forces as they influence perceptions of what opposing forces intend and are capable of. Left unattended, these small, adverse changes in our security environment can accumulate and lead to significant deterioration.

Operating as a fortress America from which we venture only to slay the most fearsome dragons, then, is not an effective strategy because it will do nothing to prevent the slow erosion of the secure and preeminent position we attained as a result of our victory in the Cold War. This slow erosion is now the principal threat we face; preventing it, our principal security task. Failing at this task will jeopardize not only our security but the attainment of our other ends as well, such as a prosperous economy and a world in which democracy and free trade are at home. If we cannot isolate ourselves, we have no other choice but to engage the world, to use our power and influence in hopes of shaping a world more hospitable to our way of life than destructive of it. That in the post–Cold War world engagement is the alternative to isolationism is not a stunning insight. When the

United States unilaterally declared the end of the Cold War in the early 1970s, it adopted a strategy of engagement. As soon as the Cold War showed signs of ending in the late 1980s, the United States returned to the idea of engagement as an organizing principle. Both the Bush and Clinton administrations have used it, for example.[42] Although what they meant by engagement was not identical in scope or spirit, both Administrations used the term to oppose isolationism. But opposing isolationism is not sufficient strategic guidance. We must decide on the level of our engagement. Should it be global or selective?

GLOBAL ENGAGEMENT

Global engagement has its advocates. They argue, as did a recent national military strategy document, that "global interdependence and transparency, coupled with our worldwide security interests, make it difficult [for the United States] to ignore troubling developments almost anywhere on earth."[43] Instability anywhere should concern the United States, according to this argument, because instability in one place helps create instability in another, encouraging nations to arm or act more belligerently than they would otherwise. This instability domino effect eventually touches our interests—the world is interdependent—so acting to curb it helps preserve our power and security. A variant of this argument would contend that if we do not concern ourselves with instability wherever it occurs, we will forfeit our role of world leadership, which would not be to our advantage.

Unfortunately for globalists, the argument that the United States should deal with instability wherever and whenever it occurs has at least three difficulties. First, it is not clear that there is an insecurity domino effect. It is doubtful, for example, that the arms race in Asia is a result of conflict in Africa or how the United States deals with it. Proponents of this domino theory will note that thugs on the docks in Port au Prince chased away a ship bringing the first unarmed elements of the U.S. military to Haiti while shouting about Somalia. To these commentators, this means that if our prestige suffers in one part of the world, our power is diminished in another. There is truth to this claim, but it does not prove that conflict anywhere should concern us. Such a claim was more plausible during the Cold War, when we faced one predominant enemy in a virtual global struggle, whose opposition was based on ideology as well as interest and who could exploit a failure occurring in one place in an altogether different place. We are no longer in such a situation. Our enemies now are not all alike, nor do they all think alike or all act for the same reasons. In resisting one, we are no longer resisting all. We now face a variety of enemies, with a variety of prejudices, capabilities, and predilections in a variety of regional settings. On the face of it, there is no reason to believe that they will all respond in the same way to a setback suffered by the United States far from their borders. If disengaging in a marginal area from an intractable problem before disaster befalls us or before we waste vast resources diminishes our prestige, we can more than recover by a strong performance in a more important area. Deterring the North Koreans did not require victory over

Aideed in Somalia. It required effective action against North Korea. Standing tall in Somalia was not the best way to handle Haiti. The best way to handle regional conflicts is to deal with them on their own merits. To do otherwise is to declare, in effect, a no concessions policy toward instability that requires us never to ignore or give in to it. This policy would be even less appropriate as a strategic principle than it is as a technique to combat terrorism.

The second difficulty with the insecurity domino effect is that the effort to suppress conflict around the globe would require intervention on an unprecedented scale. This in itself would create a climate of belligerency and insecurity. Many of these interventions would require the use of military force, since they would be undertaken against the wishes of local or regional players hoping to profit from the victory of one or another of the belligerents. The practical consequence of the argument for world stability, in other words, is a situation the exact opposite of the one it hopes to create: an increase in conflict. Finally, an effort to enforce global security would require a vast commitment of resources altogether disproportionate to the good likely to be achieved.

The commitment of resources to counter conflict worldwide might be proportionate to some achievable good if, to enter into the second argument for a global concern with stability, such a commitment enhanced our role of world leadership and if such a role actually brought us some advantage. No doubt, given the power of tautology, assuming the role of the world's law enforcer would give us a leading role in the world; but it is difficult to see how this would give us any advantage, unless there was something like an insecurity domino effect, which we have argued there is not. In some cases, our political or military power may translate into economic gain or our economic power may give us a political advantage. In these cases, this transference should be taken into account and weighed against the danger of overextension and exhaustion when deciding whether to intervene. But it does not follow from this that successful intervention anywhere will now always be to our advantage, economic or otherwise. We have played a leading role in the world and will continue to do so because of our economic strength and military power, which give us political clout, and the power of our founding ideas, which gives us moral influence. We do not have to suppress instability globally to have such a role. We may conclude, then, that we do not need to be concerned with instability everywhere it occurs because such meddling is likely to breed more conflict and have costs out of all proportion to benefits.

These arguments against global engagement are not yet conclusive. Support for this strategic orientation has come of late from those who advocate the promotion of democracy around the world. According to these advocates, this version of global engagement avoids both pitfalls of worldwide engagement against instability: promoting democracy will neither increase instability nor bankrupt us. On the contrary, democratization diminishes conflict and, by doing so, pays for itself. Promoting democracy, in other words, is a cost-free benefit. The benefits, according to its promoters, include an end to what President Clinton called "great-nation conflicts." These will end, we are told, because "democracies do not go to war with each other" or are "less likely to wage war." But promoting democracy is also touted as an effective indirect strategy to counter terrorism and the other indirect threats we face. For example, Islamic fundamentalism has inspired a good deal of violence, some of it directed against us, but in Jordan more democratic or at least representative politics has included Islamist elements, moderating them. The general adoption of this Jordanian practice in other countries with Islamic extremists would lead to a diminution of anti-American terrorism. This and other benefits of democratization come at no or little cost, according to the advocates of democratization, because enlarging the zone of democratic peace will allow us to decrease the resources we must devote to security, ultimately increasing prosperity at home. It is for this reason, as President Clinton has argued, that "all of America's strategic interests—from promoting prosperity at home to checking global threats abroad before they threaten our territory—are served by enlarging the community of democratic and free market nations." Moreover, promoting democracy is a perfect strategy for the United States because it reconciles our global, humanitarian impulses with our limited resources. It is not a crusade, the President's *National Security Strategy* tells us, but a pragmatic commitment. Consequently, America should promote a global "coalition for democracy," as President Clinton has called it, to spread the peaceful blessings of democratic rule. A member of his National Security Council Staff, arguing that "the opportunity to take a giant step toward universal constitutional democracy is here and should be seized," even advocated the "permanent or open-ended presence of an international police force" to guarantee democracy wherever it is established. Although not going this far, both President Reagan and Secretary of State Baker endorsed the idea that the spread of democracy will lead to the spread of peace.[44]

The argument that we should engage globally for democracy because democratization is a cost-free benefit is clever. Unfortunately, it is also specious. It is not necessarily the case that promoting democracy will lead to a more peaceful world, which means that the policy will not necessarily pay for itself. In turn, this means that global engagement remains a policy of ruinous costs and few benefits. To see this, we must examine the argument that democracy leads to peace. Those who argue that democracies are more peaceful than other regimes, an argument some have dubbed "democratic peace theory," offer two reasons for doing so. One is institutional. The people rule in democracies and since it is they who pay the price in a war, they use their power to limit their involvement in war. The other is attitudinal. Democratic forms of governance require and encourage compromise and cooperation as ways of resolving disputes. These attitudes also come to characterize the foreign relations of democracies. They seek alternatives to the use of force to resolve international disputes.[45]

The institutional explanation for the connection between democracy and peace does not hold up. Historically, a democracy going to war is not a rare occurrence. Proponents of democratic peace theory thus generally limit their claims to a statement that democracies do not go to war against each other. As a critic has noted, however, this qualification does not save the institutional explanation. If the institutions of democracy limited involvement in war, this should be the case regardless of which opponents democracies fight. "If citizens and policymakers of a democracy were especially sensitive to the human and material costs of war, that sensitivity should be evident whenever their state is on the verge of war, regardless of whether the adversary is democratic: the lives and money spent will be the same."[46] Since democracies are willing to spend lives and money in war, the institutions of democracy do not seem to explain why it is that democracies do not fight one another. A similar objection arises to the attitudinal explanation for democratic peace. Since democracies go to war, a willingness to compromise cannot explain why they do not fight each other. A democracy should be willing to compromise with any opponent but, according to democratic peace theory, it is only other similar regimes that democracies do not fight. If it remains true that democracies do not fight each other, there must be another explanation besides the attitudes generated by democratic practices.

The explanation, according to one analyst, lies not in the institutions or attitudes of democracy but in the principles of liberalism. Liberalism is the view that self-preservation and material well-being are most important. If a nation values these goals above all others, it will, as a matter of self-interest, deprecate war and seek to handle its international disputes with negotiation and compromise rather than threat and violence. According to the principles of liberal foreign policy, "war is called for only when it would serve liberal ends—i.e., when it would most likely enhance self-preservation and well-being."[47] It is adherence to these liberal principles that ultimately make a state pacific, not the fact that it possesses democratic institutions or is willing to compromise. Two states adhering to such liberal principles would indeed be unlikely to wage war against each other.

Democratic institutions allow liberal principles to permeate the body politic and inform all its decisions. But this should not lead us to think that it is democracy or its institutions that make for pacific international and domestic politics. Liberalism is the key, for democratic institutions and liberal ideas do not necessarily go together. Just because a state like Iran has universal adult suffrage and parliamentary debate does not mean that it is a liberal state. Other possible examples of illiberal democracies are "those arising from the ruins of the Soviet Union." If they do in fact become illiberal democracies, "democratic peace will not emerge in that area of the world."[48] Furthermore, illiberal leaders may be elected in a democracy; they may not be prevented by democratic institutions from waging war, as we know from the history of Germany in the 1930s. It is the liberalism of liberal democracies, then, that promotes peace and not the democracy.

It is hard to see in this emphasis on liberalism an improvement over previous versions of democratic peace theory. For this version is tautological, paradoxical in a way that undermines its claim to importance and ultimately no help to those who insist that promoting democracy is a benefit without cost. The emphasis on liberalism is tautological because it reduces democratic peace theory to the claim that those who want to avoid war (liberals) avoid war. It is paradoxical because it claims that liberals will wage war only for the sake of self-preservation, that is, that they are willing to risk their lives only to save them. It claims, in effect, that men have made the heroic sacrifices war demands for what are explicitly non-heroic, or liberal, reasons—self-preservation and material well-being. Of course, they have not made such sacrifices for these reasons. That people have sacrificed their lives for others both in war and in other circumstances and continue to do so, suggests that liberalism is not the force in human affairs that its proponent supposes it to be.

Even if we concede that liberalism is slowly becoming the operative understanding of human life, this would provide only cold comfort to proponents of democratic peace theory. For if the populations of democracies act on the principles of liberalism and put self-preservation and material well-being above all else, how well will they be able to defend themselves against the illberals both within and without their countries? Will they not become prey to illiberal predators? In the post–Cold War world of liberal democratic peace theory, "better red than dead" would become "better anything than dead." In this case, liberal democracy would be more likely to die out, as it became unable to defend itself, than to spread over the world. If the liberal version of democratic peace theory is right, then the proponents of this theory may be wrong to think that promoting democracy will lead to the triumph of either democracy or peace. On the other hand, if the proponents of liberal democracy remain prepared to defend it against its enemies and even use force to spread liberalism about the globe, then they will not usher in an age of peace but another age of war. This is the historical pattern seen in the development of democracy. Even if nations that are now liberally democratic are also peaceful, it is not accurate to imply that they were peaceful when becoming democratic. In fact, the road to democracy is strewn with bloody corpses. Ethnic conflict, for example, is more frequent and intense in states transitioning to democracy than in others.[49] Promoting liberalism, as opposed to democracy, is also not free of costs. In Asia and the Middle East, democratic or at least representative institutions are accepted where supposedly American values that place self-preservation and material well-being above all others are bitterly resisted. Promoting liberalism in these places for the sake of peace may well increase conflict, not to mention undermining our relations with these states.

We turned to a discussion of promoting democracy because this strategy promised a cost-free, high-gain alternative to the strategy of fighting instability on a global scale, a strategy of high costs and few benefits. The argument for promoting democracy had to be rescued in turn by the claim that liberalism was the true source of democracy's costless benefits. Yet the argument for liberalism dissolved into a paradox suggesting that liberalism is of limited significance in explaining human behavior. Furthermore, since liberalism threatens some societies, promoting it will generate conflict and thus increased costs, a result the opposite of the one we sought by promoting democracy. We are left, then, with the problem that global engagement—for the sake of stability, democracy, or liberalism—has high costs and few, if any, commensurate benefits.

The persistence and popularity of global engagement in the face of such weak arguments for it suggests that it must have means of support other than strategic reasoning. The inertia remaining from our global confrontation with the Soviet Union is part of this support, but global engagement as a way for the United States to live with the rest of the world predates the Cold War, although that war encouraged popular acceptance of such engagement. The most enduring support of global engagement comes, in fact, from a deeply rooted belief that provides its ultimate justification: the belief in progress. The costs of engagement would be easier to bear, and we would be more justified in paying them, if we knew that these costs were the price of progress toward a peaceful, prosperous world. The assumption that such a world will come about is, in fact, the implicit premise in the argument that we should promote democracy abroad. Speaking of Haiti, for example, former Secretary of State Warren Christopher said that "those who hold illegal power there should know that they're swimming against the tide of history and they will not prevail." In describing Iran and Iraq as outside "the family of nations now committed to the pursuit of democratic institutions," former National Security Advisor Anthony Lake said that both nations "remain on the wrong side of history." President Clinton has also invoked the notion of progress as an ultimate justification. In his speech on the fiftieth anniversary of D-Day, he said that "avoiding today's problems would be our own generation's appeasement, for just as freedom has a price, it also has a purpose, and its name is progress." He indicated that what he meant by progress was the spread of democracy when he went on to say, in his only reference to foreign policy in the speech, that "our mission is . . . to light the lives of those still dwelling in the darkness of undemocratic rule." The influence of the idea of progress extends, of course, beyond the Clinton administration. As allied forces rolled into Kuwait, Senator Christopher Dodd, known for his interest in such progressive causes as the Sandanista revolution, anticipated Congressman Dellum's lament noted in the previous chapter by expressing dismay that wars could still occur "as we approach the end of the twentieth century," as if by now we should have progressed beyond such primitive responses to our problems. New York Governor Mario Cuomo, who reportedly suggested ceding oil and water rights to Iraq in order to avoid fighting, explained that "before you go to war, you should pursue every reasonable alternative. That is not called surrender. That is intelligence and civility and progress." The appeal to progress, however, is not a partisan distinction. President Bush invoked the term, although in a less grandiose way than his successor. In making such remarks, these men place themselves among those who sense or wish for a pacific trend in human affairs, for growing tolerance, for the kind of liberalism that makes wars less likely. They also place themselves in a distinctively American tradition, whose first great spokesman was Thomas Jefferson. According to Jefferson, each generation "must advance the knowledge and well-being of mankind, not *infinitely*, as some have said, but *indefinitely*, and to a term that no one can fix and foresee."[50]

Proponents of global engagement, especially in the currently popular democratic version, rely, then, on the notion of progress. It is their belief in progress that also allows progressives to downplay the Defense Department's traditional role of using violence in pursuit of our national interests or leads them to act as if sovereignty has become irrelevant even before it has. Progressives can take these avant garde and risky positions because they assume that everyone will eventually share them. But how do they know that? How do progressives know that their efforts to promote democracy, for example, which may generate increased violence and slaughter in the short term, will ultimately lead to a peaceful and prosperous world? How do they know there is such a thing as progress? Before we can reject global engagement, we must consider this question.

Jefferson contended that he had to consider only the improvements in the world over fifty years to see that progress had occurred.[51] Yet if history continues, as Jefferson argued, "to a term which no one can fix and foresee," how do we know that the evidence will always continue to vindicate a belief in progress? We must be able to see or understand the term of our activity, our goal, to know if what is happening around us is moving us closer to that goal. For if we do not know where we are going, how can we claim to be making progress? To know if we are making progress, for progressivism to be something other than a blind faith, we need a standard by which to judge our movement.

Francis Fukuyama claims to have provided this standard.[52] Notoriously, Fukuyama has declared that history has come to its end. He means this in two senses. History is the story of humankind's striving to attain comfort and recognition because these are the two most fundamental desires that propel humans to act. Since they find both in liberal democracy, they cease to strive when they reach that state. Since they cease to strive, history ceases. Universal liberal democracy is the end of history because it is the goal of human desire and the point at which history stops. Disturbances may occur as fringe groups stumble along unknowingly toward the common human destination, but these are historical mopping-up actions. The campaign is over. There are no longer, Fukuyama claims, any viable competitors to liberal democracy. By explaining why history has moved as it has and that it has now come to an end, Fukuyama vindicates the progressive view of history, including promoting liberal democracy as a foreign policy objective. Those who have done so were, as former Secretary Christopher said, on the right side of history.

Or were they? Has Fukuyama vindicated the progressive view of history? In discussing the end of history, Fukuyama is following in the footsteps of Alexandre Kojève, who was, in turn, reinterpreting Hegel. In remaking Hegel's argument, Kojève recognized that examining the actual state of things was not sufficient to prove that we had arrived at the end of history. Liberal democracy was not universally triumphant in the nineteenth century and is not now. The tide of democracy has ebbed and flowed. Perhaps its high tide will coincide with its transformation into something else less liberal and democratic. If we look only at the flow of events, how do we know which are progressive (leading to the triumph of liberal democracy) and which are not? The only certain way to verify Hegel's claim that history has ended, according to Kojève, was to do it logically. By this, Kojève meant that it was necessary to show that Hegel's system was circular. Normally, circularity vitiates an argument. Kojève in effect contended that if the circle Hegel constructed was big enough, if it encompassed everything, then it would make Hegel's argument rather than destroy it. Kojève offered the following example in explanation. A wise man is one who, in answering questions, can proceed through all the questions and answers that exist and arrive at the question from which he started. If he can do this, his circle of questions and answers will contain a complete statement of knowledge. Nothing will be outside it. Nothing new can come along and make us realize, for example, that liberal democracy is not the end toward which humans have been striving. Therefore, "circularity is the necessary and sufficient condition of absolute truth, that is complete, universal, and definitive (or 'eternal') truth." If Hegel's system explains all of human history and itself, all that is essential, "to ask if there is a better [more truthful] story makes no sense." If Hegel's system is circular in this sense, then Hegel is a wise man. More important for our present discussion, to retrace toward earth the steps of our ascent toward the speculative heavens, if Hegel is a wise man, then his, Kojève's, and Fukuyama's argument about the end of history is true, which means the claim that liberal democracy is the end of history must also be true, which means in turn that we have the standard that grounds and vindicates the progressive view of history, which means further that we are vindicated in trying to spread democracy even though doing so may cause conflict now, including terrorism, because we will know that the end, universal peace, ultimately will justify these violent conflicts.[53]

Unfortunately, we have indeed come back down to earth. Remarkably, Fukuyama has not undertaken to prove that Hegel's system is the circular, absolute truth. He does not do it in *The End of History and the Last Man*. In the article that preceded this book, Fukuyama stated that he did not have the ability to do it. He is not alone. Speaking of *The Phenomenology of Spirit*, the object of Kojève's analysis, one commentator has remarked that "a thorough analysis of [it] . . . has eluded all the efforts of scholarship and philosophy." Kojève himself expressed a doubt. Hegelian wisdom may not be logically impossible, but it is apparently not available to us. We may climb the mountain, but we cannot find the wise man. While we cannot prove the negative that there is no end to history, bereft of Hegelian wisdom as we are, we do not know that there is. But if we do not or cannot know what the end of history is, then we cannot know what progress is. To put it in Delphic terms, when history does not come to an end, progress does. Progressivism is at best a blind faith or, more accurately, the secular inertia of a long-forgotten religious impulse.[54]

Inertia may be good for some things, but it provides little support for a strategy with the costs associated with promoting democracy and liberalism abroad. We must face the issue of the costs of this strategy, then, without any support from history or ideas of progress. Without this support, the strategy of promoting democracy collapses into the kind of calculations commonly made in discussions of national security. Since promoting democracy does not necessarily reduce conflict and so does not necessarily pay for itself, we must decide where to invest our scarce resources in order to make sure that we get the greatest possible security in return. Yet the strategy of promoting democracy does not, in itself, tell us where to invest. This investment guidance, the pragmatism of the democratic crusade, comes from considering factors entirely unrelated to the democratic crusade itself, such as whether the states where we want to help promote democracy have "large economies, critical locations, nuclear weapons or the potential to generate refugee flows into our own nation."[55] These are the kinds of factors that nations traditionally have considered when trying to decide where they should engage. In other words, bereft of the support of history or progress, the global strategy of promoting democracy becomes subordinate to a strategy of selective engagement.

SELECTIVE ENGAGEMENT

Despite some globalist rhetoric in both the Bush and Clinton administrations, political necessity since the collapse of the Soviet Union has compelled the United States to implement a strategy of selective engagement. Such a strategy requires or is nothing more than criteria for engagement that specify when, where, and how we engage. Such criteria provide guidance for undertaking the various activities that make up our national strategy. They help us decide, for example, when and how to intervene abroad, what trade-offs to make between our concern with human rights and our need to control certain regional balances of power, and whether to risk the cost of responding to terrorism with economic sanctions, a military strike, or the rendition of an indicted terrorist. Only with such criteria in mind can we apply our resources in a rational way.

It would be wrong to imply that other strategies do not require engagement criteria, that, for example, we did not have such criteria when our strategy was containment. In fact, we had them—in several different versions. But it is also a fact that the Soviet Union helped us write them, as it were, by the way it acted, since containment was a defensive or reactive strategy. Now that the Soviet Union has disappeared, we are much freer than we were to write our engagement criteria. Generally speaking, a country's need for such guidelines is directly proportionate to the extent of its involvement in the world. If a country has limited commercial or more general foreign interests, it can concentrate on those. Its need for criteria to guide its involvement in the world will be limited. If, on the other hand, a country has extensive foreign interests, it will have great need of such criteria. This is the case of the United States. Contrary to the assertion of the national military strategy document, precisely—and perhaps paradoxically—because our interests are so extensive we cannot engage globally. Our situation now is similar to that of Great Britain's in the second half of the nineteenth century, when a British minister grasped this paradox and explained that Britain had to be cautious in engaging its resources overseas unless its interests imperatively required it. "Imperatively, I say, because our commerce is so universal and so penetrating that scarcely any question can arise in any part of the world without involving British interests. This consideration, instead of widening rather circumscribes the field of our actions. For did we not strictly limit the principle of intervention we should always be simultaneously engaged in some forty wars."[56] For a country with global interests, commercial and otherwise, it is not enough to know that its interests are at stake in some problem or conflict, for every problem or conflict will impinge somehow on its interests. Since interests do not automatically generate the resources necessary to defend them, a country with global interests must decide which are most important to defend and at what level of resources. Failure to make such decisions might lead to squandering assets; over time, such wastefulness might prove fatal.

Our general strategic orientation will also determine the kind of criteria for engagement we need. Guidelines to help us determine when, where, and how to invest our national security resources are particularly necessary for a strategy that assumes that indirect threats have a cumulative effect that must be dealt with. Such a strategy, unlike the fortress America approach, argues for addressing threats as they emerge so that we avoid the slow erosion of our strategic position. In doing so, it lets our adversaries have the advantage of selecting when and where to fight and creates the possibility that we will exhaust and disillusion ourselves by responding to an unending series of skirmishes in hopes of avoiding the big war. The Kennedy-Johnson administration followed a strategy of addressing indirect threats as its version of containment. Doing so resulted in frustration and what one commentator has called "something approaching national bankruptcy."[57] We can avoid this outcome now because we are no longer engaged in a global struggle. Consequently, we now have greater latitude to choose where to fight. Good criteria for engagement can help us make decisions that will allow us to escape the engagement dilemma: if we restrict our engagements too severely, we run the risk that our security will be eroded in the long-term by the accumulating effects of problems that individually do not warrant a response; if we engage to solve all the problems we encounter, we risk squandering our moral and economic resources in places of marginal or no interest, such as Haiti or Somalia, frustrating and exhausting ourselves so that we refuse to engage when we should or are incapable of doing so effectively. We must respond to incremental threats, but only to those that matter. Criteria for engagement help us make these decisions.

As the Soviet empire collapsed, the Bush administration increasingly needed such criteria. But the problem has been more acute for the Clinton administration, which has had some difficulty dealing with it. To his credit, a few months before he resigned, former Secretary of Defense Aspin remarked that "we need some criteria [for the use of U.S. forces] because, clearly, the number of places that need help exceeds the number of troops we will have. . . . It's a different world and it needs to be thought through." Aspin was here echoing the remarks of the nineteenth century British Minister just cited, albeit, by speaking of places that need help, with a typically altruistic or meddling American spin. Aspin noted that the administration would be spending a lot of time developing such criteria, a process that obviously had not been finished by the time he resigned. Then, in his defense, someone described as his ally told a reporter that "we have a dilemma, which Somalia exemplified. We haven't worked out when, where, and how we are going to commit our forces in this new age. Les hasn't worked it out, nobody's worked it out. . . . The President will have to resolve that issue." Under political pressure and the pressure of reality, the Clinton administration has begun this process, slowly restricting the global rhetoric of its first election campaign. For example, the administration moderated its support of multilateral peace operations, publishing rather restrictive criteria for deciding whether and how the United States will engage in such operations. Aspin's successor, William Perry, went further and outlined some general criteria for the use of force and military forces in the post–Cold War world. In a speech in November 1994, he distinguished three categories: vital interests, those that justify going to war or the decisive and overwhelming use of force; important interests, those that justify only a selective use of force; and humanitarian interests, those that justify the use of our forces but not force. These distinctions have now become part of our national strategy.[58]

The Secretary's distinctions are helpful but not sufficient. It is not immediately clear, for example, why we should not use decisive force to handle important interests. Assuming that the problem is susceptible to decisive force, would it not better to use it and finish with the problem? More generally, it is not the case that we can rigidly associate some particular kind of military force with some particular level of national interest. We have a range of interests and a range of military options to bring to bear in support of them. Depending on the circumstances, one or another of these options may be appropriate. For these and other reasons, the currently accepted criteria for engagement need further elaboration. Notoriously concerned with global issues, such as promoting democracy, providing humanitarian assistance, and saving the environment, the Clinton administration has not devoted as much effort to the ungenerous business of specifying the limits to what we should and can afford to do. Indeed, when a ranking State Department official, in an anonymous background briefing for reporters, made the apparently silly remark that because its resources were limited the United States had to "define the extent of its commitment and make a commitment commensurate with those realities," his remarks were quickly disavowed by the Secretary of State and other officials.[59] But despite these disavowals, we do need to think through the consequences of the reduced threat we currently face and our limited resources and specify, not just for peace operations, the criteria that will govern when and how we will engage. For us, this is now the core of strategic thinking, for strategy relates means to ends. If we do not think through our criteria for engagement, we will be less likely to achieve our goals, whether lofty or mundane. This is especially true with regard to our efforts to combat terrorism and other such indirect threats. As we have noted, it is particularly important that such threats be countered within a comprehensive and effective strategy, which requires that we have appropriate and effective criteria for engagement.

CRITERIA FOR ENGAGEMENT

Our discussion of engagement criteria will begin with a discussion of the two principles that should guide us now in our foreign engagements (moderation and conservation of resources) and then address two principles that should concern us globally (promoting free trade and limiting the spread of WMD). We will then review areas of geographic interest, and discuss some guidelines particularly relevant for combating terrorism. Throughout, we will emphasize fundamental principles rather than contingent facts, noting how these contingencies affect the application of principle, and will highlight issues related to terrorism.[60]

Moderation should be our strategic watchword. Absent the restraint provided by our confrontation with the Soviet Union, the United States is freer than it has been for half a century to indulge its typical urge, felt by Secretary Aspin, to intervene in all those places where people need help. Two different administrations have felt this freedom and acted on it. We should remember, however, that our efforts abroad to promote political or economic change or to help the needy can have consequences the opposite of those we intend. Interfering in the domestic affairs of another country can generate resentment toward the United States and even terrorist attacks, or it may weaken a government in power, tainting it as subservient to the United States and thus encouraging its opposition to attack. The history of our engagement with Iran illustrates this point. Helping the needy may hurt them in the long term, if our aid disrupts market mechanisms and breeds dependence. Such considerations suggest that when we intervene, we do so with only modest objectives.

Given the complex situations we are likely to confront and our limited means, we will be inclined to intervene as part of a coalition or multinational force to conserve our resources. In these cases, we may have to contribute forces to get others to do so but, as often as possible, we should try to restrict our involvement to transportation, logistics, and intelligence and limited numbers of trainers, observers, liaison elements, and advisors. While committing things and services to a coalition rather than troops has its obvious advantages, it also has disadvantages. As we saw in Bosnia, before we put troops on the ground as part of the peace agreement implementation force, if we do not commit troops when others do, we limit our influence and authority. Conserving our resources in this way makes sense, then, only if our aims are limited or if our chief aim is to support the coalition or alliance itself and we are therefore willing to abide by its decisions, whatever they may be. In Bosnia, for example, our efforts to do everything but commit troops on the ground would have made sense if we really did mean that Bosnia was a European problem and our principal goal was to support our allies in their efforts to deal with it. Unfortunately, we have had other goals in Bosnia (punishing or containing the Serbs, protecting human rights). In this case, conserving resources meant that we committed the elementary mistake of not allocating resources commensurate with our objectives. Conserving resources, then, is not an end in itself but a means to attain our ends most efficiently. It assumes clarity about goals and a competent judgment about what resources are necessary to attain them. Only with such clarity and judgment can we hope to conserve our strength while achieving our objectives.

Competing against our need to act moderately and to conserve our resources is our urge to help others, or as Secretary of State Madeleine Albright once put it most strongly, the moral imperative that we do so. "I believe that when the United States can make a difference, that we have a moral imperative to make a difference." This imperative, which both President Clinton and former National Security Advisor Anthony Lake have accepted, is the equivalent in morality of the imperative in geostrategy to suppress instability. Both are equally incompatible with a strategy of selective engagement. If we accept this moral imperative, we will clearly be set on a course of frequent intervention abroad, since as Secretary Aspin noted, there are many places where people need help and the United States can make a difference.[61]

Does this imperative exist, however? If there were a moral imperative to help others, by definition, we would be bound morally to obey it. Since the needs of others are without limit, we would in effect be under an order to exhaust our resources in helping them. An individual might conclude that saving his honor or his soul required that he ruin himself in helping others when he was not also thereby helping himself. We recognize and admire this kind of heroic virtue. But does the United States have an obligation to be so heroically virtuous? Does the government have the right to demand that American citizens be so virtuous? The government, as our representative, can demand that we risk our lives in war but it can legitimately do so because we recognize that in defending our way of life we are doing something that is ultimately good for us and for our families. It does not follow from this that the government can demand that we exhaust ourselves for the sake of foreigners when doing so will not benefit us. If our government had this authority, it would cease to be our agent, becoming our master in a way incompatible with our liberty and the limited government that we accept as legitimate. The principal purpose of foreign policy, then, or at least traditionally of American foreign policy, has been to protect domestic freedom and thus the possibility that as individuals we can save or lose our souls or honor as we see fit. If there is a moral imperative in foreign action, it is not to help others at whatever cost to ourselves, but to do no more harm than necessary in protecting our way of life. It may be true, therefore, that with the demise of the Soviet Union we are freer to act abroad than we have been for fifty years and that, consequently, we are freer than we were to undertake humanitarian efforts. But this does not mean that we must. Confronted by the endless neediness in the world, we must decide what we are able to do that is compatible with our own well being. In the mid-nineteenth century, the British were free enough from foreign threats that they could devote significant energy to suppressing the slave trade. In the late nineteenth century, on the other hand, Great Britain's geopolitical position did not permit it to help the Armenians being slaughtered by Turks even though the British government wanted to.[62] It both cases, the British acted appropriately. Morality does not require imperatively a foreign policy of helping others no matter what the cost to us.

Morality, we are no doubt comforted to learn, does not require an immoderate foreign policy. But, one might object, American foreign policy has consistently, at least since the end of World War II, encouraged immoderation by encouraging free trade, the first of the two principles, we argued, that our national strategy should support globally. We might try to escape the dilemma of preaching moderation, while encouraging immoderation by denying the immoderate, indeed revolutionary, character of free trade. In fact, however, although we may now take economic freedom for granted, it is a revolutionary force, not just an economic principle, with social and political causes and effects, clearly evident in our own history. If promoting free trade contradicts the call for moderation in our foreign policy, we should accept the contradiction for the sake of the good that free trade does. As free trade increases, so does the well-being of those who engage in it. (People freely exchange goods because they believe they will be better off as a result.) In addition, facing foreign competition through free trade will help make our economy more productive, making us wealthier, and will do the same in other countries open to trade. From the viewpoint of national strategy, however, this wealth-making activity has other advantages. Promoting free trade has been one of the principal ways in which the United States has spread its influence. As free trade has spread, it has helped make and will continue to help make the world hospitable to fundamental U.S. principles, such as equality of opportunity and individual responsibility. It will also make the world more hospitable to democracy by making people wealthier. While not necessarily a prerequisite for democracy, increasing wealth makes building democracy easier.[63] Promoting free trade is also more compatible with the principle of moderation than other reform initiatives we might take because, as a practical matter, promoting free trade is easier and less likely to increase violence than promoting democracy. The control of a political or cultural ruling group, or at least the illusion of control, can more easily be maintained if trade is free than if elections are free. And, as economic growth builds wealth and independence in a population, the possibility opens of a transition to more democratic governance. Taiwan is slowly making this transition. China may make it as well, although the problems in such an evolution are likely to be enormous. Thus, those who wish to promote democracy should first promote free trade. Finally, unlike the strategy of promoting democracy, promoting free trade will actually pay for itself. Thus, on balance, the United States gains from promoting free trade even though by doing so it is promoting revolution.

This benign view of free trade has met with opposition recently. Recognizing that free trade is a revolutionary force, some analysts have claimed that it devours its young or at least its less well paid. In the emerging global economy of free trade, labor, and capital, these analysts argue, low-wage industrial workers are in competition with even lower-paid workers in industrializing countries and will see their jobs shift to these countries. Some effect like this, and not just for the lowest-paid industrial workers, is occurring apparently, but its magnitude and the causal role of free trade are not clear. Concerning the latter point, we should remember that while it is a stimulus to productivity and greater wealth, international trade means less for our economy as a whole than for many others because it makes up relatively less of our economic activity. Free trade, then, may be causing little of the "economic insecurity" that we may or may not in fact be experiencing. The "domestic effect" argument against free trade, then, is rather weak and becomes weaker still when we recall that the alternative to free trade is protectionism, which we know will produce domestic economic and social problems. In sum, then, while globalization may produce social and economic effects that we will have to address, free trade deserves support. It has a positive effect economically, as it spreads our influence and helps shape the world in a way that is favorable to us. We should promote it, therefore, and other activities and institutions necessary to sustain it, including freedom of the seas.[64]

Not without exception, of course. Having argued that economic sanctions, which restrict free trade, are a useful way of combating terrorism, it would be inconsistent to argue that support for free trade should be absolute. On the other hand, our support for free trade is important enough that exceptions to this rule should not be made lightly. There is no formula for deciding when an exception should be made. Research has uncovered guidelines that suggest when sanctions are likely to have an economic effect[65] but, as we noted in our discussion of sanctions to combat terrorism, factors other than economic ones must be considered when deciding whether to restrict trade with sanctions.

A similar point may be made about our efforts to stop the proliferation of WMD, which should be the second global principle of our strategy. Restrictions on trade will be necessary to hinder proliferation, even though this and other efforts to counter the proliferation of WMD are probably doomed to failure, despite even the widespread acceptance of the Non-Proliferation Treaty and the unilateral renunciation of nuclear weapons programs by a few countries. Illustrating once again that on this earth there is no good without its accompanying evil, the ubiquity and easy accessibility of information that works against repressive governments works to spread WMD. The technological and economic order in which we live requires that scientific and technical knowledge be available and that scientists and technicians communicate. The result is that the information needed to build WMD of the kind suitable for terrorist operations is available in open sources, including scientific journals and doctoral dissertations, for those who want it. We cannot limit access to such information without crippling technological advance and our way of life. Restricting access to only harmful technological or scientific information, if it were possible, would not work, since, given human ingenuity, it is impossible to determine which information can be used to harm and which cannot. In short, proliferation of WMD is the downside, as they say, of the Faustian bargain that is modern science and technology. Since the relevant knowledge is available, inspection regimes fallible, trade restrictions porous,[66] and humanity's wisdom likely to lose the race with his growing power, we must be prepared to use direct action to prevent the proliferation of WMD and their use by states, terrorists, or fanatics. This means that we must overcome the counterproliferation dilemma: direct action is considered too difficult politically when the weapon program of concern is at an early stage and the threat is hard to see yet easy to deal with; but it is considered too difficult militarily when the weapons are ready, the threat evident, and the political will available. What we have learned about the techniques of disruption and preemption in attempting to combat terrorism should enter into our calculations about the risks and benefits of direct action to counter the proliferation of WMD. On balance, these lessons should make us more willing to take direct action and allow us to do it more effectively, especially since the consequences of a WMD attack could be far more lethal than any terrorist attack we have so far suffered.

Promoting free trade and countering the proliferation of WMD should concern us everywhere. We should work to extend and improve the General Agreement on Trade and Tariffs and any global counterproliferation regimes. Inevitably, however, we will focus as well on our trade with the biggest and most powerful economies in the world and on our counterproliferation efforts against those countries most likely to export or acquire weapons of mass destruction or the components necessary to build them. Economic and military power are located in particular countries, which is why our strategy cannot reflect just global interests or concerns. When we think about what areas of the globe most concern us, we must begin, as every country must, with the area closest to our own borders. This means that maintaining good relations with Canada, Mexico, and the countries that lie in or border the Caribbean and the Gulf of Mexico should be a high priority. The internal affairs of all countries near us will always interest us because they affect us, at least potentially, more than the internal affairs of countries farther from our borders. Cooperation with Canada and Mexico must be particularly close since controlling terrorism and other problems within the United States depends to a significant extent on our ability to control our borders, which we can do most effectively with the help of the Canadians and the Mexicans. Our relations with our neighbors will vary because the countries themselves vary so much. In general, however, we should work to extend the North American Free Trade Agreement (NAFTA), recognizing that this will happen only slowly but that the effort to do so is likely to have beneficial consequences whether all countries in the western hemisphere join or not. Military and police cooperation with our neighbors should be as close as possible.

To understand which regions of the world beyond our immediate neighborhood should concern us and to what degree, we need only reflect that World War I, World War II, and World War III, otherwise known as the Cold War, all occurred for the same reason: one nation or alliance of nations tried to dominate Europe. We fought in these wars to prevent this because any nation or alliance of nations that dominated Europe would have controlled vast resources of wealth, technology, and human skill. The United States would have had to accommodate itself to a power controlling such resources. To that extent, we would no longer have controlled our own destiny and might at a later date have found our independence fatally impaired.

The principle that we should prevent any nation or alliance of nations from dominating Europe is as true today as it has ever been. Indeed, it is one of the fundamental principles of American geopolitics, as it was of British statecraft before. Thomas Jefferson adhered to it when, thinking of Napoleon, he wrote to a correspondent that "it cannot be to our interest that all Europe should be reduced to a single monarchy." Today, this principle needs to be modified. Given the extraordinary economic growth in Asia over the last forty years and the vast population and currently surging economy of China, we must now think not of Europe alone but of Eurasia. This was true to some degree at the time of World War II, when the alliance between Germany and Japan threatened to dominate Eurasia, and during the Cold War, when Russia posed the same threat. But given Asia's greater economic strength now and its likely future role in the world economy, the importance of Asia has grown. Our principle should now be that no nation or alliance of nations should be allowed to dominate Eurasia. For this reason, it is no longer sensible to argue about whether the Atlantic or Pacific worlds should dominate our concerns. Since we must now think of Eurasia and not either of Europe or Asia separately, we must also think of the seas that touch our shore as one ocean and of neither the Atlantic or Pacific separately.[67]

The principal means at our disposal for preventing the domination of Eurasia is balancing power so that no nation or group of nations attains a position of preeminence. What this means in detail for the United States depends on how the principal players in the balance of power (the European Union, Russia, Japan, and China) develop economically and politically. The Cold War pattern may reassert itself, with the United States allied with the European Union, China and Japan against the Russian Federation and its surrounding dependencies and outlying allies, such as India. Something like this pattern seems to be emerging, as Russia reestablishes its military control over the borders of the former Soviet Union, including those that touch Europe and China. Russian nationalist opinion favors this familiar pattern. In early 1995, Vladimir Zhirinovsky, a prominent and extreme nationalist, argued that "from a geopolitical point of view, it is very good for Russia if India becomes a superpower." In 1996, Russia and India renewed their defense relationship after a hiatus of five years. This reemerging Cold War pattern is not the only geopolitical line-up possible in Eurasia. One analyst has suggested that a new pattern might emerge, in which Germany or a German-led Europe will ally with China against Russia, as the United States allies with Russia and Britain as a counter. China has indeed been flirting with Europe, even as it tries to improve relations with Russia. However Eurasian politics develops, its balance of power will remain vitally important to the United States. In considering it, we are likely to ally with the second strongest power or powers to balance against the strongest, in accordance with the principle that it is not in our interest for one power to dominate Eurasia.[68]

At the moment, then, we should do our best to preserve NATO and the Japanese alliance as the best access we have to Eurasian politics. At the same time, we should pursue a policy that is both even-handed toward the Eurasian powers outside these alliances, since there is not for the time being a dominant power among them, and yet most keyed to resist the reemergence in whatever form of a new Russian empire. If the balance in Eurasia can be disturbed to our disadvantage in the near-term, it is the Russian Federation—dominating Eurasia geographically, filled with natural resources and technical expertise, armed with weapons of mass destruction, and undergoing extraordinary economic and political changes—that can do it. While the emergence of a democratic or, more precisely, a liberal Russia might be to our advantage, there is little or nothing we can do directly to bring this about. The economic and political struggles currently convulsing Russian life are beyond our power to affect. We can, however, resist the reemergence of a Russian empire. This may be the most we can do for liberalism or democracy in Russia, since those in Russia who favor empire are more or less those who do not favor liberalism and democracy. Their lack of opportunities abroad may make them less relevant at home, allowing Russia to rejuvenate itself internally. Such an event would be important to us for a number of reasons, including our potential need for powerful allies against a twenty-first century China. Even if resistance to Russian imperialism does not lead to a democratic Russia, we should still resist the reconstruction of a Russian empire. This is most critical in areas that touch most closely on the richest part of Eurasia, western Europe. Accordingly, we should incorporate Poland, the Czech Republic, and Hungary into NATO.

Critics of such an approach argue that its costs will be great and that we and the other NATO members are not ready to assume responsibility for defending these countries. This is true. It will be costly. (The Congressional Budget Office has estimated $125 billion over 15 years.) We have the resources, however, especially if the costs are shared equitably among current NATO members. It is only a question of deciding what we want to spend our resources on. The history of the twentieth century suggests that defending our position in Eurasia is most cheaply done before war starts. As for the second part of the critics' assertion—that we and our allies are not ready to assume our responsibilities—this is an accurate description of the current state of affairs but proves only that statesmanship has much work to do. Part of that work will include reassuring the Russians, but not at the expense of NATO or other allies, by offering some sort of pan-Eurasian security arrangement that would exist alongside of but, in our and our allies calculations, be subordinate to NATO. Since it will be clear to the Russians that this Pan-Eurasian arrangement is less important to us than NATO, its existence will offer little reassurance. But in the face of an evidently nonaggressive NATO, which, for example, does not station troops in the newly admitted countries, it may be enough to provide moderate, democratic elements in Russia with some protection against the attacks of their imperialist rivals.[69]

This focus on Russia as the element most likely to disturb the Eurasian balance of power assumes that for some time to come aggressive, nationalist sentiments will remain powerful politically and that a slowly reviving and modernizing economy will give Russia more power to act on these aggressive impulses. If neither of these assumptions proves well founded, and if at the same time China becomes increasingly rich and belligerent, then balancing power in Eurasia will require that we oppose China most of all rather than Russia. In the long term, assuming that it does not disintegrate, China is likely to be our major concern in the Eurasian balance of power.

Although not directly involved in this balance of power, the Middle East will remain a region of interest to us because of the role that oil plays in the industrial economies, thus affecting the balance of power in Eurasia, and because the Middle East is the home of Islam, some of whose adherents see us as a threat and will thus threaten us in return to the extent of their ability. The importance of oil means that our principle of action in the Middle East is a variant of our principle of action in Eurasia. We should endeavor to see that no nation or alliance dominates the Middle East in such a way that it threatens the supply of oil. If oil production increases in other parts of the world, then our interest in the Middle East will decline accordingly, although the Middle East's vast reserves mean that, barring the discovery of equivalent reserves elsewhere, it will retain its strategic importance. It may even be worth encouraging such alternate sources through diplomatic initiatives and other measures.[70] A tax on imported oil or oil imported from the Middle East might be one means of encouraging the development of alternative sources of energy. As always, when considering exceptions to the principle of free trade, the calculation of the economic cost of such a measure would be only one factor in deciding whether it was worthwhile. Yet even if we encourage alternative sources of energy to Middle East oil, this commodity is likely to maintain its special place in world trade, which will mean again that the Middle East will remain important to us. As with Eurasia, what we must do in detail to protect our interests in the Middle East depends on how the countries in the region develop politically and economically and on their relations with one another and with outside powers. At the moment, given German, French, and Russian interest in improving relations with Iran and Iraq and our continued efforts to isolate these two countries while supporting Saudi Arabia and Kuwait, there is a bipolar structure of external alliances developing around the Persian Gulf different from the one that prevailed during the Cold War. At the same time, in another part of the Middle East, a new axis is developing, with the encouragement and support of the United States, consisting of Israel, Jordan, and Turkey, motivated in part by closer relations between Greece and Syria.[71]

Like its predecessors, the Clinton administration seeks a balance of power in the Middle East favorable to the United States. Unlike them, it believes that it can attain this balance while it contains both Iran and Iraq. Such a "dual containment" approach may be possible for a while, but it is unlikely that the United States will have the military or political power to enforce it indefinitely. If we cannot contain both countries, we will have to deal with at least one. Although a concern with terrorism might suggest that Iran is the greater danger of the two, Iraq must receive that dubious honor because of the fragility of its regime, its remaining military power, and its unreformed intentions. In this situation, it will probably be best to work with Iran, as we work separately with the Israel-Jordan-Turkey axis (assuming it survives and matures) to see that developments in Iraq serve both our interests. Establishing such a working relationship with Iran should not require that Iran stop doing all those things we object to, as the Clinton administration demands, nor that we find "moderates" there who share some of our principles. It requires only that we find interlocutors willing to put aside hatred of the United States and what it stands for so that Iran may protect its interests. Such interlocutors may not exist or, if they do and make themselves known, they may not survive, but we should be prepared to meet them. Sooner or later, the failure of dual containment will require that we do so.[72]

Beyond our immediate border areas, Eurasia, and the Middle East, our interests decline sharply. In Africa, the southern parts of Latin America, and a vast extent of land stretching on a southern diagonal from Afghanistan to southeast Asia, our interests dictate that we promote free trade and counter the proliferation of weapons of mass destruction but little else. India is an exception to this rule because of its population, economic potential, ambitions in the Indian Ocean, and role in possible coalitions or loose alliances with Russia. Generally speaking, however, India is likely to be less important to us than the major actors in the northern part of Eurasia. If we had the ability and the resources to reengineer societies, we might want to address some of the problems or "threats" described by those who see anarchy lurking in the future of many of the countries in these peripheral areas. We have neither, however, and few of our limited national security resources should be spent there. In many of these peripheral countries, for example, we do not need to have full, permanent diplomatic representation (resident ambassadors) or any official U.S. government presence. If the independence of African countries had not been accompanied by our growing competition with the Soviet Union, we would not have opened embassies in many African countries and would not have created separate Africa regional bureaus throughout the national security bureaucracy.

One could object to this regional distribution of our interests (essentially northern Eurasia) and to the proposed strategy for dealing with it (balancing power) that the former is too narrow and the latter too limited. In both cases, the criticism would be valid. There are at least three ways that our geographic interests should or could be broadened. The first is through a sort of principle of affinity, whereby the interests of our allies become our interests. For example, southern Europeans currently worry about the Maghreb, making this area more important to us than it would be otherwise. Again, Iran should be of primary interest to us because of our interest in the Middle East and the free flow of oil, the influence of Islamic fundamentalism, and Iran's support of terrorism. This makes Pakistan, a more moderate Islamic country bordering Iran, more important to us.

This, in turn, gives us an additional interest in India because of the problematic relations between Pakistan and India. The second way our interests can expand is through activities originating in peripheral areas that directly affect us. It is quite possible, for example, that one of the states outside our area of greatest geographic interest would use terrorism against us or an important ally, since it has proven an effective way for weaker states to attack stronger ones. Sudan is a current example of a country that may be pursuing such a strategy. Afghanistan poses a similar problem, since Islamic terrorists are using its territory for training and sanctuary. Countering these threats requires an investment of diplomatic, economic, and military resources otherwise unnecessary. Similarly, the Andean countries of South America have received greater attention than they would have otherwise because their territory is the source of much of the cocaine that reaches the United States. Nigeria, because of the involvement of its citizens in drug trafficking and other criminal activity, earns through this dubious distinction more of our attention than it would otherwise. Finally, any effort to locate our geographic areas of interest is subject to revision. Geography itself changes at a rate that need not concern a strategist, but technology and politics, each changing at different rates, will alter the calculus of where a country's interests lie. Small yearly changes in economic growth rates can have dramatic cumulative effect, delaying for many years, for example, the rise of China to great power status; technological breakthroughs could render oil much less important as a source of energy; revolutions in public opinion or political power could change foreign policies, pushing Russia into authoritarian expansion or Europe to greater cohesion. All these changes, and many others, would affect the details of Eurasian politics and our response, altering the survey we have just offered. In sum, affinity and peripheral threats broaden our geographical areas of interest and change may alter them. But the analysis offered here and its central principle, that we try to prevent any one power or alliance from dominating Eurasia, still provides the means by which we can rank our interests, the means by which we know that an affinity is by marriage rather than blood, so to speak, a threat peripheral rather than central, or a political change inconsequential or significant. It is by such analysis that we can deploy our resources to best effect.

Assuming that this is so, must we also assume that balancing power will be the best means at our disposal to counter a future Eurasian hegemony? Historically, states have used several strategies besides balancing in order to address their security concerns: hiding, bandwagoning, and transcending.[73] We have already argued that "hiding" or isolating ourselves from the world would not be beneficial to the United States. In some situations, it may be desirable and possible for the United States to hide by declaring neutrality, assuming a defensive posture or letting an ally take the lead. Neither of these should be acceptable responses to the threatened domination of Eurasia, however. Jumping on the bandwagon of a strong power is generally what a weaker power does in order to protect its interests. On certain regional issues, the United States may be a relatively weak power and may jump on a bandwagon but, again, with regard to the question of hegemony in Eurasia, the United States would be ill advised to adopt this strategy, for doing so would make it all the easier for the strong power to dominate.

This leaves transcending, "attempting to surmount international anarchy and go beyond the normal limits of conflictual politics" by dealing with security problems "through some institutional arrangement involving international consensus or formal agreement on norms, rules, and procedures." An example of transcending or, more accurately, of an attempt at transcending, is the effort the United States has made over many years to limit terrorism by building an international consensus against it. This effort has taken place in a number of multilateral fora, including the Organization of American States, meetings of the leaders of the seven wealthiest economies, and at the United Nations. Examining these efforts at the UN is a good way to evaluate the strategy of transcending, since the UN is a gigantic institution dedicated to this strategy. In principle, the UN is able to transcend the international anarchy generated by sovereign powers pursuing their interests because, presumably, its actions are not based on the interests of any one nation or group of nations. The standards of international conduct incorporated into UN conventions, for example, apply to all states equally and, in principle, benefit all equally by establishing rules of the game by which all can play. In fact, as we have seen, states that support terrorism ignore these rules in practice because they do not aspire to some juridical equality with other states but to have certain advantages with respect to stronger states. They seek these advantages because they believe that the international consensus, determined by the strong states, is to the disadvantage of the weaker. Their belief is accurate. Madeleine Albright, while Ambassador to the United Nations, said, "with a chuckle," that "the UN is a tool of American foreign policy. . . . What it does is provide us an opportunity to deal with some national interests in a way where we can share the burden and the risks and costs." As the more powerful states bend the UN to their interests, the weaker states may be disadvantaged.[74]

Burden sharing through the UN has its own costs, however. The UN's effort to transcend "the normal limits of conflictual politics" disadvantages strong states precisely because the UN, in order to respect the interests of all its member states, must resist the efforts of its stronger members to use it for their ends. To attain this goal of impartiality, the UN must, to the extent its members let it, treat conflict anywhere it occurs with the same seriousness. To have taken more seriously the slaughter in Bosnia than the slaughter in Rwanda, for example, would have been to take a Eurocentric view, one unacceptable to its non-European members. The United States must take this global view from time to time—and should never speak as Ambassador Albright did—if it wants to keep other members involved in efforts that serve its interests. Every time the United States takes this global perspective, however, it means that our engagement under the UN banner (in a place like Somalia, for example) becomes much deeper than it would have been if we had considered our own interests only. Ultimately, this means that our commitment to the UN in such places becomes unsustainable, which discredits our entire relationship with the UN. Transcending, then, while it may work in some cases, is a strategy not completely acceptable to either weak or strong states because it is not completely compatible with their different interests. Nor is it the case necessarily that if all compromise, each will gain equally. Transcending is a strategy that we may be able to pursue in some cases but cannot rely on. The fact that we and others cannot rely on it limits its applicability and undermines it in those cases where it is applied. With regard to the central national security task before us (preventing the domination of Eurasia), therefore, balancing power remains the best means.[75]

A number of different developments could threaten a balance of power we wished to preserve or establish in our favor. Iraq's invasion of Kuwait is one obvious example of such a development. But shifts in a balance of power more subtle than that caused by a massive invasion of a regional ally could occur if a country's aggressive acts, including the acquisition of conventional weapons or WMD, threatened important U.S. allies or, as in the case of Iran's acquisition of submarines, lines of communications associated with U.S. interests. A regional balance of power might also begin to shift subtly if a country undertook to undermine a key U.S. regional ally through subversion or terrorism or if a regime hostile to the United States and its allies came to power. Iran and Sudan, for example, are supporting terrorism against Israel and Egypt that might produce these results. Even at a low level these subtle threats might turn a balance of power against us if the instigator is aggressive and our failure to respond encourages further actions contrary to our interests or persuades our allies that they cannot count on our support. In all of these cases, to note that our interests are affected does not mean that we must engage, nor does it determine how we should engage or at what level. Those decisions depend on a careful assessment of each situation. For example, we are unlikely to stop the proliferation of weapons of mass destruction, but there may be a particular situation in which those involved, their geopolitical position, or the nature of the proliferation require that we take action.

One might object to the strategy of selective engagement we have just outlined that while sensible in general it is useless as a guide for our efforts to combat terrorism because the violence and drama of terrorism overthrow all calculations of interest and selectivity. Casualties inflicted by terrorism can make us withdraw from places, such as Lebanon, where we have established interests. Hostage crises can paralyze and destroy an Administration, as the Tehran Embassy hostage crisis destroyed the Carter Presidency and hostages in Lebanon led the Reagan Administration into its worst foreign policy failure, Iran-Contra. Even on a smaller scale, a hostage crisis can confound a government's plans, especially given the influence of the media. The epitome of such an episode was the seizure of TWA Flight 847. As we have mentioned, the media played a prominent role in this hijacking. The publicity they gave the hijackers, through interviews with them and their hostages and assorted experts, generated a great deal of pressure on decisionmakers. It complicated their efforts because their strategy was to make the hostages less valuable to the terrorists by insisting that no concessions would be made to gain their release, while making their continued detention more costly, in hopes that eventually the terrorists would calculate that it was in their interests to let them go. Media publicity, on the other hand, made the hostages more valuable to the terrorists by generating pressure on decisionmakers to do something—anything—to get their release. This made the terrorists less willing to release the hostages. At one point, hostage-taking combined with media coverage also worked to the advantage of the Serbs in Bosnia as a way to stop NATO bombing, which suggests that we may see more of this tactic in the future.

There is some truth to the argument that terrorism and the media combine so powerfully that no criteria for selective engagement can prevail against them—but not much. In 1995, there were ninety-nine international terrorist attacks against Americans, few of which got anything more than a paragraph or two on the back pages of major newspapers, if that. Throughout 1995, a hostage-taking episode involving an American and several Europeans played itself out in northwest India but was hardly noticed. Several Americans are being held for ransom by revolutionary terrorists in Colombia, and two were killed in 1995, again with little notice taken by the press. Generally speaking, concern with terrorism follows the geostrategic and other interests we have outlined here, being higher when the event takes place in an area of greater interest to the United States (in the Middle East, for example, as opposed to Kashmir). Nor must casualties inflicted by terrorism force us to abandon a course of action. Since the October 3 battle in Mogadishu between American Rangers and Aideed's militia, in which eighteen Americans died and which led to the curtailment of our efforts there, it is common to hear people say that we are now down to a withdrawal threshold of eighteen killed in action. This belief is based on misconceptions and misunderstandings, however. When casualties are taken, the public response has usually been a desire to escalate so that we could win and then withdraw. This response depends, however, on a public perception that the intervention has some sensible purpose to begin with. This was not the case in Beirut by the time the Marine barracks was blown up. Nor was it the case in Somalia. Our purpose there was humanitarian, and no effort was made to connect this to our interests or larger purposes as a nation. Combat deaths, therefore, made no sense. Under these circumstances, the threshold in Somalia should have been one wounded, let alone eighteen dead. In other words, casualties will not force us out as long as we have some reason to sustain them and the American public is aware of the reason. We maintained a decade-long involvement in El Salvador in the 1980s, despite the deaths of American civilians and military personnel from terrorist attacks. As for hostage-taking, according to George Shultz, the U.S. government at first did not have a good way to handle the TWA Flight 847 hijacking and hostage-taking. As the crisis developed, however, it discovered that centralized control of official statements, the reiteration of the "no concessions" policy and its rationale (concessions produce more terrorism) and relative silence otherwise was effective. The Bush administration used a similar approach when dealing with the issue of the hostages taken in Lebanon and with Saddam Hussein's hostage-taking in the Gulf War, confirming that this may well be the most effective way to handle these situations.[76]

With these brief comments on the media as a threat to a strategy of selective engagement, we have finished our outline of such a strategy. In several respects its complementary military strategy already exists, replete with an explanation of the deterrent use of nuclear weapons.[77] In other respects, this strategy needs revision. Its tendency to argue that we must fight instability wherever it exists is misleading. As we have argued, global interests demand selective engagement. Its focus on having clear objectives and applying decisive or overwhelming force to achieve them also should be revised. Applying force only when objectives are clear and the enemy can be defeated with decisive force will mean either using force rarely or in a way inappropriate to the circumstances. As we have seen when discussing the use of force, terrorism, and the difference between war and peace, we face enemies who cannot be dealt with by overwhelming force in circumstances where objectives are necessarily ambiguous. Finally, our current military strategy insists that we maintain the ability to fight two regional wars at nearly the same time. If the money available for defense were unconstrained, there would not be any objection to such a requirement, because it is possible over the next several years that we might have to fight both in the Middle East and on the Korean peninsula. But with defense resources constrained as we know they will be, the requirement to fight two regional wars means that we are in danger of keeping force structure to fight today's enemies, who are weak, at the cost of preparing to fight tomorrow's, who will be stronger. We should be willing to take risks with our enemies now to avoid greater risks in the future, except for the fact that for decisionmakers present risk is more evident than future risk and a failure to respond adequately now to a war on the Korean peninsula, for example, would have wide-ranging and unpredictable repercussions in a region vitally important to us. The best we can hope for, then, is that our military strategy and spending not ignore the future as it emphasizes the current wars we may have to fight.

These revisions would bring our current military strategy into line with the selective engagement strategy that we have outlined here. This understates the need for change, however. For what the United States and its military must do is accommodate themselves to a geopolitical situation that does not play to their strengths and traditional way of operating in the world. For the time being, there are likely to be no evident threats to our vital interests, no grand reasons to go to war, few if any threats that the arsenal of democracy can overwhelm with decisive force. Nor as time passes are we likely to have the economic or military weight to tip every balance in our favor on our own. The threats and problems we confront with military resources diminishing absolutely and our weight in the world declining relatively are likely to be smaller, more difficult to assess and counter. Over the next two decades or so, we will be engaged in termite control and not the bear hunt we prefer, as children still of the frontier. To prevent the slow but sure erosion of our security, we will need patience, therefore, a willingness to accept partial and inconclusive results, an ability to absorb setbacks and to use means that take time. Maintaining favorable balances of power will require allies and thus an ability to accept compromise and ambiguity and a willingness to act for something less than the establishment of worldwide democracy. So contrary to our past ways of acting are these newly necessary attitudes that several authoritative commentators have suggested that the United States will have difficulty adapting and may not be able to do so.[78] Our campaign against international terrorism is at least somewhat reassuring in this regard, however, since over twenty-five years, under administrations of both parties, we have pursued against terrorists and their sponsors, with only occasional lapses, the modern equivalent of the Roman methods of siege warfare that one of these commentators argues we should emulate. We have been patient, accepted inconclusive results, suffered setbacks, but struggled on. We have worked with allies, and applied sanctions and other economic forms of statecraft, as well as the slow but steady pressures of criminal investigation, diplomatic cajolery, and intelligence gathering and clandestine operation. We have, in the case of terrorism, pursued our goals with the persistent application of diplomacy and force that the United States was supposed to be incapable of. To the extent that the problems we now confront resemble terrorism in its indirect, slow, but persistent method of attack, we can learn and draw some consolation from our history of combating it.

We have concluded this strategic review by suggesting the relevance of our response to terrorism to our strategy as a whole. We began it with the narrower issue of what place terrorism and our response should have in our strategy. It is to that question that we now can return.

CONCLUSION

The day may dawn when fair play, love for one's fellow men, respect for justice and freedom, will enable tormented generations to march forth serene and triumphant from the hideous epoch in which we have to dwell. Meanwhile, never flinch, never weary, never despair.
—Winston Churchill

The collapse of the Soviet Union has created a new strategic setting, providing us with greater strategic depth than we have had since the immediate aftermath of World War I. There is not currently any nation or group of nations that threatens hegemony over Eurasia. Nor is a hegemonic power likely to emerge in the near future. The threat of a nuclear attack on the United States has greatly diminished. This strategic depth has increased our freedom of action in both foreign and domestic matters, giving us greater flexibility to handle the various problems that confront us. Our task now is to assess the place of terrorism in this current setting. In what ways can terrorist attacks penetrate our strategic depth?

Terrorism could be used against us by three different enemies: autonomous terrorist groups, a regional power, and an Eurasian power. As we have noted, analysts fear that autonomous groups are capable of more unrestrained violence than other terrorists precisely because they are autonomous, not subject to the restraints of a sponsoring state's political agenda. Acting more to satisfy hate than to advance a political cause, they are not restrained by the need to tailor their use of force to a political purpose. Coming together for a single act or a brief campaign, autonomous groups are amateurish; although amateurish, they are capable of doing great damage. Some analysts have even speculated that such groups might be willing to use weapons of mass destruction (WMD).[1]

Whether such use could reasonably be tied to an effort to influence an audience and thus be called terrorism, as the U.S. government defines it, we have argued, is not an unimportant consideration. But whether we would classify such an act as terrorism or not, it would obviously have a devastating effect on the United States, as would the political use or threatened political use of a WMD in an effort to extort concessions from us. Yet in assessing the consequences of a WMD attack, we should remember that however horrendous its consequences, it would not affect the ability of the United States to recover from it. It might cost billions to do so—lost or ruined lives, obviously, would never be recovered— but our capacity to recuperate would not be implicated in the attack. Even if it occurred in an economically vital region, the economy of the United States is sufficiently diverse and decentralized that we would rebound. Indeed, such an attack, like a devastating natural disaster, would generate an overwhelming official and public response, not only to rebuild and make sure, as far as possible, that such an event not recur but to punish those responsible. This is what happened in Japan following the gas attack on the Tokyo subway. One could imagine, of course, a WMD or other technologically sophisticated attack occurring in several places at once. But such an attack, more clearly than the use of one such device, would have to be considered the equivalent of a strategic attack on the United States delivered not by missiles but by clandestine agents. Although a possibility, such an attack would be beyond the scope of what we normally consider terrorism because it would aim to destroy not to influence us.

Any WMD attack, with or without an accompanying effort at extortion, would have extraordinary and long lasting political and psychological consequences that would be difficult to estimate. Such an event might even prompt a fundamental change in the American way of life, persuading people to accept a curtailment of some civil liberties or much stricter control over immigrants and visitors in order to decrease the chance that a similar attack would recur. While it might have such effects, they would not be inevitable. Since a terrorist attack in the United States using WMD would not destroy our physical ability to recover, the basis of our independence would remain. We would remain free to respond to this calamity, to bring all our economic, political, and spiritual resources to the task of recuperating. Good leadership and what we hope would be our resilient spirit might permit a full recovery.

Although a WMD attack in the United States would not necessarily threaten our independence of action, another form of terrorism might. Whether occurring in the United States or abroad, terrorism sponsored by a state in an effort to tilt a regional balance of power against our interests or to persuade us to give up our support for a regional ally could prompt our strategic withdrawal from a region. Depending on where it took place, such a withdrawal could diminish our long-term prospects or curtail our strategic depth. For example, we have noted the importance of the Middle East for the balance of power in Eurasia, a balance upon which our own security and independence rests. A state aspiring to regional mastery could use terrorism against us during war or peacetime. It would be more likely to succeed, however, during the latter. When war threatens, as Saddam Hussein discovered, we and our coalition partners can focus our attention on the terrorism threat and take effective action to defuse it.   Additionally, threatening to use terrorism, when passions are already inflamed during a war, makes the sponsor of terrorism appear more villainous and allows his opponents to organize public opinion more strongly against him, making a strong response more likely.   In peacetime, experience suggests, a terrorism campaign can proceed for years and if its director (say, an Arafat or an Asad) is clever can contribute to the attainment of his goals.   A backlash can occur, of course, against any state or group whose support becomes clearly known or results in acts judged monstrous.   Asad and Arafat have survived and prospered, however, despite such setbacks.

The last way that terrorism could be used against us would be by a Eurasian power, which would use terrorism as part of a larger geopolitical struggle.   The Soviet Union and its Warsaw pact allies used terrorism in this way during the Cold War, supporting anti-NATO terrorism in Western Europe and anti-U.S. terrorism in the Middle East and other parts of the world.   In this case, the threat would be the same as that posed by a regional power but on a bigger scale and with greater adverse consequences for us should we not respond effectively. Terrorism would be one of the indirect political-military means for carrying on a great power rivalry, as would be such related activities as insurgency, subversion, and coups d'état.   The threat posed by these indirect means would be related directly to the threat posed by the great power that used them.   The threat would decline, for example, as the great power declined.   Individually of no great consequence from the perspective of a great power rivalry, indirect attacks can be significant collectively, as we have argued, especially if they are part of a sound strategy.   The greatest threat posed by such indirect means of aggression would be the slow erosion of our strategic position through the loss of lines of communication, trade advantages, base rights, regional allies, and other forms of influence.   The intended result of this indirect campaign would be the slowly dawning realization, when it was already too late, that the strategic balance had tipped against us to such a degree that the only choices open to us were dignified surrender or vain resistance.

In sum, then, terrorist attacks in the United States by autonomous groups, even their use of a WMD, would not threaten our independence of action as a nation but might, in the extreme case, adversely affect our character as a free and tolerant people.   Such attacks would galvanize officials and the public and assure the most effective response of which we were capable.   A terrorist campaign against the United States supported by a regional or Eurasian power, on the other hand, could threaten our independence of action but would not threaten our character.   Such campaigns and the indirect strategies of which they would be part might not generate significant reaction from us or only a delayed or misguided one.

Which kind of terrorism—autonomous or strategic—is the most dangerous? It would be difficult to decide. What is most vulnerable and hardest to repair, our character or our independence of action? Deciding is beside the point ultimately. Each terrorist threat must be carefully analyzed, prevented, and its consequences prepared for. This work is going forward with regard to a possible WMD attack in the United States by a terrorist group. The issues here are largely technical—the goals of prevention and consequence management being indisputable and the seriousness of the threat helping to override political and jurisdictional controversies—and the United States commands formidable technical power. In considering strategic terrorism, we should start with an obvious point: the threat posed derives from those who sponsor it. The threat is greatest when terrorism is the tool of another great power or of the wicked and clever, least when it is used by the weak or stupid. At its most potent, as a tool of a great power, strategic terrorism is ancillary to the main struggle. It occurs on the periphery or at the margins. "Not a single government has been overthrown as a result of terrorist action," one analyst reminds us. "Terrorism is rarely associated with political instability or with radical political change," another remarks.[2] This does not mean it is insignificant. As we have argued, the slow but steady erosion of power and of strategic position can have a significant cumulative effect. The barbarians eventually made it to Rome. Terrorism and its related forms of political violence may be a skirmish at the edge of our empire, but we cannot ignore it, particularly if we face a strong and determined foe who is willing to use terrorism as an integrated element in regional or global conflict.

Over the years, we have developed a number of responses to terrorism. Some are more effective or relevant than others or are so in different ways. As we have argued, diplomacy, economic sanctions, and disruption can work against state sponsors, while law enforcement and disruption are likely to be most effective against terrorist organizations, including the new autonomous groups. The effectiveness of these methods depends directly on effective intelligence work. None of these methods or all used together will put an end to terrorism; they will help us only to manage this and similar threats. But they will not even do this, unless they are used as part of a coherent national strategy. Given that the threat posed by terrorism is derivative, in responding to it our focus should be on that from which it derives its power. We must contend effectively with regional powers and, when the next one arises, a paramount Eurasian power. We should be able to do this, as long as we are not distracted by mistaken notions of what threatens us or misled by mistaken ideas of what morality demands of us. Ultimately, this means our best defense against strategic terrorism is a sound national strategy that maintains the proper perspective on terrorism and similar indirect threats. We cannot ignore the skirmishes, lest we be pushed imperceptibly from advantageous positions; we cannot think only of the skirmishes, lest we lose the greater battle.

No doubt it will seem odd to say that terrorism is a skirmish at the edge of our empire. Terrorists have bombed the World Trade Center in New York City. After the bombing of the federal building in Oklahoma City in 1995, the headlines screamed "Terrorism in the heartland." We have even acknowledged the possibility that terrorists might use a WMD in the continental United States. How can such things be said to occur at the edge of our empire? Answering this question requires that we reflect on the essence of our empire.

Empire means power. The result of the scientific and industrial revolutions is that power derives less and less from control over territory and more and more from ideas and innovation; in short, from knowledge. This accords with the teaching of the founder of the Enlightenment in its technical and scientific manifestation. Knowledge, Francis Bacon said, is power. The United States is the first child of the Enlightenment and still its most prodigious. Our empire is one of immense material power because this power derives from an even more powerful idea. Its essence is a belief in human equality and equal opportunity, that people should be rewarded for what they do and not for who they are, how they look, or where they worship. This still revolutionary understanding of justice inspires the openness of American life, the surging inventiveness of American economic and technological achievement, as well as America's free-wheeling democratic politics. Thomas Jefferson understood that a nation acting on this understanding would set free unprecedented human energy and power. This was the empire that Thomas Jefferson wanted to establish. Jefferson called it an Empire of Liberty.

Terrorism attacks this empire indirectly. It destroys individuals or property to get at its primary target, the human mind. It is violence intended to influence, coerce, or intimidate an audience. Terrorism, even of the most violent kind, even when it occurs in the United States, is a skirmish at the edges of our empire because it attacks the ultimate source of our strength indirectly. These skirmishes will accomplish nothing as long as we do not forget our principles, those guiding ideas that constitute us as a free people. Terrorism has caused such forgetting in other places.   While terrorism has not overthrown governments, it has led governments, in effect, to overthrow themselves by adopting repressive measures that extinguish liberty. This is now only a remote possibility in the United States, although concerns in this regard were raised about proposed extensions of police power following the bombing in Oklahoma City.[3] Part of preparing for the consequences of the most extreme terrorist attacks in the United States is to fortify ourselves in the knowledge of who we are and why.

Such fortification is necessary, for a general forgetting of our principles and their replacement by inferior ones is already well developed. Terrorism is part of this development. The arguments of terrorists and their supporters— obscuring the difference between legitimate and illegitimate government and undermining respect for the rights of the innocent—have found support in the schools and other institutions of democracies, as well as in international organizations. It was against this erosion of principle that George Shultz raised his voice as Secretary of State. His example is a reminder of the best way to combat terrorism. As the best defense against the strategic threat of terrorism is a sound national strategy that deals appropriately with peripheral threats, so the best defense against the graver threat to our principles is a conscious effort to revive them. This defense of principle is a more difficult task than implementing an effective strategy, which we managed to do during the Cold War. Our success at this easier task has given us a temporary respite. As a consequence, we are now free to focus more on domestic matters, to repair our home base before the next onslaught. Our principal task in this regard is neither economic nor technological. It is political and philosophical, strengthening the foundations of the Empire of Liberty. In doing so, we may even fortify ourselves against the calamity of a WMD attack in the United States, if we recover the proper understanding of our principles and come to realize that the threat of terrorist attack under which we live is the price we pay for our true greatness.

NOTES

INTRODUCTION

1. Robin Wright, "U.S. Worries About Iranian Unit in Bosnia," *Los Angeles Times*, December 5, 1995, 1.

2. For recent statistics on international terrorism, see *Patterns of Global Terrorism: 1995* (The Department of State, Washington, D. C., 1996), iii–v, 1–2.

3. See, for example, David B. Ottaway, "U.S. Considers Slugging It Out With International Terrorism," *Washington Post*, October 17, 1996, A25.

4. *National Military Strategy of the United States of America, 1995* (Washington, D.C.: U.S. government Printing Office, 1995), 12. On the U.S. government's difficulties with political-military problems, see Henry L. T. Koren, Jr., "Congress Wades into Special Operations," *Parameters* 18 (December, 1988): 62–74; Bernard F. McMahon, "Low-Intensity Conflict: The Pentagon's Foible," *Orbis* 34 (Winter, 1990): 3–16.

5. Andrew F. Krepinevich, Jr., *The Army and Vietnam* (Baltimore: Johns Hopkins University Press, 1986), 5; Ralph Peters, "The New Warrior Class," *Parameters* 24 (Summer, 1994), 24 and Ralph Peters, "After the Revolution," *Parameters* 25 (Summer, 1995): 7–14.

6. William Perry, "Remarks and Selected Questions and Answers at the Regional Commerce and Growth Association, St. Louis, September 29, 1995," *Defense Issues*, volume 91, number 10 (Washington, D.C.: Department of Defense, n.d.).

7. Jeffrey D. Simon, *The Terrorist Trap, America's Experience with Terrorism* (Bloomington: Indiana University Press, 1994), 9.

CHAPTER 1

1. Evan Duncan, "Terrorist Attacks on U.S. Official Personnel Abroad," *Department of State Bulletin* (DSB), 81 (April, 1981): 34–37; Jeffrey D. Simon, *The Terrorism Trap, America's Experience with Terrorism* (Bloomington: Indiana University Press, 1994), 54–57, 88–93; Stanley Karnow, *Vietnam, A History* (New York: The Viking Press,

1983), 10, 408–409; Edward F. Mickolus, *Transnational Terrorism, Chronology of Events, 1968–1979* (Westport, Connecticut: Greenwood Press, 1980), 51, 59.

2. For an example of how what we now call terrorism was treated as part of a war of national liberation, see *U.S. Army Handbook of Counterinsurgency, Guidelines for Area Commanders* (Washington, D.C.: Headquarters, Department of the Army, January, 1966), 1, 27, 205.

3. Duncan, "Terrorist Attacks on U.S. Official Personnel Abroad," 34–37; Timothy Wickham–Crowley, *Exploring Revolution, Essays on Latin American Insurgency and Revolutionary Theory* (Armonk, New York: M. E. Sharpe, 1991), 80; Christopher Dobson and Ronald Payne, *The Never-Ending War, Terrorism in the 80's* (New York: Facts on File, 1989), 309; *Patterns of International Terrorism: 1980* (Washington, D. C., Central Intelligence Agency, June, 1981), 2–3; Statement of Secretary Rogers before the Third Special Session of the Organization of American States General Assembly, Washington, D.C., January 25–February 2, 1971, DSB 64 (February, 1971), 228; Mickolus, *Transnational Terrorism,* 65, 73, 166.

4. *Patterns of International Terrorism: 1980*, 4; DSB 64 (February, 1971), 231.

5. John R. Stevenson, "International Law and the Export of Terrorism," an address before the Bar of the City of New York, November 9, 1972, DSB 67 (December 1972): 646. For the Draft Convention on Terrorism, see Ernest Evans, *Calling a Truce to Terrorism, The American Response to International Terrorism, Contributions in Political Science,* 29 (Westport, Connecticut: Greenwood Press, 1979), 93–113.

6. Dobson and Payne, *The Never-Ending War, Terrorism in the 80's,* 309–310.

7. Barry Rubin, *Revolution Until Victory? The Politics and History of the PLO* (Cambridge: Harvard University Press, 1994), 24–26, 30–31; Walter Laqueur, *The Age of Terrorism* (Boston: Little, Brown and Company, 1987), 236–238; Michael Radu and Vladimir Tismaneanu, *Latin American Revolutionaries, Groups, Goals, Methods* (Washington, D.C.: Pergamon–Brassey's International Defense Publishers, Inc., 1990), 46–49; Jean Paul Sartre, "Preface" to Frantz Fanon, *The Wretched of the Earth* (New York: Grove Press, 1963), 12, 21, 24; Dobson and Payne, *The Never-Ending War, Terrorism in the 80's,* 313.

8. Barry Rubin, *Revolution Until Victory?* 38, 214 note 42; Abu Iyad, with Eric Rouleau, *My Home, My Land, A Narrative of the Palestinian Struggle* (New York: Times Books, 1981), translated by Linda Butler Koseoglu, 96–98; Dobson and Payne, *The Never-Ending War, Terrorism in the 80's,* 315.

9. Rubin, *Revolution Until Victory?*, 24–28; Abu Iyad, *My Home, My Land,* 98.

10. *New York Times*, "U.S. Sets Up Intelligence Group to Combat Terrorism," September 9, 1972, 4.

11. The Defense Department uses the term *combating terrorism* to refer to both anti-terrorism (preventive measures) and counterterrorism (offensive measures). Since 1984, the State Department has used the term *counter-terrorism* to refer to both preventive and offensive measures. Unless otherwise specified, in this book *counterterrorism* refers to both offensive and preventive measures. U.S. Department of State, "President Nixon Establishes Cabinet Committee to Combat Terrorism," DSB 67 (October, 1972): 475–480. Presidential Memorandum dated September 25, 1972; Marc A. Celmer, *Terrorism, U.S. Strategy and Reagan Policies* (New York: Greenwood Press, 1987), 18.

12. Discussion of the activities of the Working Group is based on an interview with Ambassador Armin Meyer, November, 1994.

13. *Patterns of International Terrorism: 1980* (Washington, D.C., 1981), 21.

14. The information on the Cuban, Congolese, and North Korean hostage situations is drawn from Simon, *The Terrorism Trap*, 56–57, 92–96; David A. Korn, "'We Will not Pay Blackmail,' The Khartoum Murders and U.S. Policy on Terrorism," *Foreign Service Journal* 68 (February, 1991): 29; Dobson and Payne, *The Never-Ending War, Terrorism in the 80's*, 309.

15. Armin Meyer, "The Khartoum Tragedy" (undated typescript), 2, 3.

16. Details in this paragraph are drawn from Meyer, "The Khartoum Tragedy," and Korn, "'We Will not Pay Blackmail,' The Khartoum Murders and U.S. Policy on Terrorism." On Arafat's possible role, see Rubin, *Revolution Until Victory?*, 38; Neil C. Livingstone and David Halevy, *Inside the PLO, Covert Units, Secret Funds, and the War against Israel and the United States* (New York: William Morrow and Company, 1990), 276–288, and Mickolus, *Transnational Terrorism*, 375–378, which is a good short summary of the incident.

17. Lewis Hoffacker, Special Assistant to the Secretary of State and Coordinator for Combating Terrorism, "The U.S. government Response to Terrorism: A Global Approach," speech before the Mayor's Advisory Committee on International Relations and Trade and the Foreign Relations Association, New Orleans, February 28, 1974, DSB 70 (January–March, 1974): 277; "Kissinger, in Tanzania Case, Affirms Curbs on Ambassadors," *New York Times*, August 18, 1975, 4. See also Linda Charlton, "Kissinger Queried on Envoy's Future," *New York Times*, August 20, 1975, 5; "Kissinger News Conference," Vail, Colorado, August 17, 1975, DSB 73 (July–September, 1975): 407–408; and "Policy on Kidnapping and Terrorism," DSB 73 (October–December, 1975): 526.

18. This paragraph is based on Robert Fearey, Special Assistant to the Secretary of State and Coordinator for Combating Terrorism, "International Terrorism," An address before the World Affairs Councils of Los Angeles and Orange County, February 19, 1976, DSB 74 (March 29, 1976): 394–403. Information on the Nuclear Emergency Support Team is drawn from Larry Collins, "Combating Nuclear Terrorism," *New York Times Magazine*, December 14, 1980, 38; Walter Laqueur, *The Age of Terrorism* (Boston: Little, Brown and Company, 1987), 312–317, provides information on the efforts of terrorist groups in the 1970s to get nuclear materials and chemical and biological agents.

19. Rubin, *Revolution Until Victory?*, 39–40; Livingstone and Halevy, *Inside the PLO*, 283; Dobson and Payne, *The Never-Ending War*, 317 and 319; Henry Kissinger, *Years of Upheaval* (Boston: Little, Brown and Company, 1982), 1037. For a depiction of the pattern of terrorist attacks over the years, see *Patterns of Global Terrorism, 1995* (The Department of State, Washington, D.C., 1996), 71.

20. Kissinger, *Years of Upheaval*, 624–625, 627, 629, 1036–1037.

21. Mickolus, *Transnational Terrorism*, 389–390, 439, 506, 508; Duncan, "Terrorist Attacks on U.S. Official Personnel Abroad," 34, 35, 37.

22. Fearey, "International Terrorism," DSB 74 (March 29, 1976): 396; Laurence Gonzales, "The Targeting of America: A Special Report on Terrorism," *Playboy* (May, 1983) 180; U.S. Congress, Senate, Subcommittee on Foreign Assistance of the Committee on Foreign Relations, *International Terrorism*, Comments of Brian Jenkins, 95th Congress, 1st session, September 14, 1977, 67; Celmer, *Terrorism*, 17; and James B. Motley, "U.S. Counterterrorist Policy: An Analysis of its Strategy and Organization" (Ph. D. diss., The Catholic University, 1982), 62; American Society of International Law (ASIL), "Legal Aspects of International Terrorism," February, 1977.

23. U.S. National Security Council, *The United States Government Antiterrorism Program: An Unclassified Summary Report* (Washington, D.C., 1979), 2.

24. The State Department's management of foreign incidents is based both in law (22 USC 2651) and on Presidential decision (Presidential message of October 25, 1977 to all overseas posts); James B. Motley, *US Strategy to Counter Domestic Political Terrorism* (Washington, D.C.: National Defense University Press, 1983), 39. Information in this paragraph is taken from the testimony of Ambassador Anthony Quainton, Director, Office for Combating Terrorism, in Hearings on Federal Capabilities in Crisis Management and Terrorism, before the Subcommittee on Civil and Constitutional Rights of the Committee on the Judiciary, House of Representatives, 95th Congress, Second Session, September 15, 1978, 34–37.

25. Quainton testimony, September 15, 1978, 34–37.

26. William Regis Farrell, *The U.S. government Response to Terrorism, In Search of an Effective Strategy* (Boulder, Colorado: Westview Press, 1982), 42–43. Farrell's descriptions differ in minor ways from those given by Ambassador Quainton in his testimony cited in note 24. Information on the Working Group was provided by Lieutenant General WIlliam Odom, U.S. Army (Retired), formerly on the NSC staff, January 14, 1994 and a State Department official, October 26, 1993.

27. Mickolus, *Transnational Terrorism,* 274, 407–408.

28. Interviews with Odom, January 14, 1994, and a State Department official, October 26, 1993.

29. Consider the testimony of Secretary of State Vance before Congress, DSB 78 (January–June, 1978): 53–54, and Ambassador Anthony Quainton, "Terrorism: Do Something! But What?", based on an address before the Cleveland Council on World Affairs, May 22, 1979, DSB 79 (September, 1979): 60–64, especially 61 and 63.

30. Brian L. Davis, *Qadaffi, Terrorism, and the Origins of the U.S. Attack on Libya* (New York: Praeger, 1990), 10–14; Rubin, *Revolution Until Victory?,* 31; David A. Flores, "Export Controls and the U.S. Effort to Combat International Terrorism," *Law and Policy in International Business* 13 (1981): 573; "Deputy Under Secretary Macomber Discusses Terrorism in Interview on *Today* Program," DSB 68 (April, 1973): 401; Paul Wilkinson, *Terrorism and the Liberal State,* 2nd ed. (New York: New York University Press, 1986), 187 quotes the CIA research report as do David C. Martin and John Walcott, *Best Laid Plans, The Inside Story of America's War Against Terrorism* (New York: Harper and Row, 1988), 51; Fearey, "International Terrorism," DSB 74 (March 29, 1976): 402; John E. Karkashian, Acting Director of the Office for Combating Terrorism, "Dealing with International Terrorism," a Statement before the Subcommittee on Foreign Assistance of the Senate Committee on Foreign relations, September 14, 1977, DSB 77(October–December, 1977): 608; Secretary Cyrus Vance, "Terrorism: Scope of the Threat and Need for Effective Legislation," DSB 78 (January June, 1978): 53–54; interview with State Department official, October 26, 1993.

31. Erin Day, "Economic Sanctions Imposed by the United States against Specific Countries: 1979 through 1992," Congressional Research Service Report to Congress, August 10, 1992, 624–625; Flores, "Export Controls and the U.S. Effort to Combat International Terrorism," 553–554, 539–543, 563; testimony of Ambassador Anthony Quainton before the Subcommittee on Aviation of the Committee on Public Works and Transportation, the House of Representatives, 96th Congress, 1st Session, February 29, 1979, 86–88 and 94–96.

32. "PLF Head Regrets Klinghofer Murder, Hijacking," *Al–Diyar,* September 13, 1994, 21 in Foreign Broadcast Information Service, *Terrorism,* (FBIS), October 5, 1994,

20; "U.S. Delays Sales Made to Libyans, Curbs on Others Studied in Drive on Terrorist Aid," *New York Times*, June 24, 1978, 25.

33. Lieutenant Colonel Tom Hamrick, "The Black Berets," *Army* 27 (May, 1977): 29–31; "U.S. Is Training Units to Fight Terrorists," *New York Times*, October 20, 1977, 17; Quainton, "Terrorism: Do Something! But What?," 61 and 63; and "Antiterrorist Policy of U.S. Held Weak," *New York Times*, April 23, 1978, 1, which describes these new special units.

34. Ambassador Anthony Quainton, statement before the Subcommittee on Civil and Constitutional Rights of the House Judiciary Committee, held in Newark, New Jersey, May 19, 1980, DSB 80 July, 1980), 75–77.

35. David Binder, "U.S. Revises Antiterrorist System, but Some Question Preparedness, Congressional and Government Specialists Say New Lines of Command Are Too Diffuse," *New York Times*, January 9, 1978, A14 and David Binder, "Antiterrorist Policy of U.S. Held Weak," *New York Times*, April 23, 1978, A1.

36. *Patterns of International Terrorism: 1980*, 1, 2, 8, 9, iii, 4; Duncan, "Terrorist Attacks on U.S. Official Personnel Abroad," 34–37; Mickolus, *Transnational Terrorism*, 820.

37. Information on the achievements of the Carter administration is drawn from interviews with a State Department official, October 26, 1994, and Odom, January 14, 1995 and May 6, 1996, and from Larry Collins, "Combating Nuclear Terrorism," *New York Times Magazine*, December 14, 1980, 38.

38. Interviews with Odom, January 14, 1994, and a State Department official, October 26, 1993.

39. Zbigniew Brzezinski, *Power and Principle, Memoirs of the National Security Adviser, 1977–1981* (New York: Farrar, Straus, Giroux, 1983), 81–82, 193–194, 401–402 and "President Carter's Farewell Address to the Nation," DSB 81 (February, 1981): 22–23.

40. "U.S. Is Said to Plan a New Approach on Terrorism," *New York Times*, March 27, 1976, 3; "Comments by the DOD Working Group Representatives on the RAND Study 'Dealing with Political Kidnapping,'" DOD Memorandum, 1977; State Department official, October 26, 1993; "U.S. Asks Talks in Bogota Siege," *Washington Post*, March 4, 1980, A12. On President Carter's attitude toward negotiating in hostage situations, see Simon, *The Terrorism Trap*, 123–125.

41. John Vinocur, "Terrorism: Almost a Commonplace," *New York Times*, December 30, 1979, section 12, 3; Margot Hornblower, "More Terrorism as 'Surrogate Warfare' Seen," *Washington Post*, November 22, 1979, A19.

42. State Department official, October 26, 1993.

43. For the text of the Carter-Reagan exchange on terrorism, see *New York Times*, October 29, 1980, A27.

44. "Secretary Haig's News Conference of January 28," DSB 81 (February, 1981), Special Section, J; "Haig, Leaving NATO, Charges Communists Encourage Terrorism," *New York Times*, June 30, 1979, 3; Bernard Gwertzman, "Administration Assails Making of Hostage Deal," *New York Times*, February 19, 1981, A1, A10; State Department official, October 26, 1993.

45. Edward Walsh, "Muskie and Christopher Dispute Non-Negotiation Policy," *Washington Post*, February 20, 1981, A6; Philip Taubman, "U.S. Tries to back Up Haig on Terrorism," *New York Times*, May 3, 1981, 1; Martin and Walcott, *Best Laid Plans*, 51–56; "Senator Condemns I.R.A. as Marxist," *New York Times*, June 12, 1981, 2. For the definition of terrorism, see *Patterns of Global Terrorism: 1995*, p. vi.

46. Martin and Walcott, *Best Laid Plans,* 53; Angelo Codevilla, *Informing Statecraft, Intelligence for a New Century* (New York: Free Press, 1992), 187–239.

47. "Soviets Armed Terrorists, Russian Documents Show," *Stars and Stripes,* May 27, 1992, 1–2; Michael Dobbs, "Russian Says Soviets Aided Terrorists," *Washington Post,* May 26, 1992, A1; Wilkinson, *Terrorism and the Liberal State,* 188–189, gives other examples of Soviet support for terrorism; "Unequal Brothers in the Struggle against the Same Enemy," *Die Welt,* April 16, 1991, 3 in FBIS, June 27, 1991, 27–28; Piotr Jakucki, "Arms Trade Secrets: Polish Generals Aided Terrorists," *Gazeta Polska,* January 26, 1995, 1,3 in FBIS, March 10, 1995, 49–50; Lester W. Grau, "Supporting 'Carlos the Jackal': Recent Materials from the former 'Soviet Bloc'," *Low–Intensity Conflict and Law Enforcement* 1 (Summer, 1992): 92–101 provides a useful summary of Eastern European support for terrorism that covers more than just Carlos.

48. Claire Sterling, *The Terror Network, The Secret War of International Terrorism* (New York: Holt, Rhinehart and Winston, 1981), 10, cf. 84; "The Desperadoes' Camp," *Der Spiegel,* January 16, 1995, 72, in FBIS, March 10, 1995, 47.

49. "Mielke, Too, Did Not Know Anything About the Bomb," *Berliner Zeitung,* March 26–27, 1994 [no page], in FBIS, April 8, 1994, 47; "Syrian Diplomat to be Charged in Attack on Berlin French Center," DPA, April 29, 1994 in FBIS, May 5, 1994, 3; "Shritah: 'I Was Not the Embassy Chieftain,'" *Neues Deutschland,* February 15, 1994, 10, in FBIS, March 1, 1994, 5; "International Terrorist Leader Arrested in Vienna," *Neue Kronen–Zeitung,* October 27, 1994, 6–7, in FBIS, November 10, 1994, 6; "Terrorist Chief and Carlos' Accomplice Still Imprisoned in Austria," *Neue Kronen–Zeitung,* November 7, 1994, 15 in FBIS, November 30, 1994, 7; "Great Excitement over Suspected Syrian Terrorist," *Die Presse,* November 24, 5, in FBIS, December 12, 1994, 44–45; "Arrested Syrian Diplomat Permitted to Leave Country," Deutsche Presse Agentur, November 24, 1994, in FBIS, December 12, 1994, 44; "Government Officials Discuss Carlos' Hungarian Activities," Budapest Kossuth Radio Network, August 16, 1994, in FBIS, August 24, 1994, 25.

50. "International Terrorism," statement of Richard T. Kennedy, Under Secretary for Management, Department of State, before the Senate Foreign Relations Committee, June 10, 1981, DSB 81 (September, 1981): 65–67; State Department official, October 26, 1993.

51. *Patterns of International Terrorism: 1981,* Department of State (Washington, D.C., July, 1982), 1, 6.

52. Martin and Walcott, *Best Laid Plans,* 57–66 provide details on the Dozier rescue; Noel Koch, a Defense official involved in counterterrorism in the Reagan administration, October 1, 1993.

53. This paragraph is based on interviews with State Department officials, September 2, 1993 and October 26, 1993, and Koch and Odom, October 1, 1993 and May 6, 1996, respectively. Martin and Walcott, *Best Laid Plans,* 48, give background on the staffer.

54. This paragraph is based on interviews with a State Department official, September 2, 1993, and Koch, October 1, 1993.

55. This paragraph is based on an interview with Koch, October 1, 1993 and an intelligence official December 8, 1993. Martin and Walcott, *Best Laid Plans,* 64–65, describe one of these incidents.

56. Koch, October 1, 1993.

57. Koch, October 1, 1993; State Department official, September 2, 1993.

58. Karkashian, "Dealing with International Terrorism," DSB 77 (October–December, 1977): 609; *Patterns of International Terrorism: 1980,* 8, 21; *Patterns of Global*

Terrorism: 1989, 4; Dobson and Payne, *The Never-Ending War*, 309, 312; Edward F. Mickolus, Todd Sandler, and Jean M. Murdock, *International Terrorism in the 1980s, A Chronology of Events, Volume I, 1980–1983* (Ames, Iowa: Iowa State University Press, 1989), 233–234.

59. For two very different views of the Phoenix program, see Dale Andrade, *Ashes to Ashes: The Phoenix Program and the Vietnam War* (Lexington, Massachusetts: Lexington Books, 1990) and Douglas Valentine, *The Phoenix Program* (New York: Morrow, 1990). This paragraph is based on interviews with Koch, October 1, 1993, and an intelligence official, October 26, 1993. See also Drew Middleton, "U.S. Called Ill-Equipped to Fight 'On the Cheap' War by Terrorists, Military Seeks Solutions," *New York Times*, December 29, 1983, A1, A15; Richard Harwood, Bob Woodward, and Christian Williams, "Covert Hit Teams Might Evade Presidential Ban," *Washington Post*, February 12, 1984, A16; David Ignatius, "U.S. Readies Anti-Terrorism Policy," *Wall Street Journal*, March 12, 1984, 32; and George C. Wilson, "Risks from Retaliation Enjoin Caution," *Washington Post*, December 11, 1984, A10.

60. This paragraph is based on interviews with Koch, October 1, 1993, an intelligence official, October 26, 1993, and a State Department official, September 2, 1993.

61. Secretary George Shultz, "Power and Diplomacy in the 1980s," address before the Trilateral Commission, April 3, 1984, DSB 84 (May, 1984): 12–15; "Terrorism: The Challenge to the Democracies," address before the Jonathan Institute's Second Conference on International Terrorism, June 24, 1984, DSB 84 (August, 1984): 31–34; "Terrorism and the Modern World," Address before the Park Avenue Synagogue in New York City, October 25, 1984, DSB 84 (December, 1984): 12–17; "U.S. government and Business: Our Common Defense Against Terrorism," DSB 85 (March, 1985): 10–12.

62. Secretary George Shultz, "The Campaign against Drugs: The International Dimension," an address before the Miami Chamber of Commerce, Miami, Florida, September 14, 1984, DSB 84 (November, 1984): 31–32. For further details on narco-terrorism, including the involvement of Palestinian groups, see Rachel Ehrenfeld, *Narco-Terrorism* (New York: Basic Books, 1990).

63. George P. Shultz, *Turmoil and Triumph, My Years as Secretary of State* (New York: Scribner's, 1993), 648–651; Robert M. Sayre, "International Terrorism: A Long Twilight Struggle," an address before the Foreign Policy Association in New York, August 15, 1984, DSB 84 (October, 1984): 48–50; Leslie H. Gelb, "Administration Debating Antiterrorist Measures," *New York Times*, June 6, 1984, A6. For the legal concerns raised by preemption, see Martin and Walcott, *Best Laid Plans*, 66.

64. Information on Hizbollah is drawn from John L. Esposito, *The Islamic Threat, Myth or Reality?* (New York: Oxford University Press, 1992), 145–148, and Carl Anthony Wege, "Hizbollah Organization," *Studies in Conflict and Terrorism* 17 (April–June, 1994): 151–164. For Iran's motives in undertaking terrorism, see Shireen T. Hunter, "Terrorism: A Balance Sheet," *Washinton Quarterly* 12 (Summer, 1989): 21–23. The definition of terrorism is taken from *Patterns of Global Terrorism: 1985* (Department of State, Washington, D.C., 1986).

65. Gelb, "Administration Debating Antiterrorist Measures," A6; George P. Shultz, "U.S. government and Business: Our Common Defense Against Terrorism," an address before the American Society for Industrial Security in Arlington, Virginia, February 4, 1985, DSB 85 (March, 1985): 12.

66. *Patterns of Global Terrorism, 1993*, 69; Edward F. Mickolus, Todd Sandler, and Jean M. Murdock, *International Terrorism in the 1980s, A Chronology of Events,*

Volume II, 1984–1987 (Ames, Iowa: Iowa State University Press, 1989), 162, 163, 190, 227, 238, 248–249, 255, 270, 300.

67. Mickolus, Sandler, and Murdock, *International Terrorism in the 1980s, Chronology of Events, Volume II, 1984–1987*, 219–225, 282–288, 325–328; Piotr Jakucki, "Arms Trade Secrets: Polish Generals Aided Terrorists," *Gazeta Polska*, January 26, 1995, 1, 3, in FBIS, March 10, 1995, 49–50.

68. David Ignatius, "A Clear Plan to Handle Terrorism Still Eludes Divided Reagan Camp," *Wall Street Journal*, June 6, 1985, A1; intelligence official, October 26, 1993, and Koch, October 1, 1993.

69. Interview with Duane Clarridge, who was involved in establishing the CTC and ran it, January 6, 1994, and with other CIA officials, October 26, 1993, December 2, 1993, and December 8, 1993. These other officials were all part of the CTC effort and remain well disposed to it. Another CIA official (interviewed on February 2, 1994), who had worked in several of the Directorate of Operation's regional divisions, thought that the CTC's successes had been overrated. Among participants in interagency counterterrorism efforts, the CTC appeared to be generally well regarded.

70. This and the following paragraph are based on interviews with former members of the interagency group from all of the agencies involved who served on it at some point from 1986 to the early 1990s.

71. This paragraph is based on interviews with former civilian members of the interagency group who served on it at some point from 1986 to the early 1990s, particularly with an NSC representative, November 8, 1993.

72. Ambassador Robert Oakley, October 1, 1993, who was Ambassador-at-large for Counterterrorism from 1984 to 1986.

73. For the Nixon administration, see supra, p. 7; for background on the raid, see Robert Venkus, *Raid on Qaddafi: The Untold Story of History's Longest Fighter Mission by the Pilot who Directed It* (New York: St. Martin's Press, 1992). Accounts of the political effects of the raid are based on interviews with Oakley, October 1, 1993, and another State Department official, October 13, 1993. In this regard, see also James M. Markham, "Europe's Anti-Terrorism Tied to U.S. Libya Raids," *New York Times,* April 14, 1987, A8. The East German document was printed in *Die Welt*, April 16, 1991, FBIS, June 27, 1991, 29.

74. *Terrorist Group Profiles* (Washington, D.C., 1988), 5–8; *Patterns of Global Terrorism, 1993*, 37; William M. Carley, "Their Secrets Revealed, Abu Nidal's Terrorists Are Becoming Targets," *Wall Street Journal*, October 15, 1987, A1; E. A. Wayne, "Three Arabs Held in Peru Tied to Terrorism," *Los Angeles Times*, July 31, 1988, section I, 23.

75. This account of the ANO operation and its results is based on interviews with former CTC officials and analysts, December 8, 1993 and January 6, 1994, as well as interviews with Oakley, October 1, 1993, and another State Department official, November 23, 1993. See also William M. Carley, "Terrorist Group Has Financial Operation at Warsaw Company," *Wall Street Journal*, October 15, 1987, 24; John Tagliabue, "Poland Says It Expelled Reported Abu Nidal Aide," *New York Times*, January 26, 1988, 10A; "Poland Withdraws License of Firm Linked to Abu Nidal Terrorists," *Los Angeles Times*, January 27, 1988, section I, 10.

76. Analyst, State Department, Bureau of Intelligence and Research, June 6, 1994.

77. This paragraph is based on interviews with an FBI official, January 7, 1994, two State Department officials, October 13, 1993 and November 23, 1993, and a CIA official, December 8, 1993.

78. Interview with former Justice Department official, January 4, 1994, and an FBI official, December 15, 1994.

79. Interview with FBI officials, December 15, 1993 and January 7, 1994, and with a CIA official, December 8, 1993.

80. Stephen Engelberg, "U.S. Said to Weigh Abducting Terrorists Abroad for Trials Here," *New York Times,* January 1, 1986, A1; Stephen Engelberg, "Washington's War on Terrorism Captures Few Soldiers," *New York Times,* March 5, 1989, section 4, 3.

81. Kenneth B. Noble, "Lebanese Suspect in '85 Hijacking Arrested by the F.B.I. While at Sea," *New York Times,* September 18, 1987, A1; Engelberg, "Washington's War on Terrorism Captures Few Soldiers," *New York Times,* March 5, 1989, section 4, 3; interview with FBI official, December 15, 1993 and CIA official, December 18, 1993.

82. This paragraph is based on interviews with FBI officials, November 23, 1993 and January 7, 1994.

83. Interview with former NSC official, November 8, 1993, and with FBI official, November 23, 1993.

84. Interview with senior member of the Vice-President's Task Force, November 29, 1993. On the CIA's covert efforts, see David Ignatius, "A Clear Plan to Handle Terrorism Still Eludes Divided Reagan Camp," *Wall Street Journal,* June 20, 1985, A1 and Martin and Walcott, *Best Laid Plans,* 219–220. For typical State and Defense Department comments on terrorism as criminality, see *Patterns of Global Terrorism, 1995,* iv, and Army FM 100–20 (December, 1990), 3–6; William S. Sessions, "The FBI's Mission in Countering Terrorism," a speech given before the National Strategy Forum, Chicago, Illinois, February 15, 1990, *Terrorism* 13 (January–February, 1990): 6.

85. For the lower bureaucratic profile of counterterrorism in the Bush Administration, see Peter Flory, "Keeping Counter-Terrorism a Serious Priority," *Washington Times,* April 20, 1994, A19.

86. David Hoffman and Jackson Diehl, "Larger Trends May Help Explain Recent Hostage Releases," *Washington Post,* December 3, 1991, A12; interview with President George Bush, January 26, 1993.

87. Neil A. Lewis, "U.S. Officials Clash at Hearing on Power to Seize Fugitives," *New York Times,* November 9, 1989, A10; *Report to the President by the President's Commission on Aviation Security and Terrorism* (Washington, D.C., 1990), i; interview with a former NSC official, November 8, 1993, and a former Joint Staff officer, October 18, 1993.

88. For the decline in terrorist incidents, see *Patterns of Global Terrorism: 1995* (Department of State, Washington, D.C., 1996), 1.

89. John Dillon, "The Next Nuclear Warriors: Terrorists," *The Boston Globe,* May 5, 1996, 32; R. Jeffrey Smith, "Counter-Terrorism to Be Olympic Event for U.S.," *Washington Post,* April 23, 1996, A9. For the new terrorist groups, see David B. Ottaway and Steve Coll, "Retracing the Steps of a Terror Suspect, Accused Bomb Builder Tied to Many Plots," *Washington Post,* June 5, 1995, A1. For official concern about terrorism and the debate over how to respond, see David B. Ottaway, "U.S. Considers Slugging It Out With International Terrorism," *Washington Post,* October 17, 1996, p. A25.

90. Interviews with Oakley, October 1, 1993, and another former State Department official, October 13, 1993.

91. Jack Anderson, "Falling Oil Prices May Lessen Terrorism," *Washington Post,* May 24, 1986, E11; John F. Burns, "Andropov Assails Economic Failings of Soviet System," *New York Times,* December 29, 1983, A1; Philip Taubman, "Pentagon's

Inquiry Blames Major Marine Commanders and Faulty Policy in Beirut," *New York Times*, December 29, 1983, A1; Peter Schweizer, *Victory, the Reagan Administration's Secret Strategy that Hastened the Collapse of the Soviet Union* (New York: Atlantic Monthly Press, 1994), 31–32.

92. "Peru Gives Life Term to American," *Washington Post*, January 12, 1996, A18.

CHAPTER 2

1. Walter Laqueur, *The Age of Terrorism* (Boston: Little, Brown and Company, 1987) 72, 142–150.

2. Secretary George Shultz, "Terrorism: The Challenge to the Democracies," address before the Jonathan Institute's Second Conference on International Terrorism, June 24, 1984, DSB 84 (August, 1984): 31–34; Title 22, U.S. Code, Section 2656f(d). This section also defines international terrorism as "terrorism involving citizens or the territory of more than one country." U.S. Code, Title 18, Section 2331; Federal Bureau of Investigation, *Terrorism in the United States* (Washington, D.C., 1994), 24; Defense Department Directive 0–2000.12 [reference a]); JCS Pub 1–02, *Department of Defense Dictionary of Military and Associated Terms* (Washington, D.C., 1989), 370; *Patterns of Global Terrorism, 1995*, (Washington, D.C: Department of State, 1996), vi.

3. The analysis of definitions is in Alex P. Schmid, *Political Terrorism: A Research Guide to Concepts, Theories, Data Bases and Literature* (Amsterdam: North-Holland, 1983), 76–77.

4. Scott Bowles and Pierre Thomas, "FBI Takes 'a Look' At N.Y. Faction of Japanese Cult," *Washington Post*, March 24, 1995, A25.

5. John Lancaster, "Tourists Return to Egypt as Islamic Violence Wanes," *Washington Post*, September 12, 1995, A15.

6. For example, David C. Rapoport, "Fear and Trembling: Terrorism in Three Religious Traditions," *American Political Science Review* 78 (September, 1984): 659, 674–675.

7. David B. Ottoway and Steve Coll, "Retracing the Steps of a Terror Suspect," *Washington Post,* June 5, 1995, A15; *The Economist*, "Terror in Tokyo," March 25, 1995, 37; John Schwartz, "Chipping in to Curb Computer Crime," *Washington Post*, February 19, 1995, A1; Carin Rubenstein, "Educators Urged to Address Sexual Harassment in School," *New York Times*, July 15, 1994, B1; Tim Weiner, "U.S. Intelligence Officials Baffled over Possible Motives," *New York Times,* March 21, 1995, A12; Charles W. Hall, "Rush Hour Protest Assailed, Rep. Davis Urges D. C. to Stiffen Penalties on 'Traffic Terrorism,'" *Washington Post*, October 7, 1995, B1; Leon Panetta, President Clinton's Chief of Staff, quoted on National Public Radio broadcast, November 10, 1995 and in *Washington Post*, November 11, 1995, A1; Mark W. Edington, "Terror Made Easy," *New York Times*, March 4, 1994, A27.

8. Bruce Hoffman, "'Holy Terror': The Implications of Terrorism Motivated by a Religious Imperative," P–7834, (Santa Monica, California: RAND, 1993), describes it as less restrained and more lethal, 2–3; Rapoport, "Fear and Trembling," 660, as less rational.

9. David George, "Distinguishing Classical Tyrannicide from Modern Terrorism," *Review of Politics*, 50 (Summer, 1980): 390–419.

10. George Shultz, "Terrorism: The Challenge to the Democracies," an address before the Jonathan Institute's Second Conference on International Terrorism, June 24, 1984, DSB 84 (August, 1984), 32. For a detailed analysis of the Declaration of

Independence, see Harry V. Jaffa, *Crisis of the House Divided, An Interpretation of the Issues in the Lincoln-Douglas Debates* (Chicago: University of Chicago Press, 1959; with a new Preface, 1982).

11. Sharon Waxman, "France's Release of Iranians Triggers Swiss Complaint," *Washington Post*, January 1, 1994, A15; Steve Vogel, "Allies Oppose Bonn's Iran Links," *Washington Post*, November 6, 1993, A18.

12. Leo Strauss, *The City and Man* (Chicago: Rand McNally, 1964), 75–76.

13. *Patterns of Global Terrorism, 1990* (Department of State, Washington, D.C., 1991), 36. For similar examples, see "Cuban UN Delegates Differentiate Terrorism, Self–Determination," in FBIS, October 29, 1993, 6, quoting a Havana Radio Progreso Network report, October 21, 1993.

14. John R. Stevenson, "International Law and the Export of Terrorism," an address before the Bar of the City of New York, November 9, 1972, DSB 67 (December 1972): 646; *Washington Post*, February 3, 1994, A22. For other examples of references by U.S. officials to terrorism as violence against innocents, see Robert Fearey, Special Assistant to the Secretary of State and Coordinator for Combating Terrorism, "International Terrorism," An address before the World Affairs Councils of Los Angeles and Orange County, February 19, 1976, DSB 74 (March 29, 1976): 399, 403; Ambassador Anthony Quainton, "Terrorism: Do Something! But What?", based on an address before the Cleveland Council on World Affairs, May 22, 1979, DSB 79 (September, 1979): 60; Frank H. Perez, "The Impact of International Terrorism," an address before the Conference on Violence and Extremism, October 29, 1981, DSB 82 (January, 1982): 55; George Shultz, "Terrorism: The Challenge to the Democracies," an address before the Jonathan Institute's Second Conference on International Terrorism, June 24, 1984, DSB 84 (August, 1984): 32.

15. Michael Walzer, *Just and Unjust Wars, a Moral Argument with Historical Illustrations* (New York, 1977), 254.

16. Laqueur, *The Age of Terrorism*, 139.

17. Interviews with Noel Koch, former Defense Department official involved in counterterrorism, October 1, 1993, and another Defense Department official, November 30, 1993.

18. Donald J. Hanle, *Terrorism, The Newest Face of Warfare* (McLean, Virginia: Pergamon–Brassey's International Defense Publishers, Inc., Mclean Virginia, 1989), 115.

19. Hanle, *Terrorism*, 59.

20. Grand strategy can include efforts to destroy capabilities. A war or a series of wars may be part of a grand strategy, but the strategy is not reducible to the wars.

21. Hanle, *Terrorism*, 153.

CHAPTER 3

1. *History and Impact of U.S. Terrorism Policy, 1972–1984* (McLean, Virginia: Defense Systems, Inc., July 22, 1985), 1–2, 2–14, 2–21, 22.

2. *Patterns of Global Terrorism, 1995* (Washington, D.C.: Department of State, 1996), iv provides a rough guide to the importance that the U.S. government attaches to these methods of combating terrorism.

3. Bernard Gwertzman, "Administration Assails Making of Hostage Deal," *New York Times*, February 19, 1981, 1.

4. Richard Clutterbuck, "Negotiating with Terrorists," *Terrorism and Political Violence* 4 (Winter, 1990): 285.

5. Clutterbuck, "Negotiating with Terrorists," 285; *The Impact of Government Behavior on Frequency, Type, and Targets of Terrorist Group Activity*, (McLean, Virginia: Defense Systems, Inc., December 15, 1982), 8–15; Martha Crenshaw, "How Terrorism Declines," *Terrorism and Political Violence* 3 (Spring, 1991), 74, 79.

6. *The Impact of Government Behavior on Frequency, Type, and Targets of Terrorist Group Activity: The West German Experience, 1968–1982* (McLean, Virginia: Defense Systems, Inc., December 15, 1983), xiv.

7. *The Impact of Government Behavior on Frequency, Type, and Targets of Terrorist Group Activity: The West German Experience, 1968–1982*, xiv, 52–53; *Patterns of Global Terrorism, 1995* (Washington, D.C.: Department of State, April, 1996), iv.

8. Harvey E. Lapan and Todd Sandler, "To Bargain or Not to Bargain: That is the Question," *American Economic Review* 78 (May, 1988): 17–18.

9. Edward F. Mickolus, "Negotiating for Hostages: A Policy Dilemma," in *Contemporary Terrorism, Selected Readings*, eds. John D. Elliott and Leslie K. Gibson (Gaithersburg, Maryland: International Association of Chiefs of Police, 1978), 214–216 offers a useful discussion of these points.

10. Jonathan S. Landay, "Terrorism's Sponsors Aim at Mideast, US," *Christian Science Monitor*, May 16, 1995, 3; David E. Sanger, "U.S. Revising North Korea Strategy," *New York Times*, November 22, 1993, 5.

11. Daniel Pipes, "Why Asad's Terrorism Works and Qadafhi's Does Not," *Orbis* 33 (Fall, 1989): 501–508.

12. Martin Hughes, "Terror and Negotiation," *Terrorism and Political Violence*, 2 (Spring, 1990): 74.

13. Howard Kurtz, "Unabomber Manuscript Is Published," *Washington Post*, September 19, 1995, A1; Serge F. Kovaleski and Pierre Thomas, "Brother Hired Own Investigator," *The Washington Post*, April 9, 1996, A7.

14. Alvin Hugh Buckelew, *Terrorism and the American Response: An Analysis of the Mechanism Used by the Government of the United States in Dealing with National and International Terrorism*, Ph.D. dissertation, Golden Gate University, 1982, 186.

15. *Patterns of Global Terrorism, 1995*, 28.

16. Hughes, "Terror and Negotiation," 82, along with many insightful comments, makes the unfortunate suggestion that all issues can be compromised. It is probably no coincidence that he describes Thomas Hobbes as "the greatest philosopher of conflict," 73. Hobbes was the first and may be the only philosopher to suggest that cowardice is a virtue.

17. Every past or present official interviewed for this study, with one exception, held that the policy of no concessions was critical to dealing successfully with terrorism. All those who supported "no concessions," however, accepted that it was most relevant for hostage situations or others where a direct quid pro quo was at issue. Some expressed the fear that modifying the policy would be seen as weakness.

18. This discussion of justifications for the judicial response to terrorism is based on interviews with former or current officials from the Departments of State, Justice, and Defense and the Central Intelligence Agency. David Long, *The Anatomy of Terrorism*, (New York: The Free Press, 1990), 152 provides a good discussion of how the judicial approach encourages cooperation among nations.

19. *Patterns of Global Terrorism, 1995*, 2, 26.

20. *Patterns of Global Terrorism, 1992*, iv. *Patterns of Global Terrorism, 1995*, iv, lists "treat terrorists as criminals, pursue them aggressively, and apply the rule of law" as one of the three general rules of U.S. counterterrorism policy.

21. This discussion of the limitations of the judicial approach is based on interviews with current or former officials of the FBI and the Departments of Justice and State. See also Abraham D. Sofaer, "Fighting Terrorism through Law," an address before the American Bar Association Convention, London, July 15, 1985, DSB 85 (October, 1985): 38–42 and Alfred P. Rubin, "Current Legal Approaches to International Terrorism," *Terrorism*, 13 (July–August, 1990): 282–283. For the difficulties of investigating TWA Flight 800, see Don Van Natta, Jr., "FBI Fear: Ocean Won't Yield Bomb Clue," *New York Times*, August 16, 1996, A1 and Serge F. Kovaleski and Don Phillips, "Proof of Explosive Eludes Probers in TWA Crash," *Washington Post*, September 3, 1996, A1.

22. Interview with FBI official, December 15, 1993.

23. Information on pressure within the U.S. government to lift the sanctions against Syria derived from interviews with officials involved with terrorism at the time the sanctions were in place. On the UN and Sudan, see John M. Goshko, "UN Remains Reluctant to Impose Tough Sanctions on Sudan for Terrorist Links," *Washington Post*, November 24, 1996, A32.

24. R. Jeffrey Smith, "Iraqi Officer Recruited Suspects in Plot Against Bush, U.S. Says," *Washington Post*, July 1, 1993, A18; "Commander for a Day," *The Economist*, July 3, 1993, 25.

25. Sofaer, "Fighting Terrorism through Law," 38–42; Walter Berns, "The Case against World Government," in *Readings in World Politics* ed. Robert Goldwin (New York, 1968), 531–544; Samuel P. Huntington, "The West Unique, Not Universal," *Foreign Affairs* 75 (November/December, 1996), 28–46; Michael Reisman, "No Man's Land: International Legal Regulation of Coercive Responses to Protracted and Low Level Conflict," *Houston Journal of International Law*, 11 (Spring, 1989): 317–330.

26. Rubin, "Current Legal Approaches to International Terrorism," 290–291.

27. This definition of sanctions is based on Gary Clyde Hufbauer, Jeffrey J. Schott, and Kimberly Ann Elliott, *Economic Sanctions Reconsidered, History and Current Policy*, 2nd ed. (Washington, DC: Institute for International Economics, 1990), 2 and the discussion in Michael P. Malloy, *Economic Sanctions and U.S. Trade* (Boston: Little, Brown and Company, 1990), 12–13. David A. Baldwin, *Economic Statecraft* (Princeton, New Jersey: Princeton University Press, 1985), 55–57 cites examples of the conventional wisdom on sanctions. For examples of the conventional wisdom on terrorism and sanctions, see Edward T. Pound, "Sanctions: The Pluses and Minuses," *U.S. News & World Report*, October 31, 1994, 58–71, which reports the remark by Congressman Lantos and Henry Bienen and Robert Gilpin, "Economic Sanctions as a Response to Terrorism," *Journal of Strategic Studies* III (May, 1980), 89–98. David A. Flores offers his assessment of economic sanctions on Libya in "Export Controls and the U.S. Effort to Combat International Terrorism," *Law and Policy in International Business* 13(1981): 589. (Flores wrote this article before the U.S. government prohibited the import of Libyan oil.) For two guardedly favorable analyses of the use of sanctions to combat terrorism, see Jeffrey P. Bialos and Kenneth I. Juster, "The Libyan Sanctions: A Rational Response to State-Sponsored Terrorism?" *Virginia Journal of International Law* 4(Summer, 1986): 799–855, and Kenneth W. Abbott, "Economic Sanctions and International Terrorism," *Vanderbilt Journal of Transnational Law* 2 (March, 1987): 289–328.

28. Baldwin, *Economic Statecraft*, 104–105, 122, 121, 123, 130; Flores, "Export Controls and the U.S. Effort to Combat International Terrorism," 589–590.

29. Baldwin, *Economic Statecraft*, 130–134, 24.

30. Malloy, *Economic Sanctions and U.S. Trade*, 636–637, 634, 626.

31. References in this and following paragraphs to the numbers and dates of sanctions are taken from Erin Day, "Economic Sanctions Imposed by the United States Against Specific Countries: 1979 through 1992," Congressional Research Service Report to Congress, August 10, 1992.

32. *Patterns of Global Terrorism, 1995* (Washington, D.C.: Department of State, 1996), 24– 26.

33. Malloy, *Economic Sanctions and U.S. Trade*, 646–647. For a similar assessment, see Makio Miyagawa, *Do Economic Sanctions Work?* (New York, St. Martin's Press, 1992), 213–215. Interview Oakley, October 1, 1993, and another State Department official, October 13, 1993.

34. George Moffet, "Strain of Isolation Compels Qadafi to Approach US," *Christian Science Monitor*, November 9, 1994, 1, quoting Henry Schuler of the Center for Strategic and International Studies.

35. Some of the suggestions that follow as well as others can be found in the literature on sanctions, for example, Hufbauer, Schott, and Elliott, *Economic Sanctions Reconsidered, History and Current Policy*, 94–105 and Malloy, *Economic Sanctions and U.S. Trade*, 671.

36. Brian L. Davis, *Qadaffi, Terrorism and the Origins of the U.S. Attack on Libya* (New York: Praeger, 1990), 6–7.

37. Barry E. Carter, *International Economic Sanctions, Improving the Haphazard U.S. Legal Regime* (New York: Cambridge University Press, 1988), 25 argues that "export controls are not inherently more effective than import controls or financial controls."

38. Miyagawa, *Do Economic Sanctions Work?*, 214.

39. On the possibility of using multilateral sanctions, see Lisa L. Martin, *Coercive Cooperation, Explaining Multilateral Economic Sanctions* (Princeton, New Jersey: Princeton University Press, 1992), 242, 244, 247, 250. For the effort against Iran in 1994, see Peter Waldman, "Iranian Revolution Takes Another Turn, But Where Is It Going?" *Wall Street Journal*, May 11, 1995, A1, 13. On the declining effectiveness of U.S. unilateral sanctions, see Kimberly Ann Elliott, "Economic Sanctions," in *Intervention into the 1990s, U.S. Foreign Policy in the Third World*, 2nd ed., ed. Peter J. Schraeder (Boulder, Colorado: Lynne Rienner, 1992), 110–112. The oil sanctions example is from "A Very Crude Form of Politics," *The Economist*, May 6, 1995, 64. The advice to analyze carefully and the example of Greece are taken from Carter, *International Economic Sanctions, Improving the Haphazard U.S. Legal Regime*, 25 and 16–17, respectively.

40. *National Military Strategy of the United States of America, a Strategy of Flexible and Selective Engagement* (Washington, D.C., 1995), 8–9, 13.

41. Richard N. Haass, *Intervention, the Use of American Military Force in the Post-Cold War World* (Washington, D.C.: The Carnegie Endowment for International Peace, 1994), 91. For the continuing influence of the so-called Powell Doctrine, see Thomas E. Ricks, "Colin Powell's Doctrine on Use of Military Force Is Now Being Questioned by Senior U.S. Officers," *Wall Street Journal*, August 30, 1995, 12.

42. F. J. West, Jr., *The Village* (New York: Harper & Row, 1972).

43. Haass, *Intervention*, 93.

44. For some similar comments on the use of force in Vietnam, see Stephen Peter Rosen, "Vietnam and the American Theory of Limited War," *International Security* 7 (Fall, 1992): 83–113, especially 90–91 and 95–97.

45. The statistics are derived from information supplied by the Defense Intelligence Agency. The incidents include those carried out or thwarted by the discovery or arrest of the terrorists. "Libyan sponsored" means acts carried out by employees of the Libyan government or any group that received training, money, or any support from the Libyan government. The designation "Against Americans" means that the attack was directed at Americans or their property. Figures under this heading do not include those cases in which Americans were injured but they or their property do not appear to have been deliberately targeted.

46. For similar analyses of the effectiveness of the raid on Libya, see Walter Enders, Todd Sandler, and Jon Cauley, "UN Conventions, Technology and Retaliation in the Fight against Terrorism: An Econometric Evaluation," *Terrorism and Political Violence* 2 (Spring, 1990): 100–102, and Walter Enders and Todd Sandler, "The Effectiveness of Antiterrorism Policies: A Vectoral-Autoregression-Intervention Analysis," *American Political Science Review*, 87 (December, 1993): 829–844. Interview with intelligence official, October 26, 1993.

47. *Patterns of Global Terrorism*, 1995, 1.

48. Interview with former State Department official, October 13, 1993.

49. Tim Zimmerman, "Coercive Diplomacy and Libya," in *The Limits of Coercive Diplomacy*, eds. Alexander L. George and William E. Simons (Boulder, Colorado: Westview Press, 1994), 213, 220–221.

50. Ted Robert Gurr, *Minorities at Risk, a Global View of Ethnopolitical Conflicts* (Washington, D.C.: United State Institute of Peace Press, 1993), 98. The movement from grievance to terrorism sketched here is a simplified version of a complex process. For the more detailed picture see, for example, Gurr, *Minorities at Risk,* 34–138 and *Revolutions of the Late Twentieth-Century*, eds. Jack A. Goldstone, Ted Robert Gurr, and Farrokh Moshiri (Boulder, Colorado: Westview Press, 1991), 1–51.

51. Donald Horowitz, *Ethnic Groups in Conflict* (Berkeley: University of California Press, 1985), 196 and 563–566 and Ted Robert Gurr, *Minorities at Risk,* 290, argue that ethnic conflicts are not intractable or, in Horowitz's case, not absolutely so. Nehemia Friedland, "Becoming a Terrorist: Social and Individual Antecedents," in *Terrorism, Roots, Impact, Responses*, ed. Lawrence Howard (New York: Praeger, 1992), 83–84, and Martha Crenshaw, "The Causes of Terrorism," *Comparative Politics*, 13 (July, 1985): 383–392 note the greater prevalence of terrorism in democratic societies.

52. Benjamin Schwarz provides a useful summary of the arguments about income inequality and violence as well as a commentary on them similar to the view expressed here, "A Dubious Strategy in Pursuit of a Dubious Enemy: A Critique of U.S. Post–Cold War Security Policy in the Third World," *Studies in Conflict and Terrorism* 16 (October–December, 1993): 263–302. Gurr, *Minorities at Risk*, 129–130, is the expert quoted.

53. Jerold M. Post, "Terrorist Psycho-logic: Terrorist Behavior as a Product of Psychological Forces," in *Origins of Terrorism, Psychologies, Ideologies, Theologies, States of Mind*, ed. Walter Reich (New York: Cambridge University Press, 1990), 31, and Walter Reich, "Understanding Terrorist Behavior: The Limits and Opportunities of Pyschological Inquiry," in *Origins of Terrorism,* 266.

54. Bruce Hoffman, "The Prevention of Terrorism and Rehabilitation of Terrorists: Some Preliminary Thoughts," P–7059 (Santa Monica, California: The Rand Corporation, 1985), 4. For this argument as it pertains to Islam, see Olivier Roy, *The Failure of Political Islam* (Cambridge: Harvard University Press, 1994), 48–59, and 194.

55. Hoffman, "The Prevention of Terrorism and Rehabilitation of Terrorists," 5.

56. *Patterns of International Terrorism: 1980* (Washington, D.C.: Central Intelligence Agency, 1981), 5; *Patterns of Global Terrorism 1995,* 67. There were 93 attacks on Americans other than government employees in 1980, 92 in 1994.

57. Steven Komarow, "Perry: Saudi Terror Acts Intercepted," *USA Today,* November 29, 1996, 1.

58. Interviews with Oakley, October 1, 1993, and intelligence and State Department officials, December 8, 1993, January 6, 1994, and October 13 and 26, 1993.

59. *Patterns of Global Terrorism: 1994* (Department of State, Washington, D.C., 1995), iii–vi, 1–2. For the new terrorist groups, see David B. Ottaway and Steve Coll, "Retracing the Steps of a Terror Suspect, Accused Bomb Builder Tied to Many Plots," *Washington Post,* June 5, 1995, A1, A15. For the benefits of organization, see William J. Olson, "The Crisis of Governance: Present and Future Challenges," *Terrorism and Political Violence* 6 (Summer, 1994): 152–153.

CHAPTER 4

1. Rick Atkinson, "U.S. Delays Underlined As Disco Bombing Suspect Is Freed in Lebanon," *Washington Post,* August 3, 1994, A19.

2. Anthony Lake, *Third World Radical Regimes: U.S. Policy under Carter and Reagan* (New York: Foreign Policy Association, 1985).

3. Robert Pear and Neil A. Lewis, "The Noriega Fiasco: What Went Wrong," *New York Times,* May 30, 1988, 5; Atkinson, "U.S. Delays Underlined as Disco Bombing Suspect Is Freed in Lebanon," A19.

4. James Q. Wilson, *Bureaucracy, What Government Agencies Do and Why They Do It* (New York: Basic Books, 1989), 371.

5. Pear and Lewis, "The Noriega Fiasco: What Went Wrong," 5. For a Foreign Service Officer's testimony about his colleagues lack of concern for security, see David T. Jones, "State Goes to the Pentagon," *Foreign Service Journal,* 69 (March, 1992), 19.

6. For an example of the State/Commerce split on sanctions, see Ann Devroy, "President Will Ban All Trade with Iran," *Washington Post,* May 1, 1995, A1, 12.

7. Wilson, *Bureaucracy,* 91.

8. Raymond Tanter, *Who's at the Helm? Lessons of Lebanon* (Boulder, Colorado: Westview Press, 1990), 124–125; Cable, United States Liaison Office, Mogadishu, Somalia, April 14, 1994. For another similar discussion of the differences between diplomats and soldiers, see Todd Greentree, *The United States and the Politics of Conflict in the Developing World* (Washington, D.C.: Center for the Study of Foreign Affairs, 1990), 37.

9. Roger Cohen, "A Piecemeal Peace, Contradictions in Bosnia Agreement May Make It Vulnerable to Collapse," *New York Times,* September 28, 1995, 1; Wilson, *Bureaucracy,* 358.

10. "General Says U.S. Has Learned from Grenada Mistakes," *The Washington Times,* August 11, 1994, 8. For Panama, see Richard H. Shultz, Jr., *In the Aftermath of War, US Support for Reconstruction and Nation-Building in Panama Following Just Cause* (Maxwell Air Force Base, Alabama: Air University Press, August, 1993).

11. Tanter, *Who's at the Helm, Lessons of Lebanon,* 72.

12. Michael Dobbs, "U.S. Dragged Closer to Bosnia Involvement," *Washington Post,* May 14, 1995, A21. Pear and Lewis, "The Noriega Fiasco: What Went Wrong," 5.

13. Thomas Jefferson to John Adams, with Enclosure, July 28, 1785, *The Papers of Thomas Jefferson*, ed. Julian P. Boyd (Princeton, New Jersey: Princeton University Press, 1953), vol. 8: 315–320.

14. Dellums is quoted in Barton Gellman, "U.S. Calls Baghdad Raid a Qualified Success," *Washington Post*, June 28, 1993, A13.

15. Henry Kissinger provides a good discussion of the issues raised in this and the preceding paragraph in *Diplomacy* (New York: Simon & Schuster, 1994), 17–24 and 29–55, especially 33–34, 39–40 and 46–47.

16. Colin S. Gray, *War, Peace, and Victory, Strategy and Statecraft for the Next Century* (New York: Simon & Schuster, 1990), 48; Russell Weigley, *The American Way of War* (Bloomington: Indiana University Press, 1977), xix.

17. Bill Gertz, "Aspin's Decision on Tanks Was Political," *Washington Times*, October 3, 1995, 3; John L. Hirsch and Robert Oakley, *Somalia and Operation Restore Hope: Reflections on Peacemaking and Peacekeeping* (Washington, D.C.: U.S. Institute of Peace Press, 1995), 114, 124–129, 150–158. My discussion of policy-operations coordination is heavily indebted to Chris Lamb.

18. This paragraph is based on John Pimlott, "The British Experience," in *The Roots of Counter-insurgency, Armies and Guerrilla Warfare, 1900–1945*, ed. Ian F. W. Beckett (London: Blandford Press, 1988), 19–21. For a similar analysis, see Thomas R. Mockaitis, *British Counterinsurgency, 1919–60* (New York: St. Martin's Press, 1990), 13–14, 63, 69, 138–139.

19. R. Jeffrey Smith, "Cocaine Flow Not Slowed, General Says," *Washington Post*, January 12, 1996, A23.

20. R. Jeffrey Smith, "Ground Rules for Disputed Territory," *Washington Post*, October 26, 1995, A29 provides evidence of ongoing problems between the CIA and the FBI.

21. Thomas W. Lippman, "With Wirth in Position, Old Lines Lose Weight," *Washington Post*, June 30, 1994, A29. On the declining threat from terrorism, consider *Patterns of Global Terrorism, 1995* (Department of State, Washington, DC, 1996), 1.

22. Joe Davidson, "Clinton to Reassign 500 FBI Agents to Fight Terrorism," *Wall Street Journal*, September 4, 1996, p. A16.

23. William L. Waugh, *Terrorism and Emergency Management: Policy and Administration* (New York: Dekker, 1990), 98.

24. Roger B. Porter, *Presidential Decision Making: The Economic Policy Board* (New York: Cambridge University Press, 1980).

25. *Final Report of the Select Committee to Study Governmental Operations with Respect to Intelligence Activities,* The United States Senate, bk. IV (Washington, D.C.:, U.S. government Printing Office, 1976), 37.

CHAPTER 5

1. Robert Pear, "The Noriega Fiasco: What Went Wrong," *New York Times*, May 30, 1988, A1; James Wyllie, *Jane's Intelligence Review* (December, 1985), 554–555.

2. Fareed Zakaria, "A Framework for Interventionism in the Post–Cold War Era," in *U.S. Intervention Policy for the Post–Cold War World, New Challengers and New Responses*, eds. Arnold Kantor and Linton F. Brooks (New York: W. W. Norton and Company, 1994), 193.

3. *National Security Strategy of the United States* (The White House, Washington, D.C.:, 1991), 3–4 and *A National Security Strategy of Engagement and Enlargement* (The White House, Washington, D.C.:, 1996), 11–12.

4. *National Security Strategy of the United States* (1991), v, 13.

5. Edward N. Luttwak, "From Geopolitics to Geo-economics," *The National Interest* 20 (Summer, 1990): 17; *National Security Strategy Report* (1991), 2–3. Richard H. Ullman, "Redefining Security," *International Security* 8 (Summer, 1983), 133. For other references and a summary of their arguments, see Stephen J. Del Rosso, Jr. "The Insecure State: Reflections on 'the State' and 'Security' in a Changing World," *Daedalus* 124 (Spring, 1995): 175–207.

6. Daniel Deudney, "The Case Against Linking Environmental Degradation and National Security," *Millenium* 19(Winter, 1990): 463–465.

7. For Nunn's proposal, see *New York Times*, June 29, 1990, 1, 12; William J. Broad, "U.S. Will Deploy Its Spy Satellites on Nature Mission," *New York Times*, November 27, 1995, 1; *National Security Strategy Report* (1996), 1, 12; Robert Kaplan, "The Coming Anarchy," *The Atlantic Monthly* (February, 1994), 44–76. For the article's influence on the Clinton administration, see Jeremy D. Rosner, "Is Chaos America's Real Enemy?," *Washington Post*, August 14, 1994, C2, and "Brutal Struggle: Order v. Chaos," *Washington Post,* September 4, 1994, A42. Kaplan has modified his views somewhat in *The Ends of the Earth: From Togo to Turkmenistan, from Iran to Cambodia, A Journey to the Frontiers of Anarchy* (New York: Alfred A. Knopf, 1996).

8. In addition to the articles cited in note 5, see Nicholas Eberstadt, "Population Change and National Security," *Foreign Affairs* 70 (Summer, 1991): 115–131; Thomas, Homer-Dixon, "On the Threshold, Environmental Changes as Causes of Acute Conflict," *International Security*, (Fall, 1991): 76–116; Arthur H. Westing, ed., *Global Resources and International Conflict, Environmental Factors in Strategic Policy and Action* (New York: Oxford University Press, 1986); "Water, Flowing Uphill," *The Economist*, August 12, 1995, 36; and for an overview, Richard A. Matthew, "Environmental Security and Conflict: An Overview of the Current Debate," *National Security Studies Quarterly* 1 (Summer, 1995): 1–10.

9. Kaplan, "The Coming Anarchy," 58, 73–74, emphasis in the original.

10. Deudney, "The Case Against Linking Environmental Degradation and National Security," 470–471; "Water, Flowing Uphill," *The Economist*, 36.

11. Thomas, Homer-Dixon, "On the Threshold," 106, 108, note 91; Thomas F. Homer-Dixon, "Environmental Scarcities and Violent Conflict, Evidence from Cases," *International Security* 19 (Summer, 1994): 13, 18–20; Arthur H. Westing, ed. *Global Resources and International Conflict*, 205.

12. Nicholas Eberstadt, "Population Change and National Security," 117; Norman Myers, "Environment and Security," *Foreign Policy* 74 (Spring, 1989), 27; Thomas Kamm, "After a Devaluation, Two African Nations Fare Very Differently," *Wall Street Journal*, May 10, 1995, A1.

13. Benjamin Schwarz, "A Dubious Strategy in Pursuit of a Dubious Enemy: A Critique of U.S. Post-Cold War Security Policy in the Third World," *Studies in Conflict* 16 (October-December, 1993), 275–287 and David Tucker, "Facing the Facts: The Failure of Nation Assistance," *Parameters* 23 (Summer, 1993), 34–40 and the sources cited therein.

14. Kaplan, "The Coming Anarchy," 58; Thomas F. Homer-Dixon, "Environmental Scarcities and Violent Conflict, Evidence from Cases," 20–21.

15. The examples in this paragraph and some of its analysis are drawn from Myron Weiner, "Introduction: Security, Stability and International Migration," in *International Migration and Security*, ed. Myron Weiner (Boulder, Colorado: Westview Press, 1993), 1–35.

16. Homer-Dixon, "Environmental Scarcities and Violent Conflict, Evidence from Cases," 11–13. For another critique of Homer-Dixon's argument, see Marc A. Levy, "Is the Environment a National Security Issue," *International Security* 20 (Fall, 1995): 35–62 and the correspondence between Homer-Dixon and Levy, *International Security* 20 (Winter, 1995/1996): 189–198.

17. Kaplan, "The Coming Anarchy," 58, 70, 74; *National Security Strategy Report*, 1.

18. Ted Robert Gurr, "Peoples against States: Ethnopolitical Conflict and the Changing World System," *International Studies Quarterly* 38 (September, 1994): 358, 364. Gurr argues that the trend in ethnic conflict was evident to those who studied ethnicity but went unnoticed by those who focused on national security and the Soviet Union. Paul Goble is quoted in "Ethnic Strife Succeeds Cold War's Ideological Conflict," *Washington Post*, December 18, 1994, A36. The article provides no evidence to support the conclusion stated in its headline. It notes, however, echoing Gurr's argument, that "scholars and policymakers who for decades analyzed world events through a Cold War prism now see a world where nationalism and ethnic assertiveness have become the primary sources of armed conflict."

19. Steven Emerson, Hearing before the Subcommittee on Africa of the Committee on International Relations, House of Representatives, 104th Congress, First Session, April 6, 1995 (Washington, D.C.: U.S. government Printing Office, 1995), 5.

20. John L. Esposito, *The Islamic Threat, Myth or Reality?* (New York: Oxford University Press, 1992); Olivier Roy, *The Failure of Political Islam* (Cambridge: Harvard University Press, 1994) 3–7, 39–42 for the parallels between Islamic extremism and Marxism–Leninism; William Perry, "Leader in a New World," prepared remarks to the Euro-Atlantic Society, followed by a question and answer session, Warsaw, Poland, June 27, 1995, *Defense Issues*, vol. 10, no. 72 (Washington, D.C.: Office of the Assistant to the Secretary of Defense [Public Affairs], n. d.), 1; Roger Boyes, "Muslim Militancy Is Next Big Threat Says Nato Chief," *London Times*, February 3, 1995, 13; "Islam's Dark Side, The Orwellian State of Sudan," *The Economist*, June 24, 1995, 21–24.

21. Esposito, *The Islamic Threat*, 33, 34, 135, 122, 128–129; "Terrorism Trial," *USA Today*, February 3, 1995, 3; Roy, *The Failure of Political Islam*, 40.

22. Esposito, *The Islamic Threat*, 117, 164, 184, 211, 213; Roy, *The Failure of Political Islam*, 60, 67, 108, 112, 124, 129, 195; Michael S. Lelyveld, "Iran Extends Power in Region Via Trade Deals," *Journal of Commerce*, September 14, 1995, 1.

23. Eugene B. Skolnikoff, *The Elusive Transformation, Science, Technology, and the Evolution of International Politics* (A Council on Foreign Relations Book, Princeton, New Jersey: Princeton University Press, 1993), 142–143, 148–150.

24. Skolnikoff, *The Elusive Transformation*, 93–132; William J. Olson, "The Crisis of Governance: Present and Future Challenges," *Terrorism and Political Violence*, 6(Summer, 1994): 146–162; Martin van Creveld, *The Transformation of War* (New York: The Free Press, 1991), 198; Ashton B. Carter, William J. Perry, and John D. Steinbruner, "A New Concept of Cooperative Security," *Brookings Occasional Paper* (Washington, D.C.: Brookings Institution, 1992), 10 and 58–59; Jessica Matthews, "Redefining Security," 174; Morton H. Halperin and David J. Scheffer, *Self-determination in the New World Order* (Washington, D.C.: Carnegie Endowment for International Peace, 1992), 8; Kaplan, "The Coming Anarchy," 62–63, 70, 75.

25. Jim Mann, "Clinton Struggling to Shape Foreign Policy and America's Place in the World," *Los Angeles Times*, October 2, 1995, 5.

26. Jim Mann, "Clinton Struggling to Shape Foreign Policy and America's Place in the World," 5; Jeremy D. Rosner, "Is Chaos America's Real Enemy?" *Washington Post*, August 14, 1994, C1.

27. Stephen D. Krasner, "Compromising Westphalia," *International Security*, 20 (Winter, 1995–1996): 117, 123, 144, 150; Vincent Cable, "The Diminished Nation–State: A Study in the Loss of Economic Power," *Daedalus* 124 (Spring, 1995): 24; Bruce D. Porter, *War and the Rise of the State, the Military Foundations of Modern Politics* (New York: The Free Press, 1994); Olivier Roy, *The Failure of Political Islam* (Cambridge: Harvard University Press, 1994), 129, 108, 112, 124.

28. "The Myth of the Powerless State," and "A Survey of the World Economy, Who's in the Driving Seat?" *The Economist*, October 7, 1995, 16, 1–38; Ethan B. Kapstein, "Shockproof, the End of the Financial Crisis," *Foreign Affairs* 75 (January February, 1996): 3.

29. Skolnikoff, *The Elusive Transformation,* 111, 173; John Schwartz, "Chipping in to Curb Computer Crime," *Washington Post*, February 19, 1995, A1. For other examples of state power over the internet, see Pierre Thomas and Elizabeth Corcoran," Argentine, 22, Charged with Hacking Computer Networks," *Washington Post*, March 30, 1996, A4; Keith B. Richburg, "A Great Wall of China Slowly Gives Way," *Washington Post*, April 8, 1996, A1; and "Asia and the Internet, Not Too Modern, Please," *The Economist*, March 16, 1996, 42–43.

30. William Drozdiak, "Mob Ties Alleged to Italian Ex–Premier," *The Washington Post*, February 16, 1995, A36; "Is the Mafia in Retreat or in Defeat?" *The Economist*, July 29.,1995, 33–35; Stephen Fidler and Sally Brown, "Colombian Cocaine: Down but Not Out," *Financial Times,* October 12, 1995, 8.

31. Van Creveld, *The Transformation of War*, 198; "South Africa Reportedly to 'Play Hard Ball' With U.S. on Armscor," *Sunday Independent*, January 21, 1996, 1–2, in FBIS, *Daily Report, Sub-Saharan Africa*, January 24, 1996, 7; Roy, *The Failure of Political Islam,* 18.

32. Michael Mann, "Nation-States in Europe and Other Continents: Diversifying, Developing, Not Dying," *Daedalus* 122 (Summer, 1993): 118; "The Myth of the Powerless State," 15.

33. John H. Herz, "The Territorial State Revisited: Reflections on the Future of the Nation-State," in *International Politics and Foreign Policy, a Reader in Research and Theory,* ed. James N. Rosenau (New York: The Free Press, 1969), 76–77.

34. James N. Rosenau, *Turbulence in World Politics, a Theory of Change and Continuity* (Princeton, New Jersey: Princeton University Press, 1990).

35. Walter Berns, "The Case against World Government," *Readings in World Politics,* ed. Robert Goldwin (New York: Oxford University Press, 1959), 531–544; Francis Fukuyama, *The End of History and the Last Man* (New York: The Free Press, 1992); Porter, *War and the Rise of the State*, 299; W. David Clinton, *The Two Faces of National Interest* (Baton Rouge: Louisiana State University, 1994), 80–83; John Lewis Gaddis, "Morality in the Cold War: The American Experience," in *Ethics and International Relations, Ethics in Foreign Policy,* vol. 2, ed. Kenneth W. Thompson (New Brunswick, New Jersey: Transaction Books, 1985), 122.

36. Henry Kissinger, *Diplomacy* (New York: Simon & Schuster, 1994), 808.

37. Karl Kaysen, "Is War Obsolete? A Review Essay," *International Security* 14 (Spring, 1990), 42–64.

38. Peter Duignan and L. H. Gann, *The United States and Africa, a History* (Cambridge: Cambridge University Press, 1984), 58–79.

39. For the articulation of such a strategy, see Benjamin Schwarz's contribution to *Prisms and Policy: U.S. Security after the Cold War*, ed. Norman D. Levin (Santa Monica, California: RAND, 1994),.

40. Robin Wright, "U.S. Worries about Iranian Unit in Bosnia," *The Los Angeles Times*, December 5, 1995, 1.

41. "Report of the National Bipartisan Commission on Central America" (Washington, D.C., 1984), 108.

42. "From Containment to Engagement," an address by Secretary of State Rogers before the Council on Foreign Relations, September 28, 1972, DSB 67 (October, 1972): 470–473; President George Bush, "United States Defense, Reshaping Our Forces," delivered at the Aspen Institute, August 2, 1990, *Vital Speeches* 56 (September 1, 1990): 677; *A National Security Strategy of Engagement and Enlargement* (1996).

43. *National Military Stratgey of the United States, a Strategy of Flexible and Selective Engagement* (Washington, D. C., February 1995), 2; also 3–5, 9.

44. Bill Clinton, "A New Covenant for American Security," an address at Georgetown University, December 12, 1991; cf. Halperin, "Guaranteeing Democracy," 106; President Bill Clinton, "We Must Secure Peace, A Struggle between Freedom and Tyranny," an address to the 49th General Assembly of the United Nations, September 26, 1994, in *Vital Speeches of the Day* 61 (October 15, 1994) 4; *A National Security Strategy of Engagement and Enlargement* (1996), 32; Morton Halperin, "Guaranteeing Democracy," *Foreign Policy* 91 (Summer, 1993): 106, 121; President Ronald Reagan praised the pacific character of democracy in his address to the British Parliament, June 9, 1982; Secretary Baker claimed that "real democracies do not go to war with each other," quoted in Bruce M. Russett, *Grasping the Democratic Peace, Principles for a Post–Cold War World*, (Princeton, New Jersey: Princeton University Press, 1993), 128–129.

45. For a more detailed statement of these arguments and criticisms of them, see Christopher Layne, "Kant or Cant, the Myth of the Democratic Peace," *International Security* 19 Fall, 1994): 5–49 and John M. Owen, "How Liberalism Produces Democratic Peace," *International Security* 19 (Fall, 1994): 87–125.

46. For the statistical significance or insignificance of the "democratic peace," see David E. Spiro, "The Insignificance of the Liberal Peace," *International Security* 19 (Fall, 1994): 50–86; Owen, "How Liberalism Produces Democratic Peace," 92; and Henry S. Farber and Joanne Gowa, "Politics and Peace," *International Security* 20 (Fall, 1995): 123–146. For criticism of the institutional argument, see Layne, "Kant or Cant, the Myth of the Democratic Peace," 12.

47. Owen, "How Liberalism Produces Democratic Peace," 95.

48. Owen, "How Liberalism Produces Democratic Peace," 98–99.

49. Gurr, "Peoples against States: Ethnopolitical Conflict and the Changing World System," 361–363.   On the larger issue of the violent consequences of becoming democratic, see Edward D. Mansfield and Jack Snyder, "Democratization and the Danger of War," *International Security* 20 (Summer, 1995): 5–38.

50. Secretary Christopher is quoted in *Washington Post*, February 6, 1993, A8; Anthony Lake, "Confronting Backlash States," *Foreign Affairs* 73 (March-April, 1994), 45, 55; President Clinton, "The Biggest Gamble of the War, the Greatest Crusade, the Longest Day," *Washington Post,* June 7, 1994, A15; Senator Christopher Dodd, Governor Mario Cuomo, Interview, National Public Radio, January 17, 1991; *The National Security Strategy of the United States* (Washington, D.C., August 1991), 4; Jim

Hoagland, "Yellow Light for Croatia," *Washington Post*, August 6, 1995, C9; Thomas Jefferson, "The Report of the Commissioners for the University of Virginia," August 4, 1818, in *Writings*, ed. Merrill D. Peterson (New York: Literary Classics of the United States, 1984), 461.

51.   Thomas Jefferson, "The Report of the Commissioners for the University of Virginia," 461.

52.   Francis Fukuyama, *The End of History and the Last Man* (New York: The Free Press, 1992).

53.   On the tides of democracy, see Samuel Huntington, *The Third Wave, Democratization in the Late Twentieth-Century* (Norman, Oklahoma: University of Oklahoma Press, 1991); Alexandre Kojève, *Introduction à la Lecture de Hegel* (Paris, 1947), 288, cf. 287–291 and 355–356; Michael S. Roth, *Knowing and History, Appropriations of Hegel in Twentieth-Century France* (Ithaca, New York, 1988), 138.

54.   Fukuyama, "The End of History?," *The National Interest*, 16 (Summer, 1989): 8; Michael Allen Gillespie, *Hegel, Heidegger, and the Ground of History* (Chicago: University of Chicago Press, 1984), 63, cf. 103–115. Kojeve, *Introduction à la Lecture de Hegel*, 291, note 1. Those interested in pursuing the question of whether humans can be wise might consider John D. Barrow, *Theories of Everything, the Quest for Ultimate Explanation* (Oxford: Clarendon Press, 1991), and Stanley Rosen, *Nihilism, A Philosophical Essay* (New Haven, Connecticut: Yale University Press, 1969), 198–235.

55.   *A National Security Strategy of Engagement and Enlargement* (1996), 23.

56.   Quoted in Paul Kennedy, *The Realities behind Diplomacy: Background Influences on British External Policy, 1865–1980* (London: George Allen and Unwin, 1981), 105.

57.   John Lewis Gaddis, *Strategies of Containment, a Critical Appraisal of Postwar American National Security Policy* (New York: Oxford University Press, 1982), 353.

58.   Richard N. Haass, *Intervention, the Use of American Military Force in the Post-Cold War World* (Washington, D.C.: The Carnegie Endowment for International Peace, 1994), ix–x; Grant Willis, "1 Percent Les," *Army Times*, September 27, 1993, 3; R. W. Apple, Jr., "Wounded in Policy Wars," *New York Times*, December 16, 1993, 1; *A National Security Strategy of Engagement and Enlargement* (1996), 18; *The Clinton Administration's Policy on Reforming Multilateral Peace Operations* (Department of State, Washington, D.C., May 1994), for example, 5; "Rules of Engagement," remarks by Secretary of Defense William J. Perry before the Fortune 500 Forum, Philadelphia, Pennsylvania, November 3, 1994, *Defense Issues*, vol. 9, no. 84, Office of the Assistant to the Secretary of Defense (Public Affairs), n.d.; "Operations: 'Strict Guidelines,'" Interview with Secretary William J. Perry, *Air Force Times*, January 2, 1995, 40.

59.   Daniel Williams and John M. Goshko, "Reduced U.S. World Role Outlined but Soon Altered, High-Level Disavowals Follow Official's Talk," *Washington Post*, May 26, 1993, 1.

60.   This discussion of criteria for engagement borrows from Christopher J. Lamb and David Tucker, "Peacetime Engagements," in *America's Armed Forces, A Handbook of Current and Future Military Capabilities*, eds. Sam C. Sarkesian and Robert E. Connor, Jr. (Westport, Connecticut: Greenwood Press, 1996), 295–337.

61.   Catherine Toups, "Albright Cites 'Moral Imperative' for Bosnia Mission," *Washington Times*, December 13, 1995, 1. President Clinton and National Security Advisor Lake have made similar comments. See President Clinton, "If We're Not There, NATO Will Not Be . . . Peace Will Collapse," *Washington Post*, November 28, 1995,

A8; prepared remarks of Anthony Lake, George Washington University, March 6, 1996, *Defense Issues*, vol. 11, no. 14, (Washington, D.C., n.d.).

62. Paul Kennedy, *The Realities Behind Diplomacy,* 106.

63. Huntington, *The Third Wave*, 59, and Larry Diamond, "Economic Development and Democracy Reconsidered," *American Behavioral Scientist* 35 (March–June, 1992), 450–499.

64. Ethan B. Kapstein, "Workers and the World Economy," *Foreign Affairs* 75(May–June, 1996): 16–37; Paul Krugman, "Competitiveness: A Dangerous Obsession," *Foreign Affairs* 73 (March–April, 1994): 28–44 and Paul Krugman, "Does Third World Growth Hurt First World Prosperity," *Harvard Business Review* 72 (July–August, 1994): 113–121; "War of the Worlds, a Survey of the Global Economy," *The Economist* (October 1, 1994), 14–24. C. R. Neu and Charles Wolf, Jr., *The Economic Dimensions of National Security* (Santa Monica, California: RAND, 1994), 49–67 discuss several of the financial and commercial underpinnings of free trade. For a brief but informative review of the arguments for "strategic trade" as an alternative to free trade, see "How to Beggar Your Neighbor," *The Economist*, February 3, 1996, 68.

65. For example, Gary Clyde Hufbauer, Jeffrey J. Schott, and Kimberly Ann Elliott, *Economic Sanctions Reconsidered, History and Current Policy*, 2nd ed. (Washington, D.C.: Institute for International Economics, 1985; second edition, 1990).

66. Jim Anderson, "Iran Doesn't Need Reactor Deals to Get Nuclear Know-How," *Washington Times*, May 17, 1995, 15; Rowan Scarborough, "Russia Losing Nuke Control, Senators Told, Atomic Smuggling Expected," *Washington Times*, August 23, 1995, 1.

67. Thomas Jefferson to Thomas Lieper, January 1, 1814, *Basic Writings of Thomas Jefferson*, ed. Philip S. Foner (New York: Wiles Book Co., 1944), 720. On the balance of power in Eurasia as the primary concern of American strategists, see Eugene V. Rostow, *Toward Managed Peace, the National Security Interests of the United States, 1759 to the Present* (New Haven: Yale University Press, 1993), and Colin S. Gray, *The Geopolitics of Super Power* (Lexington: University of Kentucky, 1988). On pages 69–72, Gray explains the geopolitical basis of the balance of power and defends this concept against several typical criticisms. For the futility of an Atlantic–Pacific split, see Raymond Seitz, "From the Jaws of Victory," *The Economist*, May 27, 1995, 22.

68. Claudia Rosett, "Along Many Borders, the Russian Empire Stirs," *Wall Street Journal*, February 27, 1995, 8; "Zhirinovsky Suggests Free Arms for India," *Washington Times*, March 6, 1995, 13; "Brothers in Arms," *The Economist*, November 23, 1996, 38–39; Colin S. Gray, "Back to the Future: Russia and the Balance of Power," *Global Affairs* 7 (Summer, 1992), 51–52; "Chinas Plays the Europe Card," *The Economist*, May 11, 1996, 33–34.

69. Zbigniew Brzezinski, "A Plan for Europe," *Foreign Affairs* 74 (January–February, 1995): 26–42 discusses enlarging NATO in the context of a pan–Eurasian security plan and the difficulties involved; Alexei K. Pushkov, "NATO Enlargement: A Russian Perspective," *Strategic Forum*, 34 (July, 1995), Institute for National Strategic Studies, National Defense University, Ft. McNair, Wahsington, D.C.

70. See C. R. Neu and Charles Wolf, Jr., *The Economic Dimensions of National Security*, 52–53.

71. Amy Dockser Marcus, "Emerging Alliance, with Blessing of U.S. Israel Draws Closer to Turkey and Jordan," *Wall Street Journal*, May 30, 1996, 1.

72. On the issues raised in this paragraph, see Anthony Lake, "Confronting Backlash States," *Foreign Affairs* 73 (March–April, 1994): 45–55 and F. Gregory Gause, III, "The Illogic of Dual Containment," *Foreign Affairs* 73 (March–April, 1994): 56–66.

73. Paul Schroeder, "Historical Reality vs. Neo-realist Theory," *International Security* 19 (Summer, 1994), 117.

74. Schroeder, "Historical Reality vs. Neo-realist Theory," 117; Catherine Toups, "Albright cites 'Moral Imperative' for Bosnia Mission," 1.

75. For examples of the UN's even-handednes in dealing with conflicts around the world, see Barbara Crossette, "U.N. Chief Focuses on Africa's 'Underdog Conflicts,'" *New York Times*, July 23, 1995, A3, and John L. Hirsch and Robert Oakley, *Somalia and Operation Restore Hope: Reflections on Peacemaking and Peacekeeping* (Washington, D.C.: U.S. Institute of Peace Press, 1995), 37.

76. *Patterns of Global Terrorism*, 1; Benjamin C. Schwarz, *Casualties, Public Opinion and U.S. Military Intervention, Implications for U.S. Regional Deterrence Strategies* (Santa Monica, California: RAND, 1994); Gilbert A. Lewthwaite, "View of U.S. Deaths Depends on Mission," *Baltimore Sun*, November 28, 1995, 1; George P. Shultz, *Triumph and Turmoil, My Years as Secretary of State* (New York: Scribner's, 1993), 653–668, especially 658–660, 668; interviews with senior Bush and Reagan Administration officials, January 26, 1994, and January 5, 1994, respectively.

77. *National Military Strategy of the United States, a Strategy of Flexible and Selective Engagement* (Washington, D.C., February, 1995). For the deterrent effect of nuclear weapons, see Joseph Fitchett, "Nuclear States See Vindication, Threat of Annihilation Deterred Iraq, They Say," *International Herald Tribune,* September 12, 1995, 2.

78. Henry Kissinger, "We Live in an Age of Transition," *Daedalus* 124 (Summer, 1995): 103; Samuel P. Huntington, "America's Changing Strategic Interests," *Survival* 33 (January–February, 1991): 16; Edward Luttwak, "Toward Post-Heroic Warfare," *Foreign Affairs* 74 (May–June, 1995): 109–122.

CONCLUSION

1. John Dillon, "The Next Nuclear Warriors: Terrorists," *The Boston Globe*, May 5, 1996, 32.

2. Walter Laqueur, *The Age of Terrorism* (Boston: Little, Brown and Company, 1987), 139; Martha Crenshaw, "How Terrorism Declines," *Terrorism and Political Violence* 3 (Spring, 1991): 79.

3. Kenneth J. Cooper, "Anti-Terrorism Bill Gets Hung Up, House GOP Conservatives Object to Expansion of Federal Powers," *Washington Post*, August 6, 1995, A4.

SELECTED BIBLIOGRAPHY

Abbott, Kenneth W. "Economic Sanctions and International Terrorism." *Vanderbilt Journal of Transnational Law* 2 (March, 1987): 289–328.

Bialos, Jeffrey and Kenneth I. Juster. "The Libyan Sanctions: A Rational Response to State–Sponsored Terrorism?" *Virginia Journal of International Law* 4 (Summer, 1986): 799–855.

Bienen, Henry and Robert Gilpin. "Economic Sanctions as a Response to Terrorism." *Journal of Strategic Studies* III (May, 1980): 89–98.

Buckelew, Alvin Hugh. *Terrorism and the American Response: An Analysis of the Mechanism Used by the Government of the United States in Dealing with National and International Terrorism.* Ph.D. dissertation, Golden Gate University, 1982.

Celmer, Marc A. *Terrorism: U.S. Strategy and Reagan Policies.* New York: Greenwood Press, 1987.

Clutterbuck, Richard. "Negotiating with Terrorists." *Terrorism and Political Violence* 4 (Winter, 1990): 263–287.

Crenshaw, Martha. "The Causes of Terrorism." *Comparative Politics* 13 (July, 1985): 383–392.

———. "How Terrorism Declines." *Terrorism and Political Violence* 3 (Spring, 1991): 69–87.

Davis, Brian L. *Qadaffi, Terrorism, and the Origins of the U.S. Attack on Libya.* New York: Praeger, 1990.

Dobson, Christopher and Ronald Payne. *The Never-Ending War, Terrorism in the 80's.* New York: Facts on File, 1989.

Ehrenfeld, Rachel. *Narco-Terrorism.* New York: Basic Books, 1990.

Enders, Walter, Todd Sandler, and Jon Cauley. "UN Conventions, Technology and Retaliation in the Fight Against Terrorism: An Econometric Evaluation." *Terrorism and Political Violence* 2 (Spring, 1990): 83–105.

Enders, Walter, and Todd Sandler. "The Effectiveness of Antiterrorism Policies: A Vectoral-Autoregression-Intervention Analysis." *American Political Science Review* 87 (December, 1993): 829–844.

Flores, David A. "Export Controls and the U.S. Effort to Combat International Terrorism." *Law and Policy in International Business* 13 (1981): 521–590.

Grau, Lester W. "Supporting 'Carlos the Jackal': Recent Materials from the former 'Soviet Bloc'." *Low-Intensity Conflict and Law Enforcement* 1 (Summer, 1992): 92–101.

Hanle, Donald J. *Terrorism, The Newest Face of Warfare*. McLean, Virginia: Pergamon-Brassey's International Defense Publishers, Inc., 1989.

History and Impact of U.S. Terrorism Policy, 1972–1984, McLean, Virginia: Defense Systems, Inc., July 22, 1985.

Hoffman, Bruce. "The Prevention of Terrorism and Rehabilitation of Terrorists: Some Preliminary Thoughts." P–7059. Santa Monica, California: Rand, 1985.

———. "'Holy Terror': The Implications of Terrorism Motivated by a Religious Imperative." P–7834. Santa Monica, California: RAND, 1993.

Hoffman, Bruce, and Jennifer Morrison Taw. *A Strategic Framework for Countering Terrorism and Insurgency*. N–3506–DOS. Santa Monica, California: RAND, 1992.

Hughes, Martin. "Terror and Negotiation." *Terrorism and Political Violence* 2 (Spring, 1990): 72–82.

Impact of Government Behavior on Frequency, Type, and Targets of Terrorist Group Activity. McLean, Virginia: Defense Systems, Inc., December 15, 1982.

Impact of Government Behavior on Frequency, Type, and Targets of Terrorist Group Activity: The West German Experience, 1968–1982. McLean, Virginia: Defense Systems, Inc., December 15, 1983.

Iyad, Abu with Eric Rouleau. *My Home, My Land, a Narrative of the Palestinian Struggle*. Translated by Linda Butler Koseoglu. New York: Times Books, 1981.

Korn, David A. "'We Will not Pay Blackmail,' The Khartoum Murders and U.S. Policy on Terrorism." *Foreign Service Journal* 68 (February, 1991): 28–31.

Lapan, Harvey E., and Todd Sandler. "To Bargain or Not to Bargain: That is the Question." *American Economic Review* 78 (May, 1988): 16–21.

Laqueur, Walter. *The Age of Terrorism*. Boston: Little, Brown and Company, 1987.

Livingstone, Neil C., and David Halevy. *Inside the PLO, Covert Units, Secret Funds, and the War Against Israel and the United States*. New York: William Morrow and Company, 1990.

Long, David. *The Anatomy of Terrorism*. New York: The Free Press, 1990.

Martin, David C., and John Walcott. *Best Laid Plans, The Inside Story of America's War Against Terrorism*. New York: Harper & Row, 1988.

Mickolus, Edward F. "Negotiating for Hostages: A Policy Dilemma." In *Contemporary Terrorism, Selected Readings*, edited by John D. Elliott and Leslie K. Gibson, 207–221. Gaithersburg, Maryland: International Association of Chiefs of Police, 1978.

———. *Transnational Terrorism, A Chronology of Events, 1968–1979*. Westport, Connecticut: Greenwood Press, 1980.

Mickolus, Edward F., Todd Sandler, and Jean M. Murdock, *International Terrorism in the 1980s, a Chronology of Events, Volume I, 1980–1983*. Ames, Iowa: Iowa State University Press, 1989.

———. *International Terrorism in the 1980s, a Chronology of Events, Volume II, 1984–1987*. Ames, Iowa: Iowa State University Press, 1989.

Motley, James B. "U.S. Counterterrorist Policy: An Analysis of its Strategy and Organization." Ph. D. diss., The Catholic University, 1982.

Pipes, Daniel. "Why Asad's Terrorism Works and Qadafhi's Does Not." *Orbis* 33 (Fall, 1989): 501–508.

Post, Jerold M. "Terrorist Psycho-logic: Terrorist Behavior as a Product of Psychological Forces." In *Origins of Terrorism, Psychologies, Ideologies, Theologies, States of Mind*, edited by Walter Reich, 25–40. New York: Cambridge University Press, 1990.

Rapoport, David C. "Fear and Trembling: Terrorism in Three Religious Traditions." *American Political Science Review* 78 (September, 1984): 658–677.

Reich, Walter. "Understanding Terrorist Behavior: The Limits and Opportunities of Psychological Inquiry." In *Origins of Terrorism, Psychologies, Ideologies, Theologies, States of Mind*, edited by Walter Reich, 261–279. New York: Cambridge University Press, 1990.

Rubin, Alfred. "Current Legal Approaches to International Terrorism." *Terrorism*, 13 (July–August, 1990): 277–297.

Rubin, Barry. *Revolution Until Victory? The Politics and History of the PLO*. Cambridge: Harvard University Press, 1994.

Simon, Jeffrey D. *The Terrorist Trap, America's Experience with Terrorism*. Bloomington: Indiana University Press, 1994.

Shultz, George. *Turmoil and Triumph, My Years as Secretary of State*. New York: Scribner's, 1993.

Sterling, Claire. *The Terror Network, the Secret War of International Terrorism*. New York: Holt, Rhinehart and Winston, 1981.

Wege, Carl Anthony. "Hizbollah Organization." *Studies in Conflict and Terrorism* 17 (April–June, 1994), 151–164.

Wilkinson, Paul. *Terrorism and the Liberal State*. 2nd ed. New York: New York University Press, 1986.

Zimmerman, Tim. "Coercive Diplomacy and Libya." In *The Limits of Coercive Diplomacy*, 2nd ed., edited by Alexander L. George and William E. Simons, 201–228. Boulder, Colorado: Westview Press, 1994.

INDEX

Abbas, Mohammed Zaidan, 17, 37
Abdel-Rahman, Omar, 144
Abu Abbas. *See* Abbas, Mohammed
    Zaidan
Abu Iyad. *See* Khalaf, Salah
Abu Nidal Organization. *See* ANO
Achille Lauro, 17, 36, 37
Adams, Gerry, 63
Aideed, Muhammad Farrah, 94, 120
Albright, Madeleine, 171, 180
Andropov, Yuri, 50
ANO, attacks organized, 36, 37;
    history, 40; operation against,
    40–41, 104; planned attack, 40
Arab Communist Organization, 12
Arafat, Yasir, 6, 9, 40, 187; justifying
    terrorism, 6
Asad, Hafez, 40, 98, 187
Aspin, Les, 168–169
Aum Shinrikyo, 48, 49, 54–55, 186

Baader-Meinhof gang, 5
Baker James, 128
Balance of power, 175–177;
    alternatives to, 179–180; effect of
    terrorism on, 86–187; threats to,
    180–181. *See also* Engagement;
    Fortress America; Strategy; Threat
Baldwin, David A., 86

Barr, William, 48
Black September, disbanded by Fatah,
    11; murder of diplomats in
    Khartoum, 9–10; organized by
    Fatah, 6. *See also* Fatah
Bosnia, 170-171, 180,
Buckley, William, 29
Bush, George, 28, 37, 46, 48
Bush Administration, 46–47, 48

Cable, Vincent, 149
Camp David Agreement, 16
Carlos. *See* Sanchez, Ilich Ramirez
Carter administration, efforts against
    terrorism, 13, 16, 17–18, 18–19, 20,
    21–22; Iranian hostage crisis, 22–23;
    organization to combat terrorism, 13,
    14, 15, 20–21; and Reagan
    administration compared, 27
Casey, William, 24; definition of
    terrorism, 58; proposal for
    counterterrorism operation, 39
    support for counterterrorism, 32,
    126; support for counterterrorism
    center, 38
Central Intelligence Agency, 6, 28;
    conflict with military
    counterterrorism units, 116–117,
    130; cooperation with FBI, 45;

Counterterrorism Center, 38; covert
or clandestine efforts against
terrorism, 46, 48; finished
intelligence, 32–33; influence of
regional divisions in, 32;
interagency group, 38; lack of
cooperation with FBI, 43–44;
mandate of, 116; operation against
ANO, 40-41; opposition to
preemption, 32; report on state
sponsorship of terrorism, 16, 25.
See also Counterterrorism Center
Christopher, Warren, 24, 164, 165
Clinton, William, 171; on democracy,
161; on the future, 147; on progress,
164
Clinton administration, and strategy,
138, 143, 159, 168–169,177–178;
and terrorism, 48
Coercive diplomacy, 64, 66, 67, 68
Commerce Department, 16, 17, 18, 114
Concessions, made to terrorists, 2, 4,
8, 12, 22, 78–79
Conflict, causes of, 138–146
Congo, 1, 8
Congress, economic sanctions, 16, 18;
insists on interagency cooperation,
45
Counterterrorism Center, 38; criticism
of, 41–42; operation against ANO,
40–41. See also Central Intelligence
Agency
Cuba, 1, 8; indirect strategy, 158;
sanctions against, 88, 89
Cuomo, Mario, 164

Declaration of Independence,
legitimate violence, 57–60, 61, 64;
limits on violence, 60; purpose of
American life, 171; U.S.
government definitions of terrorism,
61–62
Defense Department, 7, 13, 15, 22, 28,
29; Achille Lauro, 37; definition of
terrorism, 52; mandate of, 115;
organization to combat terrorism
35
Definition of terrorism, common
elements 53; core definition, 53, 58,

63; as criminal, 60–62; legitimacy,
57–60, 61, 64; misuse, 56; violence
against innocents, 63–65; as
warfare, 65–69
Democracy, 160–161; liberalism, 162–
163; promotion of criticized, 161–
167
Democratic People's Republic of
Korea, 77, 88, 89, 90
Desert Storm, 47
Disruption, against ANO, 40–41, 104;
defined, 103; disadvantages, 105;
methods of, 104–105
Dodd, Christopher, 164
Dozier, James, 27–29, 74
Drug Enforcement Agency, 130
Dulles, John Foster, 8

East Germany. See German
Democratic Republic
Economic sanctions, analysis of, 85–
91; criticized, 85–86; declining
effectiveness, 93; defined, 85;
development of as method to combat
terrorism, 16; guidelines for
imposition, 91–93; reasons for
imposing, 89; against state sponsors
of terrorism, 16–17, 88–91; utility
and effectiveness, 86–88
El Dorado Canyon, 39–40, 96–
99, 122–123, 133
Empire, 189–190
Empire of Liberty, 189, 190
Engagement, global: 159–167;
criticism of, 159–160; democracy,
160–164; progress, 164–167;
selective: criteria for, 167–168, 169–
179; criticism of, 181–182;
geographic interests, 174–179;
necessity of, 167–168; principles
of, 170–174; as strategy, 158–159.
See also Balance of power; Fortress
America; Strategy; Threat
Entebbe, 18
Executive Committee, 13–14, 21, 28
Extradition, 43-44, 72, 80, 105. See
also Extraterritoriality; Rendition
Extraterritoriality, 43, 44, 48, 82–83,
85. See also Extradition; Rendition

FALN. *See* Venezuelan Army of
   National Liberation
Farabundo Marti Liberation Forces, 36
Fatah, 6, 11
Federal Aviation Administration,
   13
Federal Bureau of Investigation, 7, 13;
   cooperation with other departments,
   15, 45; definition of terrorism, 52,
   60, 62; extraterritoriality, 43;
   hostage rescue, 18, 19; interagency
   group, 38, 127; Justice Department,
   111, 121
Federalist 10, 153
Force, American attitude toward use
   of, 119–120; asymmetry in
   vulnerability to, 98–99; constraints
   on use of, 99; use of, 94–96; U.S.
   military view of, 94
Fortress America, as strategy, 156–158.
   See also Balance of power;
   Engagement; Strategy; Threat
Freedom fighters, 58, 59, 63
Fukuyama, Francis, 165–166

German Democratic Republic, 26–27,
   40
Grand strategy, 66, 67

Haig, Alexander, 24, 26, 27
Hanle, Donald, 65–67
Hegel, Georg Wilhelm Friedrich, 165–
   166
Hizbollah, 35, 36, 49, 68
Holbrooke, Richard, 115, 118, 124
Homer-Dixon, Thomas, 140, 142, 143
Hostage rescue, 16, 18, 75. *See also*
   Entebbe, Mogadishu
Hostages, 47, 76
Hussein, Saddam, 47

Immigration and Naturalization
   Service, 7
Intelligence Community, 52
Interagency cooperation, agency
   culture, 115–117; agency mandates,
   114, 124; distinguished from policy-
   operations coordination, 120–121;
   effect of Iran-Contra on, 42;

interagency group, 38–39, 127;
   limited applicability of as model,
   129; processes of, 111–112; reasons
   for failure of, 109–120; reasons for
   success of, 125–128; turf, 113,
   124; in war and peace, 117–118
Interdepartmental Group on Terrorism,
   30
Iran, dual containment, 177–178;
   negotiations with, 79, 177-178;
   release of hostages, 47; sponsor of
   terrorism, 35; target of sanctions, 88,
   90; use of terrorism, 157–158
Iran-Contra Scandal, 42
Iranian Hostage Crisis, 15, 22–23
Iraq, dual containment, 177; efforts
   against during Desert Storm,
   47; sponsor of terrorism, 17; target
   of sanctions, 88, 89; use of
   terrorism, 157–158
Irish Republican Army, 26, 44
Islamic Jihad. *See* Hizbollah
Islamic Salvation Front, 59–60, 146

Japanese Red Army, 5
Jefferson, Thomas, 61, 145, 153;
   progress, 164, 165; strategy, 175.
   See also Empire of Liberty
Joint Staff, aggressive measures
   against terrorism, 48; concern about
   retaliation and preemption, 32;
   definition of terrorism, 52, 62;
   description of, 111; interagency
   group, 38, 127
Jordan, 5
Justice Department, 13, 43, 111

Kaczynski, Theodore, 78–79
Kaplan, Robert, 138, 139, 141, 142,
   143, 147, 150
Kapstein, Ethan, 150
Khalaf, Salah, 6, 26
Khartoum, 9–10, 11, 16
Khomeini, Ayatollah Ruhollah, 145
Kissinger, Henry, on changing
   international circumstances, 155;
   meetings with PLO, 11–12; no
   concessions, 9, 10, 22; protected by
   PLO, 11; target of ANO, 40

Kojève, Alexandre, 165–166
Krasner, Stephen, 149

Lake, Anthony, 164, 171
Lead agencies, defined, 13, 20;
    problems with, 15, 21, 28–29; in
    Reagan administration, 30
Libya, closure of Embassy in United
    States, 24; sanctions against, 16, 17,
    88, 90–91; sponsor of terrorism, 16;
    talks with U.S. official, 24; terrorist
    attacks organized by, 96-97. *See also*
    El Dorado Canyon
Lincoln, Abraham, 61, 62
Long Commission, 31, 49

M-19, 19, 22, 34
McFarlane, Robert, 33, 42
Malloy, Michael, 88
Mann, Michael, 152
Marine Barracks, Beirut, 31, 35
Mbeki, Thabo, 152
Meese, Edwin, 42
Meyer, Armin, 7, 13
Military retaliation, 31, 32, 96–99
Mitrione, Dan, 2, 9
Mogadishu, 18, 31
Montoneros, 12
Munich Olympics, 6, 8, 67
Muskie, Edmund, 24

National Command Authorities, 29, 30
National Liberation Action, 2
National Liberation Army, 36
National Liberation Front, 60, 146
National Security Council, 13, 20–21;
    aggressive measures against
    terrorism, 48; effect of Iran-
    Contra on, 42; interagency group,
    38; interagency role, 131;
    opposition to preemption, 32
Nation-state, 153–155
Nixon, Richard, 6, 7, 10
Nixon Administration, 6–8
No concessions, analysis of, 73–80;
    criticism of, 24; development of
    policy, 8–10, 22; flexible policy, 79–
    80; importance of, 72; in Reagan
    administration, 24

North, Oliver, 38, 42
North Korea. *See* Democratic People's
    Republic of Korea
November 17, 12

Oakley, Robert, 33, 35
OAS, 3, 180
October 8 Revolutionary Movement, 2
Office of the Secretary of Defense,
    38, 111
Oil, 18, 50, 71, 91, 177, 178
Oklahoma City Bombing, 189
Organization, agency mandate, 114;
    changing response to terrorism, 128–
    129; culture, 115–117; effect of
    American characteristics on, 117–
    120; importance of leadership in,
    128; processes of, 111–112;
    regional/functional differences in,
    110; regional/global differences in,
    110–111; turf, 113

Palestine Liberation Front, 36
Palestine Liberation Organization, 5,
    6, 11; meeting with Vernon Walters,
    11, 79; Soviet support of, 26;
    terrorist attacks sponsored by, 6, 12;
    training of Iranian red guards by, 35
Pan Am Flight 103, 31, 40, 45–46, 48,
    53, 81, 91, 96–97
People's Democratic Republic of
    Yemen, 17, 26, 88
People's Resistance Organized Army,
    12
People's Revolutionary Armed Forces,
    12
Perry, William, 144, 169
PLO. *See* Palestine Liberation
    Organization
Poindexter, John, 42
Poland, 26, 41
Policy-operations coordination, 120–
    124; in counterterrorism, 122;
    distinguished from interagency
    cooperation, 120–121; reasons for
    failure of, 123–124; in war and
    peace, 121–122
Popular Front for the Liberation of
    Palestine, 4, 5, 6, 12, 25

Porter, Bruce, 149
Preemption, analysis of, 103; defined, 103; disadvantages of, 104–105; discussion of in U.S. government, 32; need for, 31; requirements for, 103
Presidential Review Memorandum 30, 13
Prevention, 99–102, 102–103
Progress, 164–166
Pueblo, U.S.S., 8

Qadaffi, Muammar, 16, 40, 97, 98, 104
Quainton, Anthony, 13, 18–19

Rangers, 18
Reagan, Ronald, 24, 33, 37; approval of counterterrorism operation, 39; Iran-Contra, 43; support for democracy, 162
Reagan Administration, attitude toward terrorism, 22, 24, 27; compared to Carter administration, 21, 27; criticism of, 37; efforts against terrorism, 31–32, 33, 39–40, 40–41, 42–43, 44, 46; organization to combat terrorism, 28, 29–30, 37–39
Rebel Armed Forces, 2
Red Army Faction, 26, 36
Red Brigades, 27, 28
Rendition, 43–44, 72, 80, 105. *See also* Extraterritoriality, Rendition
Revolutionary Armed Forces, 36
Rogers, William, 3, 9
Roy, Olivier, 152

Sanchez, Ilich Ramirez, 26
Sartre, Jean Paul, 5
Sayre, Robert, M., 34
Shultz, George, definition of terrorism, 52, 58; emphasis on counterterrorism, 35, 126, 128; on force and diplomacy, 120; narcoterrorism, 34; opposition to counterterrorism operation, 39; rhetorical strategy of, 64; speeches on terrorism, 33–34, 35, 190

Sinn Fein, 63
Six Day War, 5
Smith, Adam, 153
Somalia, 94, 95, 120
South Yemen. *See* People's Democratic Republic of Yemen
Sovereignty, causes of decline of, 150; decline of, 147; decline of criticized, 149–154; defined 148–149, 154; human rights, 154; nation-state, 153–155; terrorism, 147, 148
Soviet Union, 16, 24–25, 26, 33, 47, 50
Special Coordination Committee, 13, 14, 21
Special Operations Forces, 39, 116–117, 130
Special Situation Group, 28, 30
State Department, 7, 13, 20, 28–29; *Achille Lauro*, 37; attitude of toward force, 118; cooperation with FBI, 45; definition of terrorism, 52; interagency group, 38; lack of cooperation with FBI, 43–44; mandate of, 115; operation against ANO, 41; opposition to counterterrorist operation, 39; opposition to preemption, 32
Sterling, Claire, 26
Stevenson, John, R., 4
Strategic depth, 135–136, 185
Strategy, defined, 135, 169; free trade, 172–173; importance of for combating terrorism, 89, 91, 92, 99, 100, 102, 103, 105, 107, 133–134, 169; military strategy, 183; morality, 171; purpose of, 102; significance of terrorism for, 135, 157–158, 183–184. *See also* Balance of power; Engagement; Fortress America; Threat
Sudan, 83, 88
Syria, sponsor of terrorism, 5, 16, 27; target of sanctions, 88–89, 90; use of terrorism by, 68, 76, 158

Terrorism, analysis of organization to combat, 125–130; attacks on Americans, 1, 8, 11, 12, 19–20, 27, 36, 48, 181; autonomous groups,

49, 106–107, 185–186, 187-188;
causes of, 99–102; changing
methods of attack, 31, 49, 105–107;
as coercive diplomacy, 69; as crime,
3, 4, 10, 60–62; criticism of
organization to combat, 19, 20–21;
criticism of U.S. efforts against, 12–
13, 19, 37; definition of, 3, 4, 24–
25, 35, 50, 51–69; development of
methods to combat, 3, 4, 10, 12, 16,
31, 33, 37, 42, 43–44, 46–47, 49,
72–73; development of organization
to combat, 7, 13, 14, 15, 28, 30, 37,
38; diplomacy, 73; ethnic and
religious violence, 55–57; failure of,
10; guerrilla warfare, 2, 3;
guidelines for combating, 105–106;
holy terror, 56–57; international
conventions against, 3–4, 15, 16, 18,
27, 33, 43, 80–81, 82–85;
international cooperation, 61;
Islamic, 23; Latin America, 2, 3;
legitimate violence, 57–60; level of
violence used in, 54; media, 181–
182; negotiations, 73–74, 77–78, 79;
purpose of, 53; rationality, 55;
relevance of methods to combat,
106–107, 188; rhetoric, 62, 64–65;
significance of in current strategic
setting, 155–156, 184, 185–188;
state sponsorship of, 11, 16–17, 23,
26–27, 35, 49, 68, 77; strategic,
186–188; as warfare, 65–69
Threat, changing conception of, 136–
139; criticism of, 139–147; and end
of Cold War, 135–136. *See also*
balance of power; engagement;
fortress America; strategy
Title 18, 52, 60, 62

Title 22, 52, 63–64
Tupamaros, 2, 5, 9
TWA Flight 847, 36, 37, 181, 182

Unabomber. *See* Kaczynski, Theodore
United Nations, 4, 11, 12, 180–181;
release of hostages, 47; sanctions
against Libya, 46
U.S. Embassy, Beirut, 31, 35
UTA Flight 772, 31, 91, 98

Vance, Cyrus, 15, 16, 22
Van Creveld, Martin, 151–152
Venezuelan Army of National
Liberation, 1, 2
Vice-President's Task Force, 37, 38, 46
Vietcong, 1
The Village, 94–95

Walters, Vernon, 11–12
War, 65–69, 94–96
Wars of national liberation, 2, 77
Wealth of Nations, 153
Weapons of mass destruction, 10,
18–19, 20, 49, 54, 76, 103, 106; in
strategy, 173–174, 181
Weinberger, Casper, 126
Westphalia, Treaty of, 149
Wilson, James, Q., 114, 115
World government, 84–85, 154
World Trade Center, 49, 76, 82, 189

Yousef, Ramzi, 82
Yugoslavia, 41
Yunis, Fawaz, 44–45, 82–83, 113

Zhirinovsky, Vladimir, 175
Zia ul-Haq, Muhammad, 45, 46

About the Author

DAVID TUCKER is Acting Director of Policy Planning in the Office of the Assistant Secretary of Defense (Special Operations and Low-Intensity Conflict). He is coeditor (with C. Harmon) of *Statecraft and Power* (1994) and holds a Ph.D. from the Claremont Graduate School in California.

ISBN 0-275-95762-4

90000>

EAN

9 780275 957629

HARDCOVER BAR CODE